I Wish I'd Known
About Young People, Drugs and Decisions

I Wish I'd Known

About Young People, Drugs and Decisions

FIONA SPARGO-MABBS

First published by Sheldon Press in 2021
An imprint of John Murray Press
A division of Hodder & Stoughton Ltd,
An Hachette UK company

1

This book is for information or educational purposes only and is not intended to
act as a substitute for medical advice or treatment. Any person with a condition
requiring medical attention should consult a qualified medical practitioner or
suitable therapist.

A CIP catalogue record for this title is available from the British Library

Trade Paperback ISBN 9781529366365
eBook ISBN 9781529366372

Typeset by KnowledgeWorks Global Ltd.

Printed and bound in Great Britain by Clays Ltd, Elcograf S.p.A.

John Murray Press policy is to use papers that are natural, renewable and recyclable
products and made from wood grown in sustainable forests. The logging and
manufacturing processes are expected to conform to the environmental regulations
of the country of origin.

John Murray Press
Carmelite House
50 Victoria Embankment
London EC4Y 0DZ

www.sheldonpress.co.uk

To my dear Dan, with love.
Mum

Acknowledgements

As I'm sure is always the case, there are so many people on whose support, involvement and input the creation of this book rests heavily. Special thanks, however, are owed to some in particular.

To those who gave their time and professional experience and insight:

Emma Crashaw and Vicki Craik from Scottish young people's drugs and alcohol charity Crew 2000, for advice on Scottish law in relation to drugs, and for reviewing several chapters for me. Dr Cara Robinson and Nick Hickmott, for their input on Chapter 8 and advice for parents on young people's drugs and alcohol treatment. Simon Bray, recently retired Metropolitan Police Commander and drugs lead on the National Police Chiefs' Council, for checking the legal chapter was all correct. Alicia Drummond, founder of Teen Tips and specialist in adolescent mental and emotional health and well-being, for casting her eye over the chapters on decisions and conversations. Ivan Ezquerra Romano, co-founder and co-director of harm reduction non-profit organization Drugs and Me, and Guy Jones, scientist at The Loop and technical director at Reagent Tests UK, for information and advice on drugs testing, and Professor Fiona Measham for reviewing the section on the work of The Loop. DSM Foundation Youth Ambassadors at Epsom College for their advice for parents in chapter six.

And then to those without whom the book may never have seen the light of day:

My older son, Jacob, conveniently a highly skilled writer/editor in his day job, for tidying up my first few chapters so well before I sent them out into the world to see if anyone might like them. Playwright Mark Wheeller, author of the play about Dan and now our dear friend, for not giving up on nagging me to send what I was writing to his own new publisher, George Spender. George, who despite specializing in drama at Salamander Street, sent my early chapters straight on to someone he knew, who passed them on to Sheldon Press, and within less than 24 hours I was speaking to the person who was to become my editor, Victoria Roddam. Victoria, for patience with a brand-new author with far too many questions, on top of all the other work needed to straighten up my many words ready for print. And the various individuals who encouraged, cajoled and badgered me to write a book, and didn't give up.

And to my husband Tim, Jacob and Dan's dear dad, for patience, encouragement and not minding me not getting much done other than writing for a little while.

And especially to all the people who are part of our story, for not minding their parts in this being shared. And to all the parents who gave their own children's stories to this book, in the hope that they would be of help to others.

Contents

About the Author

Credit: © Photography, Julie Ludlow

Having studied English at Oxford University, Fiona Mabbs met and married Tim Spargo, became the Spargo-Mabbs, and moved to South London, where they raised their two boys, Jacob and Daniel. When Dan started school, Fiona began teaching English in adult education for her local authority, and by the time Dan died she was managing a team of around 50 teachers, coordinators and managers, working closely with other departments within the council, and in partnership with local schools and educational settings.

She was also working strategically at a national level within her specialism and first love, Family Learning. Family Learning involves working in some of the most deprived areas with parents whose limited confidence and skills are risking their children's progress and achievement. The fundamental premise of Family Learning is that the involvement of parents is vital to the impact and success of children's learning.

When Dan died, Fiona and Tim were left with a passionate commitment to do all they could to prevent any harm happening to anyone else's child. They became aware not only of the vulnerability of all young people to the risks of drugs, but also of a huge gap in the resources and support available to schools to enable them to teach this tricky topic to their students effectively. It quickly became apparent that there was little provision for parents. And so, together with their older son Jacob, Fiona and Tim founded the Daniel Spargo-Mabbs Foundation, with the aim of arming young people – and the adults in their lives – with the information, understanding and decision-making skills they need to make safer choices about alcohol and drugs.

With her personal and professional lives having collided, as a drugs educator Fiona has worked with tens of thousands of young people, parents and professionals across the country and Europe; less than a decade after setting up the DSM Foundation, she is considered to be one of the leading UK experts in drugs and alcohol education. As well as regularly being asked to talk to the media, she speaks across a range of platforms, informing and influencing policy and practice at a local, regional and national level. Fiona's resolute determination to prevent any harm coming to young people from drugs drives everything she does – quite simply, it is all about making sure young people get home safely.

Foreword

I remember speaking on the phone with Fiona shortly after Dan's death. I'm sure I did my best to comfort her but in truth her sobs were just the outward evidence of a heart that was forever broken. I recall thinking how fast life can change. One minute Fiona was saying to a typical sixteen-year-old boy going out for the night the things that as parents we always say – 'Be careful,' 'Don't do anything silly,' and 'Ring if you need us.' The next moment, the police were calling.

In 2003, Care for the Family introduced a new course for parents called 'How to Drug-Proof Your Kids.' We wrestled with that title at the time as we all knew that there can be no guarantees – as Fiona and Tim tragically found out when their son Dan died from MDMA (ecstasy). But despite there being no guarantees, every mum and dad wants their child to avoid the harm that can come with substance misuse.

Fiona and Tim felt just the same. They wanted Dan and his brother Jacob to be able to develop and grow from much-loved children, into much-loved teens, and then adults who would live healthy and fulfilling lives. Sadly, that didn't happen for Dan, and at Care for the Family, through our work with bereaved parents we know that to be the case for many other parents. No one expects to bury their own child, and as our befrienders say, this is a club no one wants to join.

In this book, Fiona has taken the tragedy of Dan's death as a motivation to help other families, as much as possible, avoid the same thing. As I said earlier, there are no guarantees but that doesn't mean that as mums and dads, grand-parents, carers – or anyone for whom the well-being of our young people matters – we shouldn't give it our best shot. Fiona and Tim have done just that. This book tells their family's personal and heart-breaking story with great honesty and vulnerability. But it does much more than that. It's full of evidence-based practical wisdom: how to talk with your child about drugs and alcohol; facts about different drugs; the role brain development plays in risk-taking and making decisions, and where to go for help and support.

The good news, as Fiona says '...is that most young people, at any age, are not using illegal drugs.' However, we may never know, just as

Fiona and Tim didn't know, whether our child is going to be one of the ones who does. This book helps us be forewarned and forearmed, with the hope that one less family will experience what the Spargo-Mabbs family did.

In the fast-changing world in which we live, it is crucial to have an understanding of the challenges that may face our children – and us as their parents – further down the road. *I Wish I'd Known* is a vital read if you have teenagers, but I would urge you to read it whatever age your children are. My grandchildren are young – all under eleven years of age – but I will be urging my children to read this book – *now*.

Rob Parsons OBE Founder and Chairman, Care for the Family

Introduction

When my younger son Dan was 16, he went to a party and never came home. The policeman who rang at the door in the early hours told us he'd been found unconscious outside a rave in Hillingdon; it was thought he'd taken MDMA and been taken to intensive care. I'd never heard of MDMA. I didn't know where Hillingdon was. I didn't know anything about a rave. I thought he was at the party he'd asked me about going to the evening before. I knew where that was, who was going, when it would finish. But I didn't know about a rave, or Hillingdon or MDMA.

What I did know, by the time the police came, was that he wasn't home, and that he wasn't picking up his phone, and I knew I was more worried and more frightened than I had ever been before. I had no idea what worry and fear might come to look like.

When he left that evening, I didn't know he wouldn't get to speak to me again. When I let him go, I didn't know he'd never come back.

That was 17 January 2014. Dan died three days later from multiple organ failure caused by MDMA toxicity.

When Dan died there was so much I didn't know. But what I did know with an absolute certainty was that if something like this could go so badly wrong for someone like Dan, then it could just as easily go wrong for someone else's – anyone else's – child. And I knew with just as much certainty that I needed to do everything I could to prevent that.

Of course, I knew that most of the time it doesn't end so badly. There were four other boys who took MDMA when Dan did who all went on living their lives. Thank goodness. However, drugs and alcohol can and do cause so many dimensions of harm and damage, and all of these are avoidable because there is always a choice involved. That's so much easier said as an adult, however, than done as a teenager, and this book is all about equipping parents for the (literally) vital role they can play in supporting their children to make safe choices about drugs and alcohol.

Some perspective

It's important as a parent, when it comes to laying out the context of young people and drugs, to hold on to a balance – navigating that bewildering spectrum between worst and best case scenarios, scathed and unscathed, and all the possible shades of scathing in between. This can be especially tricky when those young people are your own precious children, who you love more than life itself, and would do anything in your power to protect from harm.

The first thing to remember in that quest for balance, though, is that most young people, at any age, are not using illegal drugs. Most of them don't drink to excess, and larger numbers than ever don't drink at all. Very few now smoke, and even though vaping has risen in popularity it's still a minority, albeit a sizable one, who have tried it. Of those who do take drugs, most will do little more than dip a toe, remove it and move on. Very few come to lasting harm.

However, it's also important to be aware that young people's use of illegal drugs has been on the rise. Routes of access to drugs are more diverse, speedy and straightforward than possibly ever before. Prices have fallen while purity has risen, at the same time that the strength, range and riskiness of contaminants has increased. The menu of substances available has broadened. Attitudes of young people have become more tolerant and use has become less stigmatized, and even normalized, as they move through their teenage years and into their 20s.

As a parent it's important to be aware your child is very likely, at some time or other, to be in a situation where they have to make a decision about drugs. It's also important to know that their decision, in that moment – and perhaps over some period of time – could well be 'yes', but is statistically more likely to be 'no'. It's important to understand how difficult that decision could be to make safely and why. It's important to know what the risks could be, and what practical strategies they could bring to bear. It's also important to know that most of the time, if there's a beginning with drugs, there will be an ending that usually leaves them relatively, if not completely, unharmed.

Sometimes, of course, the journey from beginning to end is a long and hard one and does leave its mark, and that's incredibly difficult and painful for parents. Accessing advice and support is very important, and that is the focus towards the end of this book. Very, very occasionally the journey comes to an ending that is all too abrupt, as it did for Dan. When this happens, these parents need support, understanding and lots of patience. This is a road of unique rockiness. This is where this book ends.

On the way there we'll explore the context for young people when it comes to drugs and alcohol, the risks and effects of the substances they're most likely to come across, and the legal pitfalls that may leave their own lasting legacy. We'll have a look at what's going on in that adolescent brain in relation to decision-making and managing risk, and how those important conversations can best be approached and managed in your family through these often tricky years, both generally and more specifically if you have suspicions, concerns or know your child has some level of involvement with drugs. We'll also look at some practical strategies for staying safe, some information around reducing risk and harm, and lots of places where more information, advice and support can be found. Woven throughout are 'talking points', included here and there in each chapter to provide some ideas and practical suggestions for things to do, talk about, look at, look up and consider.

What Dan did next

When Dan died, I was working as a manager in adult education for our local authority. I had started out as an English teacher many years before, teaching GCSE, A level and Family Literacy, which involved working with parents in often vulnerable families whose limited skills in literacy were in turn limiting the achievement and future outcomes of their children. I moved through layers of management, taking on wider areas of responsibility and working more broadly across education within our local authority, in partnership with early years settings, schools and other agencies. I also had a lead strategic role nationally within my specialism of Family Learning, chairing a national network of managers from local authorities across the country. I never stopped teaching, though, because I loved it best. My last class had been in the morning of the day Dan left home for his last time.

When Dan died, I knew about teaching and learning, I knew about education and working in partnership. I didn't know enough about drugs, and knew nothing about drugs education, but I knew a lot about how to learn, how to research and how to make contacts and network. I knew the importance of evidence of effectiveness, of measuring impact, of identifying best practice. And we had a huge community of support standing with us. And so the foundations of Dan's Foundation were built – the drugs and alcohol education charity my husband Tim, our older son Jacob and I set up in Dan's name – to make sure other young people had the knowledge, understanding and skills they needed to make safer choices about drugs. Over the years we've watched this grow and grow and grow (see more below).

Both personally, as a parent for whom it had all gone so badly wrong, and as someone whose professional specialism was based on evidence that involves parents in their children's learning adds to its impact exponentially – I was passionately committed from the start to educating and upskilling parents like me. Schools, colleges and community groups will do all they can. We as a drugs education charity will do all we can. But the most important players are parents, and together, we stand the best chance of raising a generation of children and young people who are able to navigate decisions about drugs more safely.

When Dan died, there was so much I wished I'd known. The Foundation isn't founded on regret, though, but on hope. I'll never know whether knowing any of the things I didn't know, or doing any of the things I didn't do, would have been enough to keep Dan safe in that moment of decision, but if in reading this book my gaps are filled for you, and a difference is made for your children, then that will be more than good enough for me.

And I hope that Dan would be proud of (if a little embarrassed by) his mum.

Notes

Talking points: these are included at various points in each chapter to provide some ideas and practical suggestions for things to do, talk about, look at, look up and think about. Chapter 6 is all about how to make these conversations work as best you can.

Terminology: although I've used the word **'parent'** throughout, this includes anyone who has a caring role, relationship or responsibility towards a child or young person.

The term **'drugs'** is used throughout to refer to any drugs that are used for non-medical purposes. Alcohol is referred to separately at times but is also included in the broader term.

I've chosen to use the term **'addiction'** in this book to refer to drug use that has become a dominant factor in a person's life, but the question of which term to use is one that's a bit fraught with differing views. Addiction, dependence, substance misuse, problematic drug use, substance use disorder and dependence syndrome are terms that are sometimes used interchangeably and other times distinctly, and there are multiple definitions and well-argued reasons for the linguistic choices made in each case. Language is important, because it has the power to shape (and to betray) not only attitudes but also the actions, policies and priorities of nations, and it's especially influential – and its influence is especially important – in an area of human existence where stigma is arguably more rife than anywhere else. However, I have to make a choice, and to do that I know there are many who will disagree with whatever that choice will be!

Names: the names of Dan's friends have either been kept as they are or changed in line with decisions made for the play that tells his story written by Mark Wheeller, *I Love You, Mum – I Promise I Won't Die* (Bloomsbury/Methuen Drama, 2017). Some other names have been changed.

The Daniel Spargo-Mabbs Foundation is a drugs and alcohol education charity which aims to support young people to make safe choices and reduce harm, through increasing their understanding of the effects and risks of drugs and alcohol, and improving their life skills and resilience. We work with young people, families, teachers and professionals in schools, colleges and community groups across the UK and overseas.

We deliver workshops and talks to young people, workshops to parents and carers and training to school staff and professionals. We have developed an evidence-based, evaluated drugs and alcohol education programme for young people, parents and teachers, Making Safer Choices, available to schools to be delivered through Personal, Social, Health and Economic (PSHE). We have a Youth Ambassador programme which trains and supports 16–18-year-olds to be positive peer influences within their community and to support the work of the charity.

The powerful verbatim play that the charity commissioned award-winning playwright Mark Wheeller to write, *I Love You, Mum – I Promise I Won't Die* has been studied and performed around the world, and has been touring schools since 2017 as a professional Theatre in Education production, with performances followed by interactive workshops.

Every penny made from sales of this book will go straight to the charity, helping us to keep doing what we do. Saving young lives.

For more information see <www.dsmfoundation.org.uk>

1

I wish I'd known what I needed to know

Starting the story, setting the scene

Dan's story: the beginning of the end

Let me tell you about Dan.

In the days just after Dan died, our police family liaison officer asked us to write a tribute to our son for the police press bureau. It was a troubling task. How could it be possible to recreate Dan in words? Even in those earliest of early days, when our home was still so resonant with his full-of-life presence, where would we find the right words, enough words, to make Dan present for people who hadn't ever known him, when there was no Dan left to fill all the gaps with his great big Dan self? And because he died taking drugs it seemed all the more important to convey who he was. We knew the assumptions people were likely to make about who they thought he must be. We would have done the same. So, we all sat down together, the three of us and Dan's girlfriend Jenna, and made a list of all the words we could think of that fitted Dan. Somewhere to start, with something that could never be finished.

This is what we wrote: 'Dan was funny, passionate, caring, considerate, courageous and outrageous, committed, strong, charming, chatty, witty, quirky, articulate, intelligent, loving, kind, trustworthy, loyal, practical, adventurous, mischievous, cheeky, warm, energetic, silly, political, interesting and interested, humble.'

How to begin and where to end? I could talk forever and still fall so far short of Dan. I hope you'll come to know him a little, here and there, over the course of this book. Because you would have liked him if you'd known him. Everyone liked Dan. You couldn't help yourself.

The start of the story

Dan had moved up to year 12 at the Church of England school in Croydon where he'd been a pupil since year 7. After the stress of the initial adjustment to the rigours of A levels after that long post-GCSE break ('I don't know what they want from me, Mum!') he was relishing the steps into independence that sixth form brought. He was studying English Literature, History, Politics and Economics. At his parents' evening that November we heard undiluted praise from all his teachers, the first time ever. There was usually something about doing more homework, or doing less chatting, but he was doing really well all round. He was in the school production of *The Wiz* just before Christmas, playing his guitar in the band, wearing a green sparkly waistcoat with the rest of them. He'd signed up as a bone marrow donor, put an organ donor card in his wallet and was very disappointed he had to wait until he was 18 to be able to give blood. He'd enrolled on the first Alpha Youth course our church was to run – a programme designed to enable people to explore the Christian faith more deeply. It started two days after he died.

At the same time as all this exemplary behaviour (the *Daily Mail* described him as a 'perfect pupil', which would have amused him greatly, along with all his teachers) he was snaffling all the biscuits at the *Wiz* rehearsals, teasing the trumpeters, earning his nickname 'weird tie guy' with his collection of mad charity shop ties worn to make compliance with the sixth form dress code more interesting. Spending far too long on the Xbox, getting far too cross. Trying to find the best deal on Creme Eggs. Leaping out from behind the kitchen door to make me jump in the mornings. Eating too much cheese.

I can't talk about Dan without talking about Jenna. Dan and Jenna had been Dan and Jenna since they were 13 and 14, and for the next two and a bit years they chatted about anything and everything, made the most mess baking the most delicious cookies and sat on the top deck of the bus into London to play with the toys in Hamleys. I always knew if Jenna had been and gone before I got home from work because Dan would make her cheesy noodles and I'd find the debris caked on pans and bowls. They were the best of friends, and loved each other with all the intensity of teenagers. Jenna was part of our family, and Jenna was Dan's world.

Tim and I were so proud of both our boys. Jacob and Dan. We were so enjoying them as teenagers. They were funny, interesting, good company, tolerated us with great patience and good humour, and our little joke was that, despite our worst efforts as parents, they'd turned into fine young men of whom we were so proud. We thought the worst of the hazards to our boys from our bad parenting were behind us. All those infinite worries you have when they're smaller and getting bigger – being too strict, being too lenient, making them too busy, not getting them doing more, getting it wrong in such a way that only years of therapy would later be able to unravel.

Dan had come into his own. He was in a really good place. He talked endlessly, always interested to hear what you thought about something, always something to tell you about, caring hugely about right and wrong, working out what he thought about things, working out his place in the world, growing into his adult self. We were increasingly trusting him to step out further into independence. He was sensible and responsible. Meanwhile holding onto all the same worries about him being happy, being healthy, staying safe and becoming all he could be.

The last words

On Friday 17 January Dan came home from school and asked me if it was OK for him to go to a party that evening. His friend George was having a party the following day, Saturday, that Dan had been looking forward to for ages, and it was the usual sort of party – in a friend's house, close to home, parents around. But the party that Friday was a little unusual. It was going to be in Clapham, further away than parties had been in the past (though just one stop on the train so not very far). It was going to finish later than anything had before, not till 3 am, which was really late.

But Dan reassured me. There would be a big group of 15 of them travelling together to and from Croydon. It was a friend of his friend, let's call her Alice, a good friend since year 7. Alice was the one I always knew he was safe with, the one who looked out for him at parties and gigs, whose dad would often very kindly bring him back home. So, Alice's dad would be able to drop him back, then? Apparently not, he was working that night. We checked there would be public transport at that late hour to get him home safely – there's always a bus or a train on a Friday night in London – and that his travelcard was topped up. But I still had a bad feeling about it.

Those judgement calls as your children grow through their teenage years can be so hard to make as a parent. You want them to have fun with their friends, you know they need to develop independence, experience new things, and continue to learn to manage risk safely, but you also know they can't always make those judgements themselves. Dan knew I was uncertain because I remember him persuading me. 'Come on, Mum – you know I hardly ever go to parties, and you know I'm sensible and responsible.' He wasn't always off to parties, he was indeed sensible and responsible and I did increasingly trust his maturing judgement, but on this occasion I shouldn't have done. Hindsight that should have been foresight.

As he always did when he was going out, he came and found me before he left the house, bent down so I could reach to give him a kiss and a hug and say, 'I love you, Dan,' to which his reply was, with a smile as always, 'I love you, Mum – I promise I won't die!' This was our joke, a little repartee and ritual that had stuck from when the boys started going out more independently in secondary school. Before they went out, I always wanted to make sure I'd told them I loved them, just in case it was the last thing I said to them, never, ever seriously thinking it might be, but just in case.

When I was at primary school my friend Jacqueline's little brother, on the way home from the shops, was knocked off his bike and killed, and after that my mum always made sure she gave us a kiss before we left the house, just in case. Then I'd heard Margaret Mizen speaking when my own boys were a bit younger, about how much comfort it had brought her that the night before her 16-year-old son Jimmy was murdered they'd had a big hug and said they loved each other. When I told this story to a suspicious young Dan, who wanted to know why I was so insistent on telling him I loved him (at an age when kisses and hugs from your mum are there only to be tolerated), his immediate, logical, response was, 'So you're telling me you love me because you think I'm going to die?' 'Well, no,' I replied, 'but just in case...'.

'I love you, Mum – I promise I won't die.' That was the last thing Dan ever said to me. What a precious gift it was.

The last night

Dan didn't come home. It wasn't a party, it was an illegal rave. It wasn't in Clapham, it was miles away, on an industrial estate on the other side of London. It was a group of boys mostly from another school, friends of a new friend of Dan's who'd joined his school for sixth form, most of whom he didn't know. There were eight boys, and five were taking MDMA, and one of these was Dan.

I learned all of this from Dan's friend, Jack. Jack was there, but not one of the five. He had moved to Dan's school in year 9 and he and Dan had been great friends since then, but he'd been at the other school before and knew some of the boys in the group. Jack is my only source of information, apart from what I learned from the police and at the trial of the alleged supplier.

Losing a child under any circumstances ranks pretty high on the list of the most awful things that can happen to someone, and each particular set of circumstances in which a child is lost has its own unique aspects of awfulness. One of the many things that makes losing a child to drugs uniquely awful is the incomplete narrative. The most important story ever to be told, the one that tells how my son came to lose his life, is full of gaping holes that will never be filled. Jigsaw pieces forever scattered into lost corners. Swept up and thrown away long ago or carried around by people who don't know they're needed.

Jack said the first time there was any talk about going out that evening was on the Friday morning, but the word used was 'party', not 'rave'.

Dan was friends with everyone, with every social group in the school. He was voted Prom King at the end of year 11 in a landslide election – a popularity test for everyone's favourite boy and girl. Everyone liked Dan. You couldn't help yourself. He had a way of engaging people, a gift for making friends, and he liked to be friends with everyone. He liked everyone to be happy. Everything was more fun when Dan was there. Everything was more interesting. He was funny, bright, crazy. He was kind and he cared. Even at his most infuriatingly, deliberately irritating self – teasing someone endlessly about exactly the same thing – he teased with such kindness and big-hearted humour it made people feel special; picked out in the best sort of way.

Everyone liked Dan and everyone was friends with Dan, and that meant his friends included a group in which, for some, taking drugs was becoming normal. It included Alice, whose involvement in drugs had grown over the preceding summer (I had no idea). And it included the boy who joined the school for sixth form, let's call him Lewis, whose friends had a plan to go to the rave.

Alice and Lewis had been talking at school that Friday about where they could get some MDMA for the evening. Both had numbers they could call. They asked Dan if he wanted some. He said he would, but only if he could share his with somebody – he didn't want to take a full amount. We'd thought this was the first time Dan had taken anything, but we found out later this was his third time. The first was a taste of Alice's. The second hadn't been good. This third time he was being wary. In, but not completely in.

Back at home, Dan said goodbye and set off to meet the others. By the time he got to the tram stop where they were meeting, one of the boys had already called his dealer, arranged for the drugs to be dropped off, and three of them had gone off to pick them up. They came back with three little bags of white powder, two of one gram, one of a half. Jack said it was hard to tell which was the smaller because they all looked much the same, but they gave them all a shake and decided one must be the half and gave that one to Dan, sharing the others between the remaining four boys.

Dan had worked hard to earn the £20 for his MDMA. He had done a paper round every day since he was 13. His alarm went off at 6 am every weekday and 7 am at weekends. I used to worry every morning about him getting knocked off his bike. He was really fond of his 'old ladies' on his round and used to run little errands for them – posting a letter or getting something from the shop. He had a gardening job at the weekend, too, for an older lady at our church. He used to stay on after his hours were finished to have coffee, cake and a chat with her because he knew she got lonely. That week's paper round money, and a bit of his gardening wages from the weekend before, paid for his share of the MDMA that killed him.

Jack said they all emptied their little bags into the bottles of water they'd taken with them and let the crystals dissolve. The other four boys then sipped theirs all the way across London. A direct journey from where we live in Croydon across London to Hayes in Hillingdon, where the rave was held, takes two hours on various trains and tubes. However, a journey to an illegal rave is not a direct journey so it took them a lot longer than that. The organizers would have done what they usually do – broken into an empty building, set it all up at short notice, and revealed the final destination in gradual stages so the police would find out too late to prevent it from happening. By the time the police find out, all they can do is manage the situation because shutting it down and dispersing so many young people in an often unsuitable space would be too risky; by then the organizers have got their money anyway. By the end of the circuitous journey across London I don't know that Dan or any of his friends had much of a clue about where they actually were.

The choice

All the way there, Jack said, he was conscious of Dan, watching the other boys sipping their MDMA, and holding his back. Jack said he could see Dan reflected in the window against the darkness outside without actually watching him directly. He was slouched back in his seat, looking as uncomfortable as Jack felt, though he would have hidden it well from the others. But Jack knew Dan well. He wanted to tell him he didn't have to take it if he didn't want to, but he knew if he did it would risk drawing the attention of the others to the fact Dan still had his, untouched, and perhaps make it harder to lose it if he wanted to.

Jack didn't say anything, and nobody else noticed until that very last train, when someone else in the group spotted Dan's full bottle and said, 'Are you not having that then?' And with that, Dan drank it. He could just as easily have said, 'Nah, I'm alright, don't fancy it now,' or something along those lines. But he didn't. He drank it.

Perhaps he thought the other boys were all fine so he would be, too. Perhaps he thought he'd paid £20 for it so he may as well have it. Perhaps he thought it was going to be a long night and he'd need something to keep him going. Perhaps he thought if he didn't take it it'd seem like he was judging those who had. Perhaps he just thought it looked as though they were having fun. Perhaps, in that moment, he didn't really think at all. These things happen.

That decision, in that moment, was to cost Dan his life. The toxicology report at the inquest told us the amount of MDMA in his blood was 12 times stronger than had caused fatality in the past. How could he possibly have known?

A brave new world?

What the numbers say

The world of the average teenager is very different to the one their parents inhabited when they were teens themselves, and it has continued to change over the years since we began doing this work. In 2014 when Dan died, when we set out on this unexpected journey into drugs and alcohol education, we brought with us a sense that, albeit somewhat vague and anecdotal at that stage, young people's drug use was at a higher level than many of the people caring for and working with them credited, and that it was rising.

As soon as we started a charity – the Daniel Spargo-Mabbs Foundation – and got to work doing our research, we found this concern was backed up by data. Although numbers of teenagers smoking and drinking alcohol have continued to fall over many years now, use of controlled substances has been increasing, after remaining at steady levels for several years. Every other year, the government commissions a survey of school children aged 11–15 years in England, and in 2014 this found that almost half (49 per cent) of 15-year-olds had been offered controlled drugs and around one in four (24 per cent) had tried something at least once.[1] Four years later those numbers had risen to 59 per cent who reported having been offered something, and 38 per cent who had said yes. By comparison, in 2018 only 12 per cent of 15-year-olds had tried a cigarette. The average

---

[1] NHS Digital, (2015) Smoking, Drinking and Drug Use Among Young People in England-2014 [online]. *NHS Digital*. Available from: <digital.nhs.uk/data-and-information/publications/statistical/smoking-drinking-and-drug-use-among-young-people-in-england/2014> (accessed November 2020).

teenager is statistically much more likely to try controlled drugs now than tobacco.[2]

The 2018/19 data for 16- to 24-year-olds showed their use of controlled drugs has also been increasing. One in five (20 per cent) 16- to 24 year-olds had taken a drug in the last year, a relatively small but steady upward trend since 2015/16 (18 per cent). This has been led by a rise in Class A drug use, which was at the highest level since 2003, with 8.7 per cent in this age group having taken a Class A drug in the last year. This had reached an all-time low in 2013 but has seen small but steady increases since then, mainly driven by an increase in powder cocaine and ecstasy use.[3]

What's out there?

The range of substances available to young people is wide, diverse and constantly shifting. The drugs market is very fluid and responsive, and factors affecting preferences and popularity are complex, as are those affecting price, purity and supply.[4] Since 2014 when we started this work, young people's use of nitrous oxide has increased, as has ketamine. Vaping has overtaken cigarettes by many miles. The popularity of the benzodiazepine branded Xanax has risen and then begun to wane, the rise due in some

---

[2] NHS Digital, (2019) Smoking, Drinking and Drug Use Among Young People in England 2018 [online]. *NHS* Digital. Available from: <digital.nhs.uk/data-and-in-formation/publications/statistical/smoking-drinking-and-drug-use-among-young-people-in-england/2018> (accessed November 2020)

[3] Home Office, (2019) Drugs Misuse: Findings from the 2018/19 Crime Survey for England and Wales [online]. *Gov.uk*. Available from: <assets.publishing.ser-vice.gov.uk/government/uploads/system/uploads/attachment_data/file/832533/drug-misuse-2019-hosb2119.pdf> (accessed November 2020)

[4] I began writing this book in June 2020, halfway through the first year of the global crisis caused by Covid-19, which had already had an impact on the controlled drugs trade. The response to Covid-19 and restrictions on move-ment, travel and trade quickly affected the drugs people were using, the ways they were using them, and the reasons for their use. The longer-term effects remain to be seen. This was by far more rapid, dramatic and global than many factors affecting supply and demand, but contains within it many of the com-plexities that are present in other, more subtle shifts, relating to issues such as supply routes, availability of ingredients, pricing, policing, political and social changes.

part to its celebration in rap and other music, the waning in turn following the sad and untimely deaths of a number of prominent rappers, due in various degrees to Xanax. Synthetic drugs created to replicate the effects of more traditional controlled substances, known as 'legal highs' and sold on high streets in 'head shops' and other outlets, became illegal to supply following the passing of the Psychoactive Substances Act in 2016, and largely disappeared off the scene for young people.

As a drugs and alcohol education charity working with young people, we need to know what substances young people, especially older teens, might be making decisions about, in order to ensure what we do is going to be relevant and useful, and so we survey 15- to 18-year-olds before working with them, asking a range of questions including one about the main substances that people in their year group might be using. This is asking for perceptions of use, not confessions, and makes no claims to be anything approaching a robust gathering of evidence, but nevertheless it does provide a valuable picture of what is around, and a picture that varies from one place to another.

At the time of writing we had just over 4000 responses from students in the current 2019–20 academic year. The overall profile shows alcohol is, inevitably, still by far the most prevalent substance, followed by vaping, and then cannabis and cigarettes neck and neck. Coming a bit of a way behind these is nitrous oxide, with ketamine and MDMA at similar levels next, then cocaine, closely followed by LSD. Xanax, magic mushrooms and steroids bring up the rear. The 'other' category always gathers some random teenage humorous responses, but also the likes of lean, 2CB, DMT and speed.[5] This book lacks space to cover the effects and risks of these in detail, but there is more information in the next two chapters about the most commonly used substances, and some useful websites at the back of the book where more information can be found.

---

[5] Lean is a mixture of cough syrup containing codeine and antihistamine with a fizzy soft drink like lemonade; 2CB is a synthetic drug with hallucinogenic and stimulant effects; DMT is a strong hallucinogenic drug found in several plants; speed is a colloquial name for amphetamine, a powerful stimulant.

Attitudes to drugs

The government school survey shows acceptance of drug use remains fairly low among 11- to 15-year-olds, but also that tolerance has increased since 2011. Around one in three (30 per cent) 15-year-olds in 2018 thought it was fine to try cannabis to see what it was like, compared with one in five in 2014, and 17 per cent thought it was OK to use cannabis once a week. Only 6 per cent thought it was OK to try cocaine, however.

Data on the attitudes of older teens towards drugs and drug use is harder to come by, but anecdotally, from working with thousands of young people every year, and from our own team of Youth Ambassadors, we know that by sixth form attitudes to drug use have generally become increasingly tolerant, and drug use more prevalent, although it's still a minority that are using drugs. It seems the majority of sixth form parties will include drugs for at least some party-goers, and at summer festivals drug use is fairly widespread, as it is at illegal raves and other unlicensed events.

That said, young people often overestimate the risky behaviours of their peers, whether regarding drink, drugs or sex. They're likely to think that their peers are up to more than they really are. Increased exposure to drugs and drug use, in music videos, films, TV and on social media, for example, can result in a gradual shift in young people's perceptions of the acceptability of substance use, as well as the levels of use of their peers. Various studies have demonstrated the influence of 'normative beliefs' on the substance use of adolescents.[6] The more normal it seems to be, the more likely it is to be done. It is important not only for parents to hold onto the fact that the majority of young people aren't using drugs, but also for their children to do so.

---

[6] R. Scott Olds, Dennis L. Thombs, Jennifer Ray-Tomasek (2005) Relations between normative beliefs and initiation intentions toward cigarette, alcohol and marijuana, *Journal of Adolescent Health* [online]. 37(1):75. Available from DOI: 10.1016/j.jadohealth.2004.09.020

Talking point

As part of a conversation about drugs and alcohol you could ask a child under 15 how many 15-year-olds they think have done the following, possibly presenting it like a little quiz. The answers in brackets are from the NHS Digital 2018 school survey referred to above.

a) Drunk alcohol in the last week (23%)
b) Been drunk in the last four weeks (9%)
c) Took any controlled drugs in the last month (19%)
d) Took Class A drugs in the last month (3.6%)

Whether it's less or more than they thought will depend a lot on your child and their age, but a conversation that emphasizes the fact the majority of young people aren't doing any of these things, and about the differences generally in young people's perceptions is important, because misconceptions could lead their friends to take risks even if they don't themselves.

How do young people get drugs?

The main route of access to drugs for young people has always been their friends. Social supply was by far the most common source of drugs cited by 11- to 15-year-olds in the school survey, with significantly more 15-year-olds saying they got drugs from a friend on the first occasion (64 per cent) than from a dealer (16 per cent), especially cannabis. When it came to Class A drugs, slightly more went to a dealer than a friend, but it was close. Most got hold of drugs out and about, in the park or the street, but they also reported buying or being given drugs in someone's house, at school or at a party, with the numbers inevitably varying according to the social environments associated with different ages. For 15-year-olds the next most common place to have got drugs was in someone else's home (21 per cent), whereas for 11-year-olds it was at school (22 per cent).

As well as these more traditional sources of supply, buying and selling drugs online now is nothing new, and accessing the dark net isn't a challenge for most tech-savvy teenagers. Products, descriptions and prices are laid out on the screen with the familiar feel of all the major legitimate online marketplaces. Customer reviews are provided for the potential buyer. Special offers encourage bulk buying. Purchases can be delivered to your door – or to a nearby drop-box – in less time than it takes to deliver a pizza.[7] Less popular with teens than those in their 20s, this is nevertheless an easier route for some than direct contact with a dealer. It can also feel – misleadingly – cleaner and safer.

The role of social media

A more recent development in the online marketplace is the shift to social media, which was probably inevitable. The controlled drugs market is dynamic, innovative and resilient, constantly finding new ways and means to maintain sales, and moving into this wide-open online social space was a natural next step. Adverts and offers pop up in young people's social media feeds. They are open and blatant, using emojis which lack any subtlety (a nose for cocaine, a pill for ecstasy, a horse's head for ketamine), images and videos of products, menus and price lists.

In 2019 the drug policy think tank Volteface published the results of a national poll of 16- to 24-year-olds, which found that one in four had seen drugs advertised on social media, namely Snapchat and Instagram.[8] We wanted to know how this affected younger teens and carried out our own, smaller, informal survey in 2020 of around 1000 year 9 and 10 students. The data showed that one in five had seen drugs advertised, mainly on Snapchat, but also Instagram and TikTok.

I was involved in the Volteface research as part of their expert advisory panel, and over several months in 2020 I worked on a campaign with the BBC, Volteface and a group of other bereaved parents, to challenge and work with the social media platforms to address the risks to young people resulting from this exposure. Some of these parents had lost children to drugs bought on social media. Two of these children were just 13. This all resulted in a short BBC documentary released that summer (see the talking point below) which exposed the complexity of risks, the blatant and careless nature

---

[7]   Global Drug Survey (2018) [online]. *Global Drug Survey.* Available from: <www.globaldrugsurvey.com/gds-2018/> (accessed November 2020)

[8]   McCulloch, L. & Furlong, S., (2019) DM for Details: Selling Drugs in the Age of Social Media. Volteface. Available from: <volteface.me/publications/dm-details-selling-drugs-age-social-media/> (accessed November 2020)

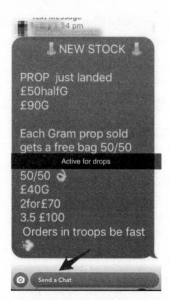

Screenshot of a suspected dealer's Snapchat story showing their drug menu for 'prop' – another term for cocaine. The suspected dealer is selling two types of cocaine in this menu – high-quality 'prop' and '50/50' 'prop'. '50/50' prop is the dealer advertising half cocaine and half cutting agent (for example, benzocaine or a stimulant). The suspected dealer is selling the high-quality cocaine for £90 per gram and the 50/50 cocaine for £40 per gram. *Credit: Volteface – DM for details 2019*

Screenshot of a suspected dealer's Snapchat story which shows cannabis in 'baggies' ready to be sold. The suspected dealer is selling the cannabis in bags of 1.8 grams '1.8s'. The suspected dealer has used UK and Canadian flags to indicate that the cannabis that they are selling is from these countries. *Credit: Volteface – DM for details 2019*

of selling on social media, and the consequences this can have. The risks of this exposure are many and various:

- **Normalization**: the use of drugs can begin to seem normal and safe through the frequency with which they're seen, and especially when they're mixed up with normal happy posts in that social space on their phones in their pockets. This can include not just the selling but also people within their wider (or closer) social networks posting images of themselves using substances on social occasions, and it's more likely to be the positive than the negative experiences that are shared. The more normal we think something is, the more likely we are to do it ourselves, however much we might know about the risks. And, of course, for those posting images of their drug-related experiences there is a digital footprint they may later come to regret.
- **Accessibility**: access to drugs becomes quick and easy through social media, and accessibility is a significant risk factor in use. The harder something is to get hold of, the less likely someone is to make the effort. Not only that, but dealers use marketing strategies to promote their wares, with special offers and incentive buys not just encouraging use, but also a greater level of use. In addition to this, a wider range of drugs becomes available to young people, and drugs of which they may not have been aware. In our survey around a third of 13- to 15-year-olds who had bought drugs had got them through social media.
- **Seeing is believing**: seeing photos and videos of drugs misled some young people considering buying something into thinking not only did they know what they were getting, but they also therefore knew it was safe, whereas of course this is no more true for controlled substances seen 'in the flesh' than seen online. Moreover, research showed many of these images had been found through regular image searches on standard search engines. There may be promises these pills are pure, or this cannabis is from California, or they've tried it themselves and can vouch it'll give other users a great experience, but of course, even if this is true, and what they see is a genuine photo of a genuine product sold by this dealer, there's no guarantee this is what they'll actually be given. Dealers are dealers online and off, and at the end of the day

it's a business, and not an honourable one, in which profit is the aim, and honesty, integrity and safety aren't priorities.

- **Selling**: the selling of drugs is a simple step, whether intentional or not entirely so (more on this in Chapter 5), and one that can leave a lot more evidence in that digital footprint than might otherwise have been available to police. In our survey, the biggest age group by far that these year 9 and 10 students had seen selling drugs on social media was 13- to 17-year-olds.

Despite these risks, the research encouragingly showed that seeing drugs for sale on social media didn't change the vast majority of young people's behaviour. Only 6 per cent said it resulted in them using controlled drugs, 3 per cent in buying them and 2 per cent in considering selling them, and none of those polled had actually got involved in supply. However, the risks exist and need to be navigated, and we'll look at some strategies to make this social space safer in Chapter 7, because neither social media use, nor substance use, is going anywhere any time soon.

Talking point

If your children use social media, depending on their age, you might ask if they have come across drugs, either being used or being sold, or just talked about. If so, how did it make them feel? What did they do? Did they report it? Block the post or the account?

If this is something your children are coming across, have a look at Chapter 7 for some advice on staying safe on social media.

Watch the documentary *Dealers in Your DMs*, available on BBC iPlayer, for more of an insight.

What harm can it do?

Cannabis is the most commonly used controlled drug in the world, and the most seriously underestimated drug in terms of risk when it comes to adolescents, and sometimes their parents, too. There has been extensive research undertaken into the risks of cannabis, with often varying findings. There has also been ongoing debate around drug policy reform exploring a huge range of related issues from diverse viewpoints. Whatever the answers may be, the fact of the matter is that cannabis remains the substance that results in more young people needing specialist treatment than all the other substances combined.

In 2018–19, 88 per cent of young people accessing drugs and alcohol treatment were there for cannabis use, and most of these were 15–16 years old.[9] The next highest substance – alcohol – was responsible for only half as many (44 per cent). Both cannabis and alcohol are substances to which some young people turn to help them manage their stress, anxiety or depression, which is a concern. Sadly, both can make mental health matters significantly worse, even if they might provide brief respite. After cannabis and alcohol, the numbers accessing treatment dropped considerably to 14 per cent who reported ecstasy use and thereafter 10 per cent who reported powder cocaine problems. Chapter 3 explores both short and longer term risks of the drugs more commonly used by young people, as well as a giving a detailed focus on cannabis, alcohol and MDMA.

The worst possible risk posed by drugs is, of course, fatality. Drug-related deaths in the most recent report were the highest on record.[10] The majority of fatalities due to illicit drug use are from older drug users, but the numbers had risen across all age groups. Of additional concern is the fact that the rate of increase of drug-related deaths has been far outstripping the increase in the rates of those using drugs. This suggests either riskier substances, riskier use or both.

---

[9]   Public Health England, (2019) Young people's substance misuse treatment statistics 2018 to 2019: report [online]. *Gov.uk*. Available from: <www.gov.uk/government/publications/substance-misuse-treatment-for-young-people-statistics-2018-to-2019/young-peoples-substance-misuse-treatment-statistics-2018-to-2019-report> (accessed November 2020)

[10]   ONS, (2019) Deaths related to drug poisoning in England and Wales: 2018 registrants [online] *ONS*. Available from: <www.ons.gov.uk/peoplepopulationandcommunity/birthsdeathsandmarriages/deaths/bulletins/deathsrelatedtodrugpoisoninginenglandandwales/2018registrations> (accessed November 2020)

Talking point

Ask your child which drugs they think cause the most problems for teenagers. They may (or may not) be surprised to hear what they are. This can be a useful starting point for a conversation about the risks of cannabis and alcohol.

Depending on the age of your child, this could also lead into a conversation about whether anyone they know, or someone in their year group they think – or know – is having problems with their drug use, and how this is affecting them, their friends, their family, the wider group of students. Witnessing, and reflecting on, the impact of drug use on someone they know can be an effective way for young people to consider the impact their own choices might have when they come along.

What about drugs education?

Many parents understandably assume that their child's school or college will be providing sufficient drugs and alcohol education. They also assume this is a statutory requirement. However, this only became the case from September 2020 – and only for schools in England and Wales, and only up to the end of GCSEs.[11] Some schools and colleges are doing drugs education well already, but many aren't – not because they doubt its importance or relevance, but for a range of perfectly valid and understandable reasons.

Pressures on school timetables are huge, and consequently the PSHE part of the curriculum has been forced out of lessons in many schools and squeezed into short and often busy form-time sessions at the start of the day, or into a few off-timetable days during the year when all those important subjects are studied in one intense hit. Pressures on school budgets are equally huge, meaning specialist support and teacher training that comes at a price is outside most budgets. A lack of evidence-based drugs and alcohol education resources and support

[11] Department for Education (2019) Relationships and sex education (RSE) and health education: statutory guidance [online]. *Gov.uk*. Available from: <www.gov.uk/government/publications/relationships-education-relationships-and-sex-education-rse-and-health-education> (accessed November 2020)

available to schools and colleges has meant that even if the budgets were there, effective education for young people is hard to find. This is precisely why we started the Daniel Spargo-Mabbs Foundation, and why I am writing this book.

The advent of mandatory Relationship, Sex and Health Education in secondary schools has coincided with the first full academic year under Covid-19, when pressures on schools, their staff and their budgets have been unlike any other, and the challenges of effective delivery of drugs education never greater. And yet young people have never more needed to be well armed with knowledge, understanding and life skills to make the choices that come their way safely, just at a time when schools are finding drugs and alcohol education most challenging to deliver to their students.

I wish I'd known I needed to know more about drugs these days

By Angela Nichols, mum of Joel (17)

Looking back at my son Joel's little life of not quite 18 years, he probably took more risks than the average child, but as parents we encouraged him to. The risks he was taking were ones we looked on as 'healthy risks', and we thought these healthier risks would counteract the more dangerous ones, like taking drugs.

A keen sportsman from the age of nine, Joel could be seen flying up and down a half pipe at the local skate park before moving on to judo, winning medals and certificates. And then it was rugby union. By the age of 11 Joel had taken up the position of hooker – arguably the most dangerous position in the team. You take both the weight of your own team on your shoulders in the scrum, as well as the pressing weight of the opposing team, but Joel was built physically and mentally for this position and he relished it. He became captain of both his school team and local RUFC club.

I had certainly taken a few less healthy risks in my own teenage years. The world was a very different place for me as a teenager. Growing up in the 80s and 90s on a deprived council estate, drugs and alcohol were normalized, and I did my share, but as soon as I could, I got out of there. I wanted better for my son.

Thirty years on, though, and drugs are not just 'normal life' on council estates, they are normal in all young people's lives, wherever they live. I wish I'd known more about what young people are taking these days. I wish I'd educated myself. I only found out on the night of Joel's death that MDMA came in powder form and could be put in a drink. I knew about ecstasy pills, but I'd never talked to Joel about the risks because he had an aversion to taking tablets and I knew he'd never touch them. I wish I could just rewind and have that conversation with him, leave some leaflets lying about for him to notice, discuss the 'start low, go slow' rule, just in case.

I wish I knew more, too, about the rising death rates in recent years from taking a party drug like MDMA. Here in the northeast of England, all the funding and focus is directed towards heroin and crack cocaine. These were the only drugs I thought you could lose your child to, not to a party drug taken for only the second time in a very short life. I wish I could have armed myself with the statistics, because Joel and I would have debated it over the dinner table like we did so many other things.

I wish every day that I could rewind to that last time I saw him alive. If I'd known more, perhaps I wouldn't now be dealing with the agony that ecstasy can bring.

Joel Nichols, with permission from Angela Nichols

2

I wish I'd known what drugs can do

Effects and risks

Most of us have, at some time or other, taken a psychoactive substance, whether it was our early morning cup of tea, a cold beer on a warm summer evening, or a sneaky teenage cigarette. Most of us have also used psychoactive substances specifically in order to change the way we feel in some way or other. A strong coffee after a rough night's sleep to help us make it through the morning. A glass of wine after a stressful day to help us relax. Even a bar of chocolate to take us to a better place when we're feeling down.

And this is nothing new. Historical evidence points to the use of psychoactive substances – from alcohol to ritualistic hallucinogens – across many cultures and many centuries stretching back thousands of years. Most of us won't have taken controlled drugs, but statistically, according to the most recent data (2019), around one in 11 people aged 16–59 years in England and Wales had done so during the previous year.[1]

This chapter begins to look at what drugs do and how they do it. It starts with what they began to do to Dan.

Dan's story: the rave

As the boys got off the last train, Jack said they could hear the beat of the bass coming from the rave. Leaving the station, they became merged into a crowd of teenagers, teeming along the streets towards the Silver Lane industrial estate.

It was around midnight when they got there. The rave organizers had commandeered two big empty industrial units adjacent to each other.

---

[1] Home Office, (2019) Drug misuse: findings from the 2018 to 2019 CSEW [online]. *Gov.uk*. Available from: <www.gov.uk/government/statistics/drug-misuse-findings-from-the-2018-to-2019-csew>
(accessed November 2020)

Jack said they were all directed into one of these and that when they stepped inside it appeared to be almost empty. Neither he nor Dan had been to a rave before, and he said he thought, 'Is this it?'

It wasn't, it was just security. Security at an illegal rave didn't mean age or ID checks, and it didn't mean drug checks. It meant taking their money, giving them wristbands, checking their bags for weapons. All the boys had made up stories for their parents, most of them saying they were staying over at a friend's house, including Jack, who'd carried his overnight bag all the way there with him. The bouncers confiscated his deodorant.

They went into the next building, an enormous dark space packed with people, with strobe lights and music at massive volume. Jack said as soon as they got there he wanted to go home. It didn't feel right. But they had no idea where they were, and he felt responsible for the others. He was one of the few with a sober head. They found a corner to set up a base, and Jack said he spent pretty much the whole night there, mostly with Dan. Dan was very talkative and affectionate, telling Jack his life story, telling everyone how much he loved them, how much he loved his family, how much he loved Jenna and how he was going to marry her. Looking back, Jack says that time with Dan was very special, but at the time it was disconcerting, and a little disturbing. Dan, but not Dan.

Most of them had taken their shirts off because it was so hot in there. Apparently, Dan was waving his around in the air. Dan and one of the other boys, Joel, went off from time to time, to explore or to dance. They were trying to find some water but without success. Then Joel came back without Dan. He'd lost track of him. They decided to go and look for him, but not in a rush or with concern because they didn't know there was anything to be concerned about. Just because that's what you do, you look out for your mates.

Jack said it felt like it took forever. It was so dark, there were all these flashing lights, teenagers crammed in dancing and all these different spaces, and no sign of Dan. In the end he went outside the building, and there he was, on the ground, in the rain, unconscious.

One of the boys from their group was there, and one of the rave staff was trying to get Dan to respond. Apparently, Dan had been dancing against a pillar, incoherent and not responding to questions, so someone had taken him outside to get some air and he'd collapsed so they'd propped him up against the wall. The boy that was with him didn't really know Dan, or Jack, and he thought Dan was Jack, and so they were calling out, 'Jack! Jack!' but he wasn't responding. Jack said, 'I'm Jack. His name's Daniel.' Jack was the only one who always called him Daniel – not Dan. So, they tried that, and he did respond a little, just the once. Someone had called for an ambulance, so they waited, in the dark and the rain.

This next little bit of my very incomplete jigsaw comes from the police officer who was first on the scene. I met him working in a school in Hillingdon some time after Dan had died, when he'd moved from the front line to become a Safer Schools police officer. I hadn't known this piece of the jigsaw even existed, and he didn't tell me about it till more than four years after Dan died. It was hard for him.

What he told me was that earlier that day they'd had intelligence there may be a rave in the borough later, but at that stage they had no idea where. They'd been out and about in the van anyway during the day, and were keeping an eye out, but saw no signs of anyone setting up or of people gathering. It wasn't until much later that night they heard it was on the Silver Lane industrial estate. The police have to gather sufficient forces before they can attempt to tackle something like an illegal rave because there are such big numbers there, made up of people who don't always have a cooperative attitude to the police breaking up the party, and a venue that may not be safe for mass evacuation.

By the time they'd been able to call enough officers in, got all the vans and cars over to the estate (which is huge) and started driving the streets to find the exact location, things had already started to go badly wrong for Dan. It was only when the paramedics' call came in that the police knew precisely where to go. This officer was trained in emergency response first aid, which is why it was he who was first out of the van, and first to get to the crowd of teenagers. They were standing around something on the ground. It was Dan. I could see as he was telling me this that the fact they hadn't been able to get there sooner was still difficult for him. It would have made little difference, but I guess a little difference may have helped, just a little.

Here's another jigsaw piece, this time from the report the paramedics wrote. Two weeks before Dan's inquest, around the time of his first anniversary, the coroner's office sent us a big brown envelope full of very upsetting reports from all the professional players in the processes surrounding his death. The paramedics' was the most upsetting of all the inquest papers. Most of the others didn't make much sense to someone not medically trained, and the interpretation necessary to understand them made them a little more distant, and softened the blow, just a little. The paramedics' report describes the very end of Dan's very last journey from conscious to unconscious. Impossible not to have that picture in my head. Impossible to shake away the question, what must that journey have felt like for Dan?

This report told me when they reached him Dan was unresponsive to voice or painful stimuli. He was moaning. His eyes were open, his pupils wide, and not responsive to light. There are lots of numbers here, which I was told meant his breathing was rapid and shallow, his blood pressure and his oxygen levels were both dangerously low, his pulse was dangerously fast, his temperature was dangerously high. They were unable to get a tube into his veins to get anything into his system fast, or even to get a spot of blood to check his blood sugar levels because his blood could no longer get that far. He was 'peripherally shut down'. They were unable to get a tube into his throat to get his oxygen levels up because his mouth was clamped tightly shut. By the time they got to the hospital they were unable to get a reading on his blood pressure.

The paramedics asked Jack if he knew our phone number, but of course he didn't. Why would he? He called Alice, who thought he was joking around. *Dan in an ambulance? Oh really? Hahaha! How could that possibly be serious?* But it was. She didn't have our number, but she did have our address.

The paramedics asked if Jack wanted to come in the ambulance, but Jack didn't feel he could leave the others there, and how would he get home when he didn't know where he was, and how would he explain it to his parents? And in any case, it never occurred to any of them that Dan wouldn't be alright. He was in the ambulance, being looked after and off to hospital where they'd sort him out. That's what they all thought. And, of course, that's almost always what happens.

And he was right not to go. He was just a lad, and what was happening to Dan was serious, it was going to get worse, and seeing it get worse at close quarters would have been deeply scarring. But that decision has been very hard for Jack to bear.

Back in Croydon, I'm ashamed to say I hadn't waited up for Dan to get home. If it'd been midnight, or even 1 am, I would have done but this was going to finish at 3 am – one of the reasons I was uncomfortable about the whole thing and needed some persuading. It was so late. I wasn't expecting Dan home till around 4.30 am, with buses and trains running infrequently in those early hours, which isn't far ahead of when we'd be getting up anyway. I woke around 2.30 am, though, and his room was still empty. It was what I was expecting, but I'd been hoping he'd be back, safe and sound and fast asleep. I started worrying – what if he wasn't OK, what if something had happened? – and trying to reassure myself in turn – he wasn't due back for a while yet, he was with his friends, Alice would look out for him and make sure he got home in one piece. But I couldn't switch off the worry, and it was a long while before I found I'd dozed off again.

Then it was 5 am. He still wasn't back. Now I really was worried. He'd never been back later than expected, and never been out so late before. I tried his phone. No answer. I left it a few minutes in case it was too noisy wherever he was to hear the phone, and tried again. Still no answer. I left a voicemail. I waited. I didn't know what I could do. I didn't have any of his friends' phone numbers. It was really late but not late enough to start calling the police and say my great big 16-year-old son was half an hour late home from a party.

I did have the number of the mum of one of his friends I had assumed (wrongly) would be there, and I made a plan. I like to have a plan because it makes me feel more in control, and I needed to try to control the panic. It was too early to call now, but I'd call at 8 am if he wasn't back by then, still early for a weekend but hopefully not too early, and anyway he'd surely be back by then. In the meantime I made a cup of tea and went back to bed with some marking from my class the previous morning, to try to make the time pass until I could make that call, or until Dan got back.

All the time, my head was racing – fear and panic interspersed with attempts at reassurance – his phone must just have run out of charge, the party must have overrun, they'd gone on to someone's house, they hadn't seen the time. A stream of reasonable explanations trying to batter down the increasingly overwhelming anxiety.

Where was he? Why wasn't he back?

At 5.30 am I heard the sound of a car pulling up outside, and our porch door opening. Thank goodness, he must have got a lift. Jumped out of bed, raced down the stairs, opened the door. But it wasn't Dan, it was a policeman, saying those words that are the beginning of every parent's worst nightmare. 'Are you the parents of Daniel Spargo-Mabbs?'

In that split second I thought, *either he's got caught up in something stupid and ended up getting in trouble with the police, or something very terrible has happened to him*, and in that split second I hoped it was the first and not the second. The first was probably more likely to be fixable than the second. The first may not mean my boy had been so badly hurt that the police were having to come and knock at my door.

Tim had also come down the stairs, ready to give a piece of his mind to whoever it was running their engine and slamming their doors in our road so early on a Saturday morning and waking him up. He had no idea Dan wasn't fast asleep in bed. I hadn't woken him. No need for both of us to worry. But there was this policeman saying all this stuff that didn't make any sense. Dan had been found unconscious outside a rave in Hillingdon, they thought he'd taken ecstasy, he had been taken to Hillingdon Hospital, he was in intensive care.

He couldn't tell us any more.

How had they got to Hillingdon from the party in Clapham? Where was Hillingdon, anyway? Ecstasy? I didn't understand. It didn't make any sense.

We had to get there. Panic. Think. *Right, get some clothes on, put some cereal bars and juice in a bag because we might be there a while, get Jacob up* (he was meant to be going back to university for his second term that weekend). *Work out where the hospital is, find the postcode, find the satnav, put the postcode into the satnav* (Tim did that bit). *Why is it taking so long to get out of the house?* We needed to get there and it felt as if everything was stuck in slow motion. I'd had nightmares – probably a standard mum nightmare – where I could see something awful about to happen to one of the boys and just couldn't make myself move quickly enough to get to them in time. It was like that, apart from that in the nightmares I always woke up before the awful thing happened.

Tim drove to the hospital while I texted everyone I could think of asking them to pray for Dan. He was in intensive care. He'd taken ecstasy. That was all we knew, but we knew that was very serious. We remembered Leah Betts. We knew one pill could kill.

How do drugs work?

Put simply, psychoactive drugs do what they do by making alterations to the brain's natural functioning, and consequently in order to understand how drugs work it helps to have a basic understanding of how the brain works first. This is also useful for understanding how drugs can cause harm, and again in Chapter 4 when we come to consider teenage decision-making and the role of the developing adolescent brain.

The brain is the most complex part of the human body, and the extent of this complexity is being more fully understood on a continual basis, as technology develops that enables it to be studied in greater detail. What follows is my attempt to simplify something very complicated for anyone like me whose own brain goes into fog mode when it encounters anything remotely like a biology lesson (apologies to all science teachers).

A (very) basic guide to how the brain works

The human brain contains around 100 billion nerve cells (**neurons**). Each neuron has a long tail-like part (**axons**) and lots of branches (**dendrites**). Neurons send messages to other neurons by passing electrical currents along their axon into the dendrites of other neurons across very tiny gaps in between them (**synapses**). In order to cross the gap, the electrical current needs a chemical (**a neurotransmitter**), which connects to specific sites on the second neuron (**receptors**). It's this communication network that is responsible for all our activity – how we think, how we feel, how we experience the world, what we do. Much of this is totally subconscious but vital to life, like breathing or keeping our heart beating.

There are many different types of neurotransmitter, and many different corresponding types of receptor, that need to fit together in order for the communication to take place. The metaphor of a key in a lock is often used for this. Once correctly connected, this sets up an electrical current in the second neuron, that process is repeated into a third neuron, and so on, at lightning speed. Neurotransmitters fall into two basic categories: some increase the likelihood of the next neuron generating an electrical current and others reduce this. The ones that amplify the current are called **excitatory**, and the ones that dampen it down are called **inhibitory**.

This happens not just along individual chains of communication but more often incredibly complex networks of communication (**neural networks**) and junctions between several networks will meet at a single synapse. The synapse at each junction acts as a gatekeeper, allowing or preventing signals from getting through. On the massive scale and speed at which the brain is operating, these individual gates being opened or closed can speed up or slow down activity across whole networks.

How drugs do what they do

Psychoactive drugs change people's feelings, thoughts and mood, and their behaviour and levels of consciousness, by taking over and making alterations to these natural communication systems inside the brain. It's generally at the synapse, that junction between neural networks where the signal between neurotransmitters and receptors can be tuned up or down, that psychoactive drugs do their work. How individual drugs do what they do in relation to different neurotransmitters and receptors is complex. On a basic level they can tune the signals up or slow them down, but they can do this in relation to different neurotransmitters, each of which has a different range of functions, some of which overlap. In the process they disturb their natural balance and functioning.

Drugs fall into four broad categories based on the primary way in which they influence these messaging systems. **Stimulants** speed things up, **sedatives** slow things down, **hallucinogens** create distortions and **dissociatives** detach the body from the mind. These effects often overlap, for example MDMA is primarily a stimulant but can also affect sensory perceptions and can have hallucinogenic effects. Sometimes categories are divided up further to reflect the unique ways in which individual drugs affect the user, for example, MDMA can be categorized as an empathogen because of the way it increases users' capacity for empathy and social connectedness, and cannabis is often put into a category of its own because it operates on the brain in a different way to any other substance.

The differences and similarities in the ways drugs affect the person using them is largely down to the particular neurotransmitters they affect, as well as the way in which they affect them. The primary neurotransmitters that psychoactive drugs can affect include: **dopamine,** responsible for pleasure and reward (cocaine, amphetamines); **serotonin** which helps us manage mood, appetite, libido and sleep (MDMA, cocaine, LSD); **cannabinoids**, responsible for learning, memory, concentration, motivation, mood and appetite (cannabis); **noradrenalin**, which also affects memory and mood, as well as sleep and levels of anxiety (cocaine, amphetamines); **glutamate**, responsible for learning, memory and cognition (ketamine, alcohol); **GABA**, which affects levels of anxiety, memory, and can act as an anaesthetic (benzodiazepines, alcohol); **opioid**, which provides pain relief and sedation and affects our mood (heroin, morphine, codeine).

As Dan's is a story of MDMA, let's use this as an example. MDMA (3,4-Methylenedioxymethamphetamine) is a synthetic drug with a stimulant effect which alters mood and perception and makes users typically feel energized, euphoric, empathetic and with heightened sensory awareness. It does this by acting on neurotransmitters to increase the release of the chemicals **serotonin** (regulation of mood), **dopamine** (pleasure and reward) and **norepinephrine** (alertness and arousal). MDMA also has the effect of increasing the levels of **oxytocin**, the hormone that promotes feelings of love, bonding and well-being, and also the hormone **vasopressin** which plays a role in social behaviour, sexual motivation and bonding.

Norepinephrine also creates a stimulant effect by increasing the heart rate and raising both blood pressure and body temperature. Too much can take these to dangerous levels, however. An excess of serotonin does the same, and this also causes muscle rigidity and muscle spasms – the jaw grinding and 'gurning' effect often seen in people who have taken MDMA, and the locked jaw Dan experienced. The release of excessive amounts of serotonin causes the brain to become seriously depleted of this important neurotransmitter and it takes a few days for them to be restored, leading to low moods following use. Vasopressin also has antidiuretic effects, and this causes urine retention and reduces the concentration of sodium in the body, which can be very risky and cause kidney damage.

There is much more than this going on, and all these effects in themselves can lead to a whole heap more trouble and complications.

It's beyond the scope of this book to explore more than a few individual drugs in detail, but below is a table which brings together some headline information specifically for parents who want to know a bit more about the drugs that their children may find themselves making decisions about. What does it look like if you were to find it in a pocket or lying around after a teenage gathering at your home? What effects are people looking for when they take it? How is it taken? What signs might you see if someone had been using it? How long would these last? What are the side effects, and the risks in the short and longer terms, to both physical and mental health? Alcohol isn't included in the table only because most parents will be more than aware of the answers to these questions for that particular substance, but it has its own focus further on in the chapter. More detailed information about individual drugs can be found on the websites referenced at the back.[2]

A parents' inside guide to drugs

Stimulants: cocaine and MDMA

	Cocaine	Ecstasy/MDMA
What does it look like?	Fine white powder. Crack cocaine appears as tiny yellowish, shiny 'rocks', but is rarely used by young people in this form.	Pills (ecstasy) come in various shapes and colours, often with designs and logos which appeal to young people. MDMA powder is slightly off-white and crystalline.
Paraphernalia?	Mirror, razor blade, small tubes of rolled up paper/straws. Often supplied in tiny plastic ziplock bags.	Often supplied in tiny plastic ziplock bags.
How is it taken?	Powder cocaine is generally snorted in lines or piles through a straw or rolled up piece of paper.	Ecstasy tablets are swallowed. MDMA powder is also generally swallowed, often in a gel cap or wrapped in cigarette paper known as 'bombs', or dissolved in water. Sometimes people dab it on their gums. It can also be snorted, either by crushing pills or as powder.

---

[2] Information sourced from Talk to Frank <www.talktofrank.com/>, Drug Science <drugscience.org.uk/> and Drugs and Me <www.drugsand.me/en/>

Onset and duration?	Onset: 1–3 mins Duration: 30 mins	Onset: 20–70mins Duration: 3–5hrs After-effects: up to 24hrs
Signs of use?	Unusually energetic, talkative, confident. Pupil dilation, decreased appetite, insomnia, headaches, runny nose/ congestion/nasal bleeding. Feeling tired, low and anxious in the hours or days following use.	Unusually upbeat, energetic, affectionate, talkative. Dilated pupils. Raised body temperature, jaw clenching, dehydration, vomiting. Insomnia. Depression or low mood 2–3 days after use. See 'down sides' below.
What's the appeal?	It can make users feel euphoric, alert, energetic, talkative, happy, super-confident.	It can make users feel ecstatically happy, uninhibited, affectionate, energetic. It also causes alertness, meaning people feel very 'in the moment' and attuned to their environment. It can increase sensitivity to touch and enhance appreciation of music, which is why it's often used at music events.
Down sides?	It can make users feel anxious, impulsive, agitated, aggressive.	It can cause jaw clenching and teeth grinding, hallucinations, raised body temperature, nausea and vomiting, erectile dysfunction, insomnia. MDMA use often causes 'come downs' which can last a few days, sometimes longer. The effects of these can include depression, anxiety, panic attacks, confusion, paranoia and, very rarely, psychosis.

Short-term risks?	Cocaine can make people over-confident, impulsive, arrogant and aggressive which can lead to uncharacteristically argumentative and even violent behaviour. Mixing with other drugs, particularly with alcohol, risks damage to the heart and liver. Bingeing on cocaine can cause episodes of psychosis and paranoid delusions. Cocaine raises body temperature, blood pressure and heart-rate, and narrows blood vessels, all of which can result in strokes, organ failure, seizures and heart attacks, all of which can be fatal.	Short-term risks relate primarily to overheating and dehydration. Raised body temperature and increased heart rate can lead to strokes and heart attacks, damage to internal organs and fatality. Dehydration can be caused in part by raised temperature and by MDMA stopping the body releasing a hormone it needs to make urine. Drinking excess water can also cause health risks and fatality.
Long-term risks?	Regular use can lead to depression, anxiety, paranoia and psychosis, damage to membranes, cartilage and even bone in the nose and head through snorting cocaine, and to addiction.	Regular use can lead to problems with memory and concentration, sleep, energy levels, appetite, mood and immunity. It can also lead to depression and anxiety. Reduced levels of sodium can damage kidneys.

Cocaine powder *Credit: © Shutterstock.com*

Ecstasy pills *Credit: © Shutterstock.com*

Depressants/sedatives: cannabis and benzodiazepines

	Cannabis	Benzodiazepines
What does it look like?	Dried grass or furry green leaves/buds (herbal cannabis), golden liquid (liquid cannabis), black or brown lump (hash or resin), translucent golden sheets or pieces (shatter). Edibles come in a variety of foods.	Tablets or capsules in a variety of colours. Includes diazepam, temazepam, Valium, Rohypnol, Xanax.
Paraphernalia?	Grinders, tiny plastic ziplock bags or various plastic pots smelling of cannabis, cigarette papers, small rolls or pieces of card/filters, pipes, bongs.	Could be sold in tiny plastic ziplock bags, bottles or blister packs.
How is it taken?	Usually smoked with tobacco but can also be used with a pipe or bong. Oils can be put into vaping devices. Edibles are eaten.	Swallowed. Less commonly used as suppositories.
Onset and duration?	Smoking/vaping: Start: 2–10 minutes Duration: 2–8 hours After-effects: up to 24 hours Edibles: Start: 20–120 minutes Duration: 3–9 hours After-effects: up to 24 hours	Depends on the type of benzodiazepine, dose and individual, but broadly: Onset: 15–40 minutes Duration: 5–8 hours After-effects: 6-24 hours
Signs of use?	Giggly, chatty, hungry. Lethargic and demotivated. Anxious and paranoid.	Unusual levels of relaxation and calm, loss of coordination, slurred or slowed speech, confusion, drowsiness.

What's the appeal?	Cannabis can make people feel relaxed, giggly, chatty and sociable. Some people use it to self-medicate to manage their anxiety.	Benzos can induce periods of calmness, relaxation and drowsiness. Used as 'chill-out' drugs. Some people use them to self-medicate to manage their anxiety. They're sometimes used to 'come down' or sleep after using stimulants or hallucinogens.
Down sides?	Can affect learning, memory, concentration, mood, motivation. Can cause nausea, anxiety, paranoia and panic attacks. Can also lead to dependency, and some cases to psychosis.	Can cause poor concentration and memory, dizziness, slurred speech, confusion, loss of coordination, amnesia, loss of consciousness. Can also cause depression and suicidal thoughts.
Short-term risks?	Impairment of learning and memory can negatively affect functioning at school, college or work. Loss of coordination and impairment of judgement can lead to accidents, especially if driving.	Risks of accidents and assault because of loss of coordination and control and impaired judgement. If taken with other sedative drugs, including alcohol, breathing can be supressed or stopped, leading to severe harm and fatality.
Long-term risks?	Mental health risks from cannabis include anxiety, paranoia, panic attacks, and more extremely it can cause, or trigger, psychotic episodes or illnesses. Smoking cannabis can affect breathing and worsen conditions like asthma. Smoking with tobacco will carry the same long-term risks including cancer.	Regular use can lead to increased tolerance, higher levels of use and addiction. Withdrawal can be dangerous and must be managed carefully.

Cannabis hash *Credit: © Shutterstock.com*

Cannabis bud, joints and grinder *Credit: © Shutterstock.com*

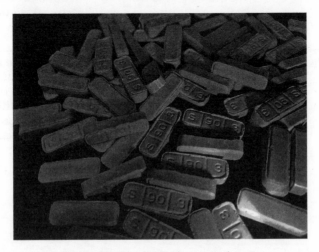

Xanax pills *Credit: © Shutterstock.com*

Hallucinogens: LSD and magic mushrooms

	LSD	Magic mushrooms
What does it look like?	Small squares/tabs of paper with pictures on. Also found as a liquid or as tiny pellets known as microdots, but less commonly used by young people in these forms.	Magic mushrooms is a term usually used to describe mushrooms that contain the psychoactive chemical psilocybin. The most common type in the UK are called 'liberty caps', which are small and tan coloured. They can be picked from fields in the autumn time. They are sold in raw or dried forms, although liquid psilocybin is also available.
Paraphernalia?	n/a	n/a
How is it taken?	Tabs are swallowed, usually after being placed under the tongue for around ten minutes. Liquid is dropped onto the tongue. Microdots are swallowed.	Liberty caps are usually dried and eaten. Sometimes they are cooked, for example in an omelette. Dried mushrooms can be made into tea.
Onset and duration?	Start: 30–90 minutes Peak: 2–3 hours Duration: 9–14 hours	Start: 20 minutes Peak: 30–45 minutes Duration: up to 6 hours
Signs of use?	Hallucinogenic effects will be experienced by individuals very differently. They may be clearly hallucinating, or may just be euphoric, giggly or excited. They may also be anxious, withdrawn, agitated or paranoid.	These will be similar to LSD, depending on dose. Mushrooms can also cause nausea, stomach aches and headaches and feeling generally wiped out.

What's the appeal?	LSD can create altered sensory experiences, including distortions and intensification of visual and auditory effects, and changes in the sense of time and place. This can lead to feelings of euphoria, connectedness and self-awareness. Some people report intense spiritual experiences.	Mushrooms can cause visual and auditory hallucinations, changes in consciousness and mood, and can create distortions in colours, sounds, objects and time. This can lead to feelings of euphoria and self-awareness. Some people experience this as spiritual, and others as interesting and fun.
Down sides?	A 'bad trip' can be very frightening, disturbing and overwhelming and can last several hours without any escape until the effects wear off.	As with LSD, the experience can be frightening and disorientating. Physically, people can also experience nausea and stomach pains, headaches and exhaustion, which can last for a couple of days.
Short-term risks?	Having an accident or hurting someone else under the influence of hallucinations.	The biggest immediate risk is eating a poisonous mushroom by mistake. There's also a risk of having an accident because of the effect on coordination and judgement.
Long-term risks?	Mental health problems can be exacerbated. Flashbacks or ongoing visual distortions can be experienced, and some users experience symptoms of post-traumatic stress disorder (hyphen and lowercase) caused by traumatic hallucinations.	Mental health problems can be exacerbated. Flashbacks can be experienced that can be frightening.

LSD tabs *Credit: © Shutterstock.com*

Magic mushrooms *Credit: © Shutterstock.com*

Dissociatives: nitrous oxide and ketamine

	Nitrous oxide	Ketamine
What does it look like?	Clear gas inside small silver cannisters approximately 6 cm long.	Mostly a grainy or fine crystalline powder that can be white, off-white or brown. Also available in tablets and as liquid but liquid ketamine is less common for young people.
Paraphernalia?	Balloons, 'chargers' or 'crackers' (metal cylinders approximately 2–3 cm diameter and 8 cm long which unscrew to fit a cannister inside)	Powder and tablets often supplied in tiny plastic ziplock bags. Liquid in small clear bottles.
How is it taken?	Gas is generally extracted from cannisters into balloons, from which it can be inhaled. Less commonly it can be used directly from a full-size gas cylinder, sometimes used to fill a confined space such as a car or a plastic bag.	Powder is usually snorted in little piles, often referred to as 'bumps'. Powder can also be swallowed, often in a gel cap or wrapped in a cigarette paper known as a 'bomb'. Tablets are swallowed. Liquid is injected, which is why it's uncommon for young people.
Onset and duration?	Start: immediate Duration: 2–3 minutes (or up to 20–30 minutes if larger amounts are taken)	Snorted: Start: 5–15 minutes Duration: 40–60 minutes After-effects: 1–3 hours Orally: Start: 5–20 minutes Duration: 90 minutes After-effects: 4–8 hours
Signs of use?	Euphoria, calmness, giggles (hence the nickname 'laughing gas'). Numbness and tingling in limbs.	Chilled, relaxed, dream-like. People may move and speak more slowly and may not make sense.

What's the appeal?	It can make people feel very happy and laugh a lot. It can also make people feel disconnected from themselves, and feel calm and relaxed.	It can make people feel calm and serene, euphoric and more connected to the world. For some the appeal is also the distortions of sensory perceptions and perceptions of time and reality, and the sense of dissociation of their mind from their body, which can be very intense and, for some, a spiritual experience. Complete dissociation of the body and mind is sometimes referred to as a 'k-hole'.
Down sides?	It can cause dizziness and headaches, tingling and numbness, and, less commonly, hallucinations and paranoia.	Distortions of reality, hallucinations and dissociation can be confusing and disturbing. For some people the 'k-hole' experience is terrifying. Loss of control of body movements and balance. Loss of consciousness.
Short-term risks?	Having an accident because of the way it affects balance and coordination and causes numbness. Compressed gas can cause explosions if it's in faulty dispensers. When the gas is released both it and the metal become very cold and this can cause frostbite of the lips, mouth and vocal cords if inhaled direct from a charger or cylinder. The gas prevents oxygen reaching the brain and so if too much is consumed over too long a period of time this can cause unconsciousness, and potentially brain damage and fatality.	Loss of balance and coordination can lead to accidents, and because ketamine is an anaesthetic people may injure themselves without knowing. Loss of feeling, paralysis of muscles, disconnection with reality and risk of unconsciousness makes people vulnerable to injury and assault. Ketamine can be fatal if used with other drugs, especially alcohol.

Long-term risks?	Use of nitrous oxide inactivates vitamin B12 reserves in the body, which can lead to mental health issues such as depression, and to nerve and brain damage. Symptoms can include severe weakness of arms and legs, and in some cases paralysis.	Tolerance builds up quickly leading to higher levels of use. Some people develop addiction to ketamine and experience withdrawal. Long-term use of ketamine can affect memory, learning and concentration. It can cause urinary problems and damage the kidneys and bladder. This can lead to pain urinating and incontinence, and in extreme cases require a stoma or bladder transplant.

Nitrous oxide canister, balloon and charger *Credit: © Shutterstock.com*

Ketamine powder and liquid *Credit: © Shutterstock.com*

The world's most widely used legal substance: alcohol

Alcohol is one of the psychoactive substances which is most readily available to young people. It's enjoyed by many of their parents, its use is culturally accepted in the UK, and its misuse tolerated often with wry amusement. However, alcohol also does a lot of damage, and in a lot of ways. According to NHS England data, 12–15 per cent of A&E attendances are alcohol-related and over 1.1 million hospital admissions a year are due to alcohol. The average age of people dying from an alcohol-specific cause is 54.4 years, compared to 77.6 for all other causes.[3] Its use is linked to liver disease, heart disease, diabetes and various cancers, as well as mental illnesses.

However, the average teenager is likely to be no more concerned about any of these longer-term risks for themselves than they are about their pension prospects. Conversations with teenagers can more usefully focus on the immediate risks to them, from which there are also plenty to choose.

The good news is that more young people are making healthier choices about alcohol now than they have in many years. A study looking at the drinking habits of 16- to 24-year-olds, published in 2018 to great rejoicing from the media, showed that around one in three described themselves as non-drinkers, 17 per cent had never touched a drop in their lives, and half of those who did drink hadn't done so in the past week. With school-age children only 9 per cent of 11- to 15-year-olds had drunk alcohol in the past week, and more than half had never tried alcohol at all.[4]

However, heavy drinking is still an issue, with around a third of 16- to 24-year-olds who had drunk alcohol in the past week having drunk relatively heavily, consuming between 9 (women) and 12 (men) units

---

[3]   NHS England, Alcohol Care Teams [online]. NHS. Available from: <www.england.nhs.uk/ltphimenu/prevention/alcohol-care-teams/> (accessed November 2020)

[4]   NHS Digital, (2019) Smoking, drinking and drug use among young people in England 2018 [online]. *NHS*. Available from: <digital.nhs.uk/data-and-information/publications/statistical/smoking-drinking-and-drug-use-among-young-people-in-england> (accessed November 2020)

on average on their heaviest drinking day.[5] This is where the risks come from for young people, because of the way alcohol works on the brain, and the way it affects balance, coordination, decision-making and judgement. The risks to young people fall into three key areas: emergency admissions, violent or property crime and high-risk intercourse. And at the worst end of harm, alcohol poisoning is something children and young people are much more vulnerable to than adults, because their levels of tolerance are lower and their livers are underdeveloped and unable to cope if they are overloaded.

The most recent guidance from the UK Chief Medical Officer is that an alcohol-free childhood is the best and safest option, and children should not drink alcohol until they are at least 15 because of the lasting damage it can do to their developing brain, bones, liver and hormones. Drinking at an early age is also associated with a range of risky behaviours as well as poor mental health, including suicidal thoughts and attempts.[6] Studies have shown that drinking below the age of 14 also increased the risk of developing alcohol dependency in later life, and often before reaching mid-twenties.[7] And yet a Drinkaware survey revealed that the average age for a first drink is 13.4 years and the average age for getting drunk for the first time is 14.2 years.[8]

Parents play a vital role in helping their children develop a healthy and responsible relationship with alcohol. Parents are the most influential role models to their children in so many things throughout

---

[5] ONS, (2018) Adult drinking habits in Great Britain [online]. *ONS*. Available from: <www.ons.gov.uk/peoplepopulationandcommunity/healthandsocialcare/drugusealcoholandsmoking/datasets/adultdrinkinghabits> (accessed November 2020)

[6] NHS, Should my child drink alcohol? [online]. *NHS*. Available from: <www.nhs.uk/common-health-questions/childrens-health/should-my-child-drink-alco­hol/> (accessed November 2020)

[7] Hingson, R.W. et al (2006) Age at drinking onset and alcohol dependence. *Archives of Pediatrics and Adolescent Medicine* [online]. July, 160(7):739–46. Available from: DOI: 10.1001/archpedi.160.7.739

[8] IPSOS MORI (2015) Drinkaware Monitor 2014: Young people's and their parents' drinking behaviour and their attitudes [online]. *Drinkaware*. Available from: <www.drinkaware.co.uk/research/research-and-evaluation-reports/drinkaware-monitor-young-people-report> (accessed November 2020)

childhood and adolescence, and parental attitudes to alcohol and their own drinking behaviours can make a big difference to their children, for better or worse. Some useful advice and guidance can be found on websites at the end of the book.

Talking point

The Alcohol Education Trust Talk About Alcohol website has a tool – 'How much is too much' – that you can use with your child to look up how many units of alcohol there are in different alcoholic drinks, work out together how much a unit would be, and use fruit juice or water to measure this into a tumbler to see what it looks like, so they would know how to gauge how many units they may be consuming when they are out with friends.

Talk through possible scenarios with your children where people have become drunk and the various harms that they may have experienced or risked experiencing. There may have been situations your teenagers have been in where friends have drunk too much, and there are often scenes in films or TV dramas you might be watching together that could be a prompt for a conversation.

There are some useful resources for 11- to 16-year-olds you can explore together on the Talk About Alcohol website, including videos and interactive games like the 'alcohol clock' game.

The world's most widely used (mostly) illegal substance: cannabis

As we've seen (Chapter 1), cannabis is the most widely used controlled drug around the world, by young people as well as adults. It is also the drug responsible for the vast majority of young people in treatment needing it. Public attitudes towards cannabis and its perceived risks and benefits have undergone significant shifts over recent years. Global as well as national debates have been taking place about drug policy reform, and laws have been passed legalizing cannabis for treating certain medical conditions in many parts of the world, including the UK. Laws have also been changed in fewer, but increasing numbers of parts of the world, allowing recreational use of cannabis for adults. CBD, a cannabis product, is being sold legitimately in many well-known high street shops and online, and marketed – with not always the same legitimacy – as a health product able to do much good in many different ways to many people.

All of this sends a confusing message to teenagers when it comes to estimating the risks to them of using cannabis, and in adolescence these risks can be significant. These relate in particular to the strength of the cannabis being used and the use of it when their brains are undergoing such an important stage of development.

The two main chemicals of significance in the cannabis plant are tetrahydrocannabinol (THC) and cannabidiol (CBD). THC is responsible for the psychoactive effects of cannabis, and CBD mitigates some of these, and so the balance of these two chemicals is important in relation to the effect cannabis can have on the person using it. One of the major concerns with cannabis in the UK in recent years is that levels of THC have increased dramatically, since the days when parents were young and may have experienced it themselves.[9] At the same time, levels of CBD have fallen. It's this shifting balance that's largely responsible for the negative impact cannabis is having on young people. The rising popularity, and availability, of cannabis concentrates, including edibles, has taken this to another level still, and branding often specifically targets a young consumer.

The adolescent brain is undergoing a crucial stage of development (we'll look at this more closely in Chapter 4) and is consequently particularly vulnerable to the harmful effects of all psychoactive drugs, and cannabis more than some others. In parts of the world where cannabis is legal for recreational use, this is always only the case for adults for this reason. Cannabinoids in cannabis copy the effects of the brain's natural endocannabinoid system, which plays a role in learning, memory, concentration, mood and motivation. This is why cannabis can affect all of these things just at a time in life when they are all particularly valuable to young people who are taking exams and making decisions that can affect future life opportunities. Heavy or daily use in adolescence can make people prone to paranoia and panic attacks and can lead to mental illnesses including depression and

---

[9] Potter D.J. et. al., (2018) Potency of Δ9–tetrahydrocannabinol and other cannabinoids in cannabis in England in 2016: Implications for public health and pharmacology. *Drug Testing and Analysis* [online]. 10(4), 619–627, i, 628–795. Available from: DOI: 10.102/dta.2368

anxiety, and more seriously to psychosis. One in five of all new cases of psychosis are associated with daily cannabis use, according to recent research, and one in ten with the use of high potency cannabis.[10] An estimated one in ten teenagers who use cannabis will develop cannabis dependency, and the more frequently they smoke, and the stronger the strain, the greater this likelihood is.[11]

One of the tricky things with teenagers and cannabis is that its harmful effects take some time to become apparent, by which point the harm can be hard to recognize for the individual user. The good news is that much of this harm can be undone when cannabis use is reduced or stopped. Most groups of parents to whom we speak, however, will include at least one person who knows somebody whose life, or whose child's life, will never be the same because of their use of cannabis in adolescence. In Chapter 8 we will hear from one of these parents.

For more detailed information about the effects and risks of cannabis, have a look at the websites provided at the end of this book.

Talking point

A conversation about medicinal cannabis is useful to dispel any myths or misconceptions your child may have. Illegally produced and sourced cannabis can seem 'safe' by its association with a product that's used by doctors to make people better. The conversation about the risks of medicines generally comes in here, and it's also worth highlighting the fact that the time it has taken for medicinal cannabis to begin to be more widely prescribed after the UK law changed demonstrates how seriously the risks of cannabis in particular are taken by the medical profession and government. At the time of writing, access to medicinal cannabis is still very limited, to the frustration of many.

---

[10] Di Fiorti, M. et. al., (2019) The contribution of cannabis use to variation in the incidence of psychotic disorder across Europe (EU-GEI): a multicentre case-control study. *The Lancet Psychiatry* [online]. Available from: DOI: 10.1016/S2215-0366(19)30048.

[11] Volkow N.D. et. al. (2016) Adverse health effects of marijuana use. *The New England Journal of Medicine* [online]. 370: 2219–2227. Available from: DOI: 10.1056/NEJMra1402309

Smoking and vaping

According to the World Health Organization, the smoking of tobacco is responsible for eight million deaths around the globe every year.[12] That said, it's encouraging to know the numbers of children and teenagers smoking in the UK has fallen steadily over the years, thanks to education, public health messaging and legislative changes that have made it increasingly difficult and expensive for under-18s to get hold of cigarettes or tobacco. In 1996 a third of 15-year-olds in England described themselves as regular smokers in the government's school survey, the highest level since it began. By 2018 this had fallen to just one in 20, but that's still more than is ideal for the leading cause of preventable death the world over.

Tobacco smoke contains over 5000 chemicals, including nicotine, but it's not the nicotine that causes the cancers and all the other smoking-related health harms. That's down to the tar and other chemicals, some more than others. What the nicotine does is to make people want to keep smoking, because it's a highly addictive psychoactive substance, and that's how the damage is done. Consequently, many alternatives to smoking have been developed over the years that still contain the nicotine people's brains have become primed to need but without all the harmful components of tobacco. One of the most recent of these alternatives is e-cigarettes, or vaping, and this is the one that has proved most popular with pre-teens and teens, whether smokers or not.

'Popular' may be an exaggeration, however, despite the concerns of many schools. According to the government school survey data, only 4 per cent of 15-year-olds were regular vapers, although 41 per cent had tried it. The vast majority of these were current smokers, though 14 per cent were vaping without ever having smoked a cigarette in their lives. However, attitudes to vaping in this age group are certainly more tolerant than those towards smoking. Whereas less than half thought it was OK to try a cigarette to see what it's like, when it comes to vaping it shoots up to almost two thirds who

---

[12] World Health Organization. Tobacco: key facts [online]. *World Health Organization.* Available from: <www.who.int/news-room/fact-sheets/detail/tobacco> (accessed November 2020)

consider it acceptable to give it a go. This is possibly to do with the positive health messages around vaping as a smoking cessation device, in contrast to the years of negative publicity around smoking. It is indeed better in many ways than burning tobacco, but there is still so much that remains unknown about this relatively new player in the substance use field, and the damage it might be doing, especially to adolescents.

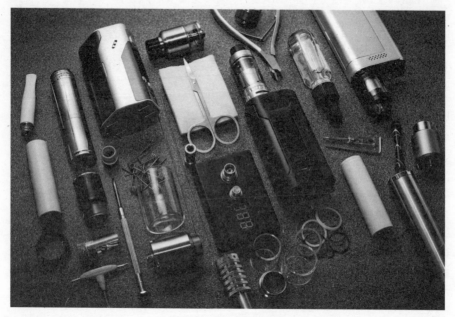

Variety of vaping devices *Credit: © Shutterstock.com*

In many ways vaping is like smoking in its early years, in terms of public health. E-cigarettes arrived in the UK less than 15 years ago, and so no longitudinal health studies are available because it hasn't been around long enough, and there is very little research into the risks specific to adolescents because they're not supposed to be doing it. However, there are considerable concerns in the medical profession about the effect on people's hearts and lungs, and for adolescents there are additional issues with vaping, one of which is the fact that the majority of vape liquids contain nicotine.

There is strong evidence to show that exposure to nicotine in the sensitive stage of neurological development that is adolescence can lead to a 'gateway' effect when it comes to other drugs. Nicotine acts on receptors in the adolescent brain, which stimulate reward-related neurotransmitters, which in turn create functional changes in the brain that primes it to seek the rewards that substance use can bring.[13] In addition to this, the fact that the data shows just as many teenagers are getting their products online as from shops, means they're likely to be using substances that are unlicensed and unregulated, as well as vaping products that contain illegal substances, especially cannabis, and that in itself is cause for concern. Too much is unknown, and there are many years of research ahead before the risks and benefits, and the balance of the two, are fully understood.

Talking point

It can be difficult to spot if your child is vaping because liquids come in so many flavours that can smell just like sweets, they can emit very little smoke, and devices come in all sorts of shapes and forms so they can look just like familiar items such as memory sticks or pens.

Bringing the risks into your conversations is probably the most useful approach. Talk about the fact the risks of vaping are not yet known, especially to under-18s, and about the fact nicotine makes changes to the developing adolescent brain that can genuinely lead to that ('yeah mum/dad such a cliché!') gateway effect with other drugs. Look at adverts around and about and talk about whether vaping is being promoted as a healthier alternative to smoking or as a lifestyle choice. Knowing the tobacco industry is so heavily invested in making a profit from people vaping might help build resistance in a cynical teenager unwilling to be manipulated by big business, especially one that does so much damage worldwide.

---

[13] Ren, M. & Lotfipour, S., (2019) Nicotine gateway effects on adolescent substance use. *Western Journal of Emergency Medicine* [online]. 20(5): 696–709. Available from: DOI: 10.5811/westjem.2019.7.41661

Prescription medication

Just as many of the drugs listed above were originally developed for medicinal purposes, prescription drugs are also used recreationally, and sometimes problematically, by some young people and adults. Prescription drug misuse has been defined as 'taking a medication in a manner or dose other than prescribed; taking someone else's prescription, even if for a legitimate medical complaint such as pain; or taking a medication to feel euphoria'.[14] For adults these are more commonly opioid and sedative drugs, but for young people this can also include stimulant drugs, for example Ritalin, which is used to treat ADHD. It can also include drugs which are sold over the counter in other parts of the world but that may not be available in the UK, such as the cough syrup used to make lean (a cough syrup drink usually containing codeine and promethazine, anantihistamine. All of these are of course available online, though inevitably more commonly acquired through friends.[15]

For young people aware of the risky nature of illegally produced 'street' drugs, prescription drugs can seem like a safer option. However much they may be aware in theory that medicines have risks, there can be an underlying sense that because we get them from doctors, figures of authority and guardians of public health, that in and of itself provides protection from harm. Young people can assume they'll have been produced under strict and safe conditions, but unless they've been able to get hold of someone else's medication, or they've been sold prescription drugs that have been lifted from the legitimate pharmaceutical supply chain at some point along the way, this is unlikely to be the case.

Supplying controlled drugs to anyone off-prescription is illegal in the UK, and so even if a drug has the name and appearance of

[14] National Institute on Drug Abuse, (2020) Misuse of Prescription Drugs Research Report [online]. *NIDA*. Available from: <www.drugabuse.gov/download/37630/misuse-prescription-drugs-research-report.pdf?v=add4ee202a1d-1f88f8e1fdd2bb83a5ef> (accessed November 2020)

[15] Novak, S. et. al., (2016) Non-medical use of prescription drugs in the European Union [online]. *BMC Psychiatry*. 16, Article number: 274. Available from: DOI: 10.1186/s12888-016-0909-3

something they'd expect to have come from a pharmacy, it was most likely produced in a back-street pill press with the same degree of unpredictability of its contents and potency as any illegally produced drugs. Online pharmacies can seem like a safer option, but many of these are unregulated, as are the medicines they supply, and anything sold off-prescription is done so illegally. And even if young people get a product that was produced under strict conditions by the UK pharmaceutical industry, and it's exactly what it's meant to be, they are self-medicating with a drug which is intended to be available only on prescription because of the risks involved in its use, and which would be prescribed for a condition they almost certainly don't have.

Practical points

Make sure you're aware of any prescription medication around the house, and keep anything you have somewhere safe, especially if there's a party or friends of your child are coming over, just in case. Anything no longer needed should be taken to a pharmacist for safe disposal.

- Ongoing conversations about the risks of medicines are, again, important.

I wish I'd known the dangers of prescription drugs
By Kim Webster, mum of Will Horley (17)

My son Will was tall and handsome, mad on sports, and a couple of months before he died he'd heard he'd achieved his long-term ambition and been accepted into the Royal Artillery. He was due to join the army that autumn and was making the most of being with his friends over the summer and working in a local restaurant waiting tables, before he got stuck into his new life.

Will was a sensible boy and we'd talked about drugs. He always told me: 'Mum, I'm not stupid. I'm going into the army which has a zero tolerance drugs policy.' There was one occasion when I caught him smoking a joint and gave him a real rollicking, but overall I had no

51

fears about my son getting involved with drugs because I believed he'd never put his future in the army in jeopardy.

The day Will died I was due to pick him up after his shift, but he called and said he was going to the beach with some mates to drink a few beers. I didn't think anything of it. My last words to him were: 'Have a good time and don't be too late – the key's under the mat.'

Will died before we could get to the hospital. He had accidentally overdosed on tramadol, a strong prescription painkiller. He had made some new friends at the restaurant, and it seems one of these had got hold of tramadol on the dark net. Will probably assumed that because it was a prescription drug it was safe, but he paid the highest price in learning that it isn't.

What Will did was totally out of character. It wasn't that he hadn't thought it through, or was being reckless, but he was sadly naïve, as so many teenagers are, and as we were as parents. This naivety cost him his life that night.

Will Horley, with permission from Kim Webster

3

I wish I'd known how complicated risk is

Drug, person, place

Risk factors and variables

When it comes to managing the risks of drugs, most parents know more than they realize, and that includes the variable factors that affect risk. It's easy to be bewildered by this very different world our teenagers inhabit, and to believe the messages coming from various directions telling us we have become somewhat redundant, a bit of an irrelevance, once our children reach a certain age, especially about something like drugs. But this is very far from the case. Not only do parents remain the most important influence in their teenage children's lives, they also have a lot of transferrable knowledge, and just need to know how and where they can usefully transfer it to drugs.

As I said in the last chapter, most of you reading this book will have had your own experiences of taking medication, many of you will have drunk alcohol, and some of you may have used controlled drugs. From these experiences you will know how many variable factors can affect the effect a substance can have on an individual. In the drugs and alcohol sector these variable factors are referred to as drug, set and setting. We like to talk about them as drug, person and place, partly because the words make more sense to the average person, and also because there are many more factors that affect the effect on an individual than the mindset (set) they may be in when they use a substance.

Think about a glass of wine. It could be small, medium, large or enormous. It could be sparkling. It could be a higher than average strength. On an empty stomach its psychoactive effects will be experienced more quickly than if drunk with a meal. If drunk over the course of an evening its effects will be experienced differently than if downed in a few gulps. If drunk in a relaxed and happy mood its effects will be different than if it was drunk at the end of a long and stressful day.

Four people sharing the same bottle will each experience their glass differently. For one person a few sips will have an effect very quickly, while another may be able to drink their way through a bottle or two without losing the ability to walk in a straight line, or hold a coherent conversation without giggling, picking an argument or bursting into tears. The risks to an individual of a glass or two (or more) of wine drunk sitting on the sofa at home will be different than if the same amount was drunk sitting on a wall above a 100-metre drop on to the rocks below. I could go on.

These are all scenarios familiar to most of us, and just the same variability of risk is true of any psychoactive substance. These dimensions of risk are often not something young people have thought about, however, when it comes to substance use, and so their parents can be a valuable resource in helping them think through scenarios, whether experienced, anticipated or hypothetical. The last part of Dan's story showed some of these variable factors at work. The end of this chapter shows the aftermath.

Risk factor #1: the drug

There is no such thing as a risk-free drug. This is just as true for drugs produced under strict regulation and licensing conditions by the pharmaceutical industry as for the sort of drugs that did it for Dan, drugs that have been knocked up in someone's kitchen or a back street underground lab for the illegal supply chain. Parents will be familiar with the risks of medicines and how these are managed, and most children will to a certain extent as well, even if only having had Calpol as a baby or toddler.

Talking point

With younger children especially, talking about the risks of medicines can be a useful basis for understanding the risks of illicit drugs, which are basically the same broad band of risks:

Look together at the information provided on a packet and inserts of over-the-counter medicines, such as where it was made, expiry date, dosage, side effects and interactions.

Talk about how long it takes for a new drug to be approved for public use because of the rigorous testing required to understand the risks and whether, or how, they can be managed.

Think through together how these risks are managed more closely by the medical profession as the medicines themselves become riskier.

You could also talk about how tolerance to some medicines can be built up and a higher dose needed to have the same effect, and the risks of some medicines being more addictive than others.

What's in it, and how much?

With all drugs, there are two vital pieces of information needed before anyone planning to take them can begin to make decisions about how to manage that inevitable risk as safely as possible: what's in them, and how much. When it comes to alcohol, we're given this information because its production and supply are regulated by law. If it was made in the UK the bottle or can will state the percentage volume of alcohol, so you know how strong it is. It may also tell you how many units will be in a glass, bottle or can, and possibly also the recommended weekly maximum number of units for adults (14 for both men and women). You need to know what all that means, of course, when it comes to managing the risks, but it gives you a good start.

With drugs from an illegal source there is none of this helpful information. You start with an unknown quantity, which makes managing risk tricky from the outset. The process of production, manufacture and supply is a messy, criminal business, motivated by profit and without any quality control. The end product sold to someone using controlled drugs will generally have passed through lots of pairs of hands before it reaches theirs, without any regulation, at any stage of the journey, of any of the fiddling around done to it in order for each pair of hands to make a decent profit. And so five boys can get three bags of white powder in exchange for their cash, one of which has an amount of MDMA that could, and did, cause fatality, with no way for any of the five boys, or the one who dropped them off on his bike, or the one who took the call and organized the drop off, to have any idea that this was the case.

A victimless crime?

One of the many lessons we have learned since losing Dan is that drug dealing is perceived by those in the business as a victimless crime. It can be useful for young people to know that there is no, or limited, sense of responsibility for the end-user's welfare. Of course they don't want to kill off their customer base, and do want to be known as someone who sells good stuff, but if anything goes wrong, that isn't something they would generally feel was down to them. Why would they? They're just providing a service. They didn't force the person to take it. Mostly, though, if something goes wrong, they would never know. They would only know if they got caught in relation to something going wrong. The man convicted of selling the drugs who killed Dan was sorry that Dan had died, we heard, but didn't feel he should bear any blame. Chapter 5 has more on drugs and the law, and the criminal justice side of drugs and drug use.

Talking point: letter from a drug dealer

One of the things Tim and I have been able to do over the last few years is to speak in prisons on a victim awareness programme run by Prison Fellowship called Sycamore Tree.[1]

Inevitably, a number of people on every course are serving sentences for charges relating to the supply of drugs, and as a result, we've been able to have some very interesting, moving and eye-opening conversations with dealers. This is an extract from a letter written to us by a young supplier, which speaks not only of his heartfelt regret but also how it had never occurred to him before we told Dan's story that he had no idea what he was actually handing over. It may be useful to read with your teenagers:

Dear Fiona and Tim,

I write this letter with the most sincere of apologies for my involvement in an industry which stole your son from you. I always saw what I did as providing a service, not much different from selling alcohol or cigarettes, the only difference being those drugs are legal and the

---

[1] Prison Fellowship. Sycamore Tree [online]. *Prison Fellowship*. Available from: <prison-fellowship.org.uk/our-work/sycamore-tree/>

ones I peddled are not. I would justify my deeds with the thoughts that these users wanted, in some cases needed, the drugs and I was providing them with a fair, pleasant service compared to that of other dealers. At first I put their personal frailties and vulnerabilities to the back of my mind, and later stopped caring altogether what state they were in. 'It's their own fault,' I would think. 'Nothing to do with me what they do with their lives.'

...Your story brought to life the reality that I can't be sure of the contents or potency of what I was selling, nor can I be sure what effect this drug will have on the user. I do still see the drug scene as an industry but not one I would want to have any more to do with. Apart from being illegal it is totally immoral and although I suppose it is providing a good or service, it is also providing death, despair, addiction and an anarchic lifestyle I wouldn't wish on anyone, let alone continue to facilitate. If I could turn back time I would...

Thank you for triggering this feeling in me and making this victim awareness course truly worthwhile.

Many thanks.

So how can you tell what's in it?

Different drugs have different effects, as we have seen, and knowing their effects is important information for anyone planning to use a substance and manage its risks. However, although a drug may contain the substance the purchaser is expecting, it may well not, and if it does, there may be a lot more of it than they're expecting, or a lot less. It will always have other ingredients as well as the one they think they're paying for. These could be harmless, used as bulking or colouring agents, cheap fillers to make the expensive bits stretch further to increase profits. They could, however, be harmful, whether a cheap substance used to cut the drugs which also happens to be potentially harmful, or a strong and risky substance used to replicate the effects of the drug by using a cheaper, or more available, substance.

These change constantly, depending on all sorts of factors, often when a key ingredient is in short supply. In the late 2000s, law enforcement made several large seizures of an MDMA precursor called safrole, resulting in a worldwide shortage of ecstasy. As a consequence, substances such as PMA and PMMA started being mis-sold as MDMA, and did a lot of damage. Fatalities from PMA/PMMA rose from just one in 2011 up to 29 in 2013, then started to drop until it was back to one in 2017 when supplies were restored,[2] and meanwhile deaths from MDMA, which was now back on the market, were on the rise.

What can drug testing tell us?

The only way to tell what's in a drug from an illegal source is to get it tested. We'll explore this more in Chapter 7 when we look at harm reduction options, but it's useful here to look at what the results of some of this testing shows us about the actual contents of substances young people have been sold. The most reliable test is one carried out by a recognized drug testing service such as The Loop.[3] The results of testing they have done at music festivals has shone a sharp spotlight on the extent of the randomness of drugs from an illegal source. The primary three drugs they are asked to test at festivals are MDMA, ketamine and cocaine. In 2016, their first summer of front-of-house, publicly accessible drug checking, they found that one in five substances were not what the person thought they were getting at all. They also found a wide variation in strengths and risky adulterants. In 2017 at Boomtown, and throughout that summer and the next, some of The Loop's biggest concerns were finding high-strength MDMA, and also N-Ethylpentylone, a stimulant that can keep users awake for up to 36 hours, being mis-sold as MDMA pills and powders, leaving users suffering anxiety, distress and paranoia.[4] Without the benefits of testing, people using these services would have been taking unknowable risks with unknown substances.

---

[2] Statista. Number of drug-related deaths due to PMA and PMMA use in England and Wales from 2011 to 2019 [online]. *Statista*. Available from: <www.statista.com/statistics/470828/drug-poisoning-deaths-pmma-in-england-and-wales/> (accessed November 2020)

[3] <https://wearetheloop.org/>

[4] VICE (2017) All the Dodgy Stuff Found in the Drugs at Boomtown This Year [online]. *VICE*. Available from: <www.vice.com/en_uk/article/vbbexd/all-the-dodgy-stuff-found-in-the-drugs-at-boomtown-this-year-safe-sesh> (accessed November 2020)

Talking point

There have been several campaigns running to encourage people who use untested drugs to take time and take care, on the basis that they will be testing them on themselves. These could also be useful sideways conversation points – what do your older teens think about how effective these campaigns might be? See The Loop's 'Crush, dab wait' campaign <wearetheloop.org/crush-dab-wait> and 'Don't be daft, start with a half' run by MixMag and Global Drug Survey <mixmag.net/feature/were-launching-a-campaign-to-promote-safer-ecstasy-use/>

How has it been taken?

The way in which a drug is consumed affects the speed with which it will reach the brain, and this is important in determining the effect it will have. There are a variety of ways in which drugs can be taken, and the same drug can often be consumed in different ways, as described in the previous chapter.

Drugs that are smoked, vaped, inhaled, snorted or injected get to the brain the fastest, which leads to a rapid effect that may not last that long. Drugs that are swallowed as pills, liquids or edibles, or 'bombed' as powders wrapped in cigarette paper, have to be absorbed by the stomach and intestines before they can reach the brain. This is a longer process, resulting in an effect which takes more time to come on and can be less intense, but is often longer lasting.

There can be risks to young people who are more familiar with one method of use but then taking a drug a different way. Cannabis is a classic example of this. People who smoke cannabis are used to the psychoactive chemical (THC) hitting their brain fairly quickly. If they then try an edible form of cannabis, such as cookies or sweets, they may initially be disappointed because it can seem to be having no effect on them. There is risk then in consuming more in order to make that effect happen, and then finding larger amounts than the person is used to in their system, resulting in a stronger and longer-lasting effect than they've experienced before. However, risks from edibles can be seen at lower doses too. A recent study of hospital admissions in Colorado, one of the US states where cannabis has been legalized for recreational use, showed that although sales of edibles were much lower than those of herbal cannabis, hospital admissions were much higher for people who had used edibles, even when the amount of THC consumed was relatively low.[5]

Talking point

With older teens especially, a conversation about differences in the ways in which drugs can be taken and how these can increase or reduce effects and risks is valuable. As always with these discussions, distancing can make these conversations easier on both sides, by talking theoretically about people you or they may know, or stories they have heard.

Mixing it up

Mixing substances complicates a complicated risk even further. Drugs interact differently with each other, changing the effect and the risk, often in unpredictable ways. There are people who only ever use one substance recreationally, but many who use one will also use another. Some of these will deliberately use substances with different effects, taking one in order to counter the effect of another. A common example is using a drug with a sedative effect to chill out and perhaps get some sleep after experiencing the influence of a stimulant perhaps still in the system.

There are certain substances that are particularly risky when taken together, and one of the riskiest mixers is alcohol. This is important to know, because it's not only by far the easiest to get hold of and most widely available, but also because one of the effects it can have is to impair the judgement and decision-making skills of the person drinking it. After a few drinks have been downed, someone might take risks that they would never have taken when sober.

However, alcohol can enhance the euphoric effects from many substances because of the specific way it acts on the brain, and so it is sometimes used in combination with other drugs for this specific purpose. Cocaine and alcohol is one example. Around three quarters

---

[5] Monte, A.A. (2019) Acute illness associated with cannabis use, by route of exposure: an observational study. *Annals of Internal Medicine* [online]. Available from: doi: 10.7326/M18-2809

of people who use cocaine drink alcohol at the same time.[6] Sometimes this is just seen as a sociable thing; two substances that are used on a night out, more by twentysomethings than teens. Sometimes people use both specifically in order to improve or prolong the night out, alternating each substance to enhance or counteract the effects of the other. In addition to the risks of not being aware of how much alcohol or cocaine you may have consumed and using excessive amounts, or doing something risky and not realizing the full effects, this combination has recently been linked to some high-profile suicides.[7] It also produces another risky psychoactive substance, cocaethylene, which has been associated with seizures and fatalities.

There are certain substances that should always be avoided with alcohol, including ketamine, MDMA, nitrous oxide, benzodiazepines, amphetamines, and GHB. However, the safest option is to avoid mixing anything with anything. This also includes prescription medication.

I wish I'd known that the combination of ketamine and alcohol can be lethal

By Wendy Teasdill, mum of Ellie Rowe (18)

I knew ketamine was bad news, but I didn't know what it looked like, how it was ingested or indeed why anyone would want to take it. Before El's death, my main information came from a hitch-hiker from the Glastonbury festival site. He was working on the clear-up team after an especially muddy year. The rain hadn't stopped in weeks.

'It's really bad up there,' he told me. 'It's a hell-hole. The mud's so bad, everyone's taking ketamine.'

In 2013 my daughter, Ellie Rowe, snorted high-grade ketamine in combination with a couple of cans of lager. She was not in a hell-hole, she was at Boomtown Festival, and had just come off her first shift as an Oxfam steward. She was happy – and dead before the festival began.

---

[6] Liu, Y. et. al. (2018) The importance of considering poly drug use: lessons from cocaine research. *Science Direct* [online]. Available from: doi: 10.1016/j. drugalcdep.2018.07.025

[7] BBC News (2019) Cocaine and alcohol, a 'deadly combination' [online]. Available from: <www.bbc.co.uk/news/health-49814269> (accessed November 2020)

Ketamine and alcohol both act as depressants on the central nervous system. Whilst unconscious she had a heart attack and there was no way she could be revived, though a whole team of people tried valiantly for hours.

Information is powerful. Telling young people not to do drugs is simplistic and unrealistic, because the forbidden fruit is especially alluring. But – had we known she was courting death, had we had a conversation about the dangers of combining two depressants - I am certain that Ellie would be alive today.

Ellie Rowe, with permission from Wendy Teasdill

Risk factor #2: the person

There are many variable factors relating to an individual that can affect the effect a substance may have, so many that it would take too long to explore them all here. These are just some of the ones that are perhaps most useful to bring into conversations with your children. Some of these variables are fixed for an individual but may vary from those of their friends, such as genes, family history, biological sex and metabolism. Others can vary for that individual from one occasion to another, such as their mood, their expectations, their physical or mental health and even their body mass. Remember that glass of wine at the start of the chapter.

Health matters

The relationship between both physical and mental health and substance use is complicated, but in this context there are a couple of factors that are useful to build into conversations at home. On a down day, or in a down spell, when someone is feeling below par physically, mentally or emotionally, or even if they're short of sleep, they are likely to have a different experience taking a substance than when they're feeling healthy and happy. A classic example is a drug like LSD, which can have its effect by feeding off the imagination. Being in a bad place (mind set-wise), or feeling anxious or depressed, may not only make these feelings worse but also lead to a bad trip, which can in turn trigger or exacerbate mental illness.

Some physical conditions make taking particular substances especially risky. Someone with asthma or a chest condition that affects their breathing will be at greater risk from inhaling substances. Someone with a heart condition – and sometimes teenagers, and their parents, are unaware they have one until it's triggered – will be at greater risk from taking a stimulant like cocaine, speed or MDMA that increases their heart rate and raises their blood pressure.

When it comes to drug use and mental illness there is a chicken and egg element which research continues to try to unravel. The relationship between the two is clearly complex. Psychoactive substances operate by making changes to our brain chemistry and communication networks, and continued use of most varieties of these will begin to have some degree of impact on the mental health of the person using them. But it is also the case that having a mental illness can mean someone is more likely to choose a particular substance, or use psychoactive substances generally, possibly as a coping mechanism, or as a form of self-harm, or because it has made them more prone to reckless behaviour. A pre-existing mental illness will then often be made worse, whether in the shorter or longer terms, by taking drugs – which has a tragic irony if the reason the person was using it was in an attempt to relieve the burden of their depression or anxiety.

Boys and girls

Whether someone is biologically male or female can affect the effect drugs have on them in multiple ways. Some of these are cultural factors relating to ways drugs are more likely to be used, and accessed, by males and females, but there is increasing evidence that psycho-active substances can affect a female differently than a male for physiological reasons as well.

Your teenagers may not be aware that alcohol affects women differently to men. This is partly because a female body is generally of smaller build and so the same amount of alcohol will have a greater effect. This would be the case to a certain extent for boys of a smaller build out with bulkier friends, though in both cases other factors can be at work. More significantly, regardless of build, a girl drinking the same amount of alcohol as a boy will end up with more alcohol in her blood. This is because alcohol is held in the body in water, not in body fat; because girls and women tend to have a higher proportion of body fat and less of water than boys and men, any alcohol consumed is more concentrated in the female body.[8]

Evidence for anything is always more scarce when it comes to drugs used illegally because funding is inevitably harder to come by for research into something people shouldn't be doing in the first place. There is, however, some evidence that shows the physical toll certain drugs take seems to be greater on female than on male users, and that oestrogen can play a role in at least some of this. The effects of stimu-lants, such as cocaine or amphetamines, can vary in women because of changes in the levels of female hormones during their menstrual

---

[8] National Institute on Alcohol Abuse and Alcoholism, (1999) Are Women More Vulnerable to Alcohol's Effects? [online] No. 46. US Department of Health and Human Services. Available from: <pubs.niaaa.nih.gov/publications/aa46. htm> (accessed November 2020)

cycle.[9,10] Generally speaking, MDMA produces a stronger response in women than men regardless of body size and weight,[11] but there is an additional risk to women relating to hormones. One of the risks of MDMA is the way its use can deplete sodium levels in the blood, a condition known as hyponatremia. This can cause disorientation, convulsions, loss of consciousness and fatalities. Girls are much more vulnerable to this because of the essential role oestrogen plays in the transfer of water across the membranes, which exacerbates the effects of hyponatremia.[12]

Talking point

Talk to your older teens, both boys and girls, about the need to be aware that their female friends (or they themselves) may not only respond differently to some drugs, as well as to alcohol, than their male friends will, but that their response may vary from one day to another depending on where they are in their menstrual cycle.

Expectations

The expectations we have will often shape the experiences we have, for better or for worse. Many studies have shown, over many years of research, that our expectations of a drug can affect its effectiveness – the well-known 'placebo effect'. Indeed, recent studies have demonstrated

---

9   Justice, A. & de Witt, H., (2000) Acute effects of d-Amphetamine during the early and late follicular phases of the menstrual cycle in women [online]. *Pharmacology, Biochemistry and Behavior.* 66(3): 509–15. Available from: DOI: 10.1016/S0091-3057(00)00218-5

10   Ewens, H., (2016) How your menstrual cycle can affect your reaction to MDMA [online]. *VICE*. Available from: <www.vice.com/en/article/exkzj4/why-are-young-british-girls-dying-from-mdma> (accessed November 2020)

11   Liechti, M.E., Gamma, A., Vollenweider, F.X. (2001). Gender differences in the subjective effects of MDMA. *Psychopharmacology (Berl)* [online]. 1; 154(2): 161–8. DOI: 10.1007/s002130000648

12   Soleimani Asl, S., Mehdizadeh, M., Hamedi Shahraki, S., Artimani, T., Joghataei, M.T. (2015) Sex differences in MDMA-induced toxicity in Sprague-Dawley rats. *Functional Neurolology* [online]. 30(2): 131–137. Available from: DOI: 10.11138/fneur/2015.30.2.131

that even when patients know the medicine they are taking is a placebo, it can still reduce the level of pain they experience, such is the power of mind over matter.[13] The power of placebo can, in just the same way, shape the experience of a psychoactive substance used recreationally. Expectations can also influence the effect of a substance in the other direction. High expectations followed by a reaction that disappoints can lead to taking more of something, or taking something else, which then increases the risk of harm. Without the high expectations there may have been no disappointment.

Talking point

A school we visited some time ago told us about a group of year 9 students who had been rushed to hospital from school under the influence of what they thought was ecstasy, given to them by another student. It turned out to have been harmless sweets, intended as a joke. Their reaction was genuine, and just as they had expected to behave after taking ecstasy, but without any chemical cause.

This could be a useful conversation starter with your children about the role of expectations in the effects of drugs or alcohol. Do your children think that could really happen? Why would the year 9s have faked it knowing it would let people at school, and then at home, know they had taken drugs that would get them into big trouble?

Group variables

Something young people need to be alert to when making decisions out and about are the variables that can exist within the group of people they're with. Young people who use psychoactive substances are generally more likely to do this with others than alone, and the group itself can present its own risk factors because of the variable factors at play for each person there. Differences between the biological sex, body mass, genetics and metabolism of the individuals

---

[13] Locher, C. et al. (2017) Is the rationale more important than deception? A randomized control trial of open-label placebo analgesia. *Journal of the International Association for the Study of Pain* [online]. Available from: DOI: 10.1097/j. pain.0000000000001012.

within the group mean that before the evening starts the playing field is far from even. And then there's more.

Starting with the original use of the word 'set' in this context, the group mindset may seem as one, but beneath that, individuals may be in a different place mentally and emotionally. They may be looking for the substance to do something different, which will affect the effect. It may be that the communal plan is to get totally smashed, but one person may be doing this for fun, another to celebrate a great test result, another to switch off the pain in their head or their heart. Another may be terrified – of the effect, of their parents' reaction if they find out – but has overcome their terror in order to feel they have secured their place within the group. We'll consider decision-making and the role of the group dynamic in adolescence in Chapter 4.

Another factor that can affect the risk to an individual within a group is the varying levels of tolerance to whatever may be being taken that can exist within any bunch of friends heading off to a party or gathering, or hanging around in a park. Tolerance can build up very quickly with some substances, including alcohol, MDMA, benzodiazepines, ketamine and hallucinogens. Friends with more experience may not only be able to cope better with a higher amount than someone newer to it, they may also need to use more to try to achieve the effect they're looking for, and there are risks to others trying or expecting to keep up. Understanding this is important.

Talking point

Thinking through different possible mindsets within one group of teenagers can be a good way of reminding your child that what their peers may show on the outside may not be how they're really feeling on the inside. Have you got an example from your own experience that you can share, such as concentrating hard at work to appear confident doing something while feeling terrified inside? Have they got an example?

Addiction

There is still limited understanding as to why some people will develop an addiction to a substance and others, with similar levels of use, at least initially, won't. There are various theories, most of which are contentious, but whatever the reason, within any group of young people using drugs or alcohol, some may develop problems and others won't. Family history and genetics may play a role here. Addiction seems to run in families, whether that's to do with genetic or environmental factors, or both. We will explore addiction in more detail in Chapter 8.

Talking point

The role of family history in the development of problems relating to drugs and alcohol is complex, but there are a couple of factors it would be good to talk to your children about, if they're relevant to you, because they may place them at greater risk:

- If your family has a history of mental illness, and particularly of psychotic illnesses.
- If you have family members (even going back a generation or two) who have struggled with addiction to drugs or alcohol.

Risk factor #3: the place

Finally, we get to the last dimension of risk. What hazards could there be in that particular place, at that particular time, relating to both the physical and human environment? Psychoactive substances can impair our judgement and cognitive processing, they can make us disorientated or uncoordinated, they can slow down our movements and make us feel numb. They can also cause seizures, convulsions and unconsciousness. The interaction between the effects of the substance and the place a person is in if they've taken something can alter the level of risk significantly, both in potentially increasing the risk of harm and also reducing the likelihood of getting help if harm happens.

Anyone who is planning to use drugs or to drink excessive amounts of alcohol needs also to plan to have someone with them with a sober head to look out for them – someone who knows them well enough to spot possibly subtle signs of behaviour that may be out of character; someone who knows them well enough to check in on them regularly even if they look OK; someone who will make sure the people around them won't harm them in any way; and ideally someone who has the individual's parents' phone number to call if needs be.

Your children may not have thought through the fact that taking substances on your own is very risky, as is getting separated from the people you came with, because help is harder to get if your mental or physical capacity has become limited, or you're becoming unwell. Just as risky, however, is ending up around people who may hurt, assault or rob you. Drugs that may cause immobility, such as ketamine or GHB, or that may cause a user to experience reality very differently, such as LSD, are especially needy of a safe and friendly pair of eyes and hands to stick around.

Equally obvious to a clear and adult head are potential hazards in the physical environment for anyone no longer thinking or behaving in an orderly manner – busy roads, open water, high-up places being just a few. Thinking through the place they'll be in before they head off there, and the journey there and back, can be really valuable. All these conversations can often be more comfortably framed in relation to friends they'll be with and how they can help them to stay safe if one of them ends up using drugs or alcohol there, and your child needs to be their safe pair of eyes and hands for the evening. Your child then also has these measures in their own back pocket should they need them.

Let's take an illegal rave as an example. The organizers will have done some initial scouting around and found a building, or an open space, suitable for a gathering of young people, where they can set up their sound system and take entrance fees as people arrive. 'Suitable' will mean somewhere relatively remote, quiet or unlikely, so they can get the necessary setting up done before anyone notices and reports it to the police. 'Suitability' doesn't necessarily mean somewhere with sufficient exit points to evacuate the building safely if there was an emergency, or adequate ventilation, or access to free water to avoid dehydration and overheating – a legal requirement in all UK licensed venues. Their planning and intended profit margins are unlikely to have stretched to ensuring there would be the correct number of first aiders and on-site ambulances a licensed event of a similar size and nature would require, nor suitable supervision of under-18s and under-16s, or security in place to check for drugs being sold or used. There is unlikely to be any limit on numbers coming through the doors to avoid the dangers of overcrowding, because why would they limit the ticket sales?

Talking point

The previous part of Dan's story showed many of these variable factors at play, across all three dimensions of risk. You could talk about these with your children and consider what could have made the situation less risky for Dan.

Think through other scenarios together, changing just one of the variables at a time.

Talk about different risk factors if you see these at work in TV programmes or films.

So, risk when it comes to substance use is complicated, because there are so many variable factors at work, which can combine in such a wide variety of ways, to make managing risk something that requires much thought, planning and preparation, and can never be totally eradicated without steering clear altogether.

And so we come back to Dan, to see how some of these complicated risk factors combined in the worst ways. A group of boys with different levels of tolerance and experience of using MDMA, one with very little. A bag containing a lethal amount of MDMA. An illegal rave, in an unsuitable venue, and unfamiliar place, where nobody knew where they were. It was hot, dark, crammed with teenagers, easy to lose track of people you're with, no water to drink for those whose body temperatures were rising and who were getting dehydrated. Drugs freely being used and sold inside, resulting in high levels of people not able to look out for signs of someone being in trouble. Variable factors that conspired against Dan surviving the experience.

Dan's story: The hospital

It took us an hour to get across London through the empty early Saturday streets. We never, ever drive through central London. We got to the hospital, and then we had to find intensive care, and then we had to wait. For ages. From time to time we tried to find someone to ask, and I'm sure a nurse came out once or twice to say someone would be with us soon, but it was a few hours before the very kind consultant came and sat in the little waiting room with us, and told us Dan's organs were shutting down. He said he was fighting for his life.

His temperature was far, far too high. He had had at least one heart attack and his heart function was still very unstable. He had pneumonia on one of his lungs from having inhaled vomit. His blood was clotting abnormally. He had acute kidney injury, acute renal injury, and lots of other things were going badly, rapidly wrong.

I did already know that this was incredibly serious – the police had knocked at my door, my son was in intensive care – but much as I had been experiencing levels of anxiety higher than I ever had in my life, it was only at this point that I actually, really thought, oh my goodness, he could actually, really die. This might be it for Dan.

Finally, we were able to go and see Dan, and there he was, propped up in a hospital bed, in a hospital gown, deeply unconscious, on a ventilator and with all these wires and tubes and machines attached to him. He had tissues sticking out of his nose which had blood soaking into them. His legs were wrapped in bandages and were enormously swollen. Dan but not Dan. Dan being Dan, though; it would have been perfectly in character for him to open his eyes, sit up and laugh his head off for having fooled us. But he didn't, he just lay there, deeply, deeply unconscious. The very kind nurses brought us tea and chocolate biscuits.

It felt as though it was hardly any time before we had to leave again. Back in the waiting room, a surgeon now sat with the consultant. The surgeon told us that one of the many things going badly wrong for Dan was something called compartment syndrome. We'd never heard of this before. She explained it meant there was swelling in the compartments around the muscles in his legs which was cutting off the blood supply and if they were unable to release

71

the pressure through surgery his legs would have to be amputated. Then it was back to the consultant, who told us Dan was continuing to deteriorate, despite their very best efforts.

We knew their efforts were the best they could be. Everyone was working so hard to save him. Everyone was so kind. We found out later that even at that early stage they knew it was very, very unlikely he'd make it home, but nevertheless they worked as hard as they could, just in case, to save the life of this boy of ours.

Dan was too unstable to take to theatre so they had to operate in the intensive care ward. I couldn't stay in the waiting room. I couldn't stay still. Other people had arrived by then to be with us, to be with Dan – friends, family, Jenna and her mum, lovely people – and so lovely that they were there but I needed to be able to think, to will Dan well, to pray as hard as I could that he'd make it, and make it intact. Dan with no legs? I paced up and down the corridor outside the ICU, praying and praying and praying.

He made it, his legs made it, thank goodness. But now they needed to find a bed for him in a specialist liver ICU. This was his best chance of getting through it. So, I prayed and prayed and prayed some more, and at some point that afternoon a bed came up in the liver intensive care unit at Kings College Hospital, one of the best places in the world he could be. Thank goodness. Off he went in the ambulance, the consultant warning us he was so unstable he may not survive the journey. So, I prayed and prayed and prayed some more. He made it. And we followed. We found the hospital, and then we found the liver intensive care unit, and then we waited. For ages.

It took me months and months to piece back together what happened next, over those two days at Kings. When Dan died my head was left full of great gaping holes, and in those days and weeks and months after we came home without him it couldn't rest from racing and racing, round and round and round, trying to remember everything, every little detail of everything that had happened, everything anyone had said, or done, in trying to make sense of this thing that made no sense. I'd spend hours going back through texts to friends and family, finding what I'd written, and what they'd written. Talking to everyone I could and asking them what I'd said and when. What the consultant had said when they'd been there. What the other doctors had said. What had been happening for Dan. I even managed to find a photo of the consultant on the hospital website and stared at it, trying to remember what he'd said, because I couldn't remember a single time he spoke to us apart from that very last time, when he told us there was no choice, they had to switch the machines off that were keeping him alive. The time he told us our son would die that morning. That, I remember.

But I know he'd kept telling us things over those two days Dan spent in his unit, and I needed to know what they were because none of this made any sense. It wasn't that I could remember him talking to us but not what he said. I had not a single memory of having any conversations at all, apart from that very last one.

A couple of months after Dan died, Tim and I went back to Kings, because the consultant had very kindly agreed to go through everything in his notes with us. I needed to know everything. Tim didn't. For him Dan was dead, and knowing things wouldn't bring him back, and that was all that mattered. That made sense, but I needed to know everything there was to know. And two years after this we went back and spoke to him again. What was the last machine they'd switched off? I really needed to know. What machine was the last in turn, that that kept Dan alive for those very last moments until it was switched off? All I've learned, in all my hard work trying to make this make sense, is that nothing can ever make sense of Dan being here, and then not being here.

But I do now remember, having pieced those two days back together in the makeshift manner I did, that the consultant had told us that first night when he was finally able to come and speak to us, when they'd finally been able to get Dan set up on all the equipment and machinery he needed to make his tiniest of chances the best it could be – that we have five systems. Something like that, anyway. Heart, circulation, liver, lungs, kidneys. He told us if someone came to his unit with one of these in trouble he'd be really concerned. He told us all five were in trouble for Dan. But, he said, they would do all they could, there was hope, he was young, fit and healthy. We held on to that important 'but', and that precious hope, as hard as we could.

I still don't remember much of what he said over those next two days, or what any of the other doctors, or the nurses, who worked so hard to try to save our son, had said. But I remember that room. I remember Dan in that bed. I remember the thing over his mouth that connected the tube in his throat to the ventilator. The tubes up his nose and the plugs to stop the bleeding from his nostrils, which they never quite did. The square blue pads over his eyes so they didn't dry out because they never totally closed. The noise of the ventilator, that constant wheezing as it breathed in and out for Dan. The bags of blood, plasma and fluid that the nurse kept changing; unhooking the empties and replacing them with fresh new full ones. The kidney dialysis machine that kept churning, doing the work of Dan's kidneys and trying to get rid of all those toxins in his body. The bank of machines that went beep with his heart and had all the numbers that went up and down that I never managed to work out. Which was good, up or down? I asked one of the nurses, who explained what they all meant, but I couldn't really take it in.

The first night we waited in the public waiting area in the unit. We were the only ones there once visiting ended. Friends had come, family had come, had brought food, tea, love. Jenna and her lovely mum. She was just 15. Dan and Jenna. Jenna and Dan. But here he was, Dan but not Dan, dying.

I remember Tim's brother and our big nephew went off to try to find pizza in the middle of the night. I remember Tim's sister had given Jacob a big bar of mint Aero, and he fell asleep with it in the back pocket of his jeans, lying along the chairs in the waiting room, and when he woke it was completely molten inside the packet and we laughed. I remember the toilets were miles away, down two flights of stairs, along a load of corridors: past the café, past the shop and back to the main entrance. It seemed like an epic journey every time.

At some point the next day, perhaps when the unit opened up for visitors again, we were given a little private waiting room, just for us. They had to ask another family to move back to the public waiting room. I felt bad for them, but also for us. It meant we were the family with the least hope.

But we did have hope. We kept losing it, but then we'd find it again. Up, then down, along with the numbers on the machine that I never worked out. We were able to be with Dan most of the time once he got to Kings, after that first night. There wasn't much space in his little room, what with all the stuff he needed to keep him alive, but there was a bit of space on one side of his bed and they'd put a chair there so someone could sit and hold his cold, stiff, blue hand. Why was it so cold, and stiff, and blue? I tried to rub the cold and blue away. The bed was a bit away from the wall and they'd put a tall chair there as well, so someone could sit at his unconscious head. His beautiful unconscious head, with the hair that I'd always cut. I found myself wanting to say to everyone, I cut that hair. I always cut his hair. Looking at it, stroking it, I felt it was my hair. It was my boy.

I sat there, all the time I could. I did sometimes give it up for Tim, but mostly I'm afraid I stuck there, and Tim, in his great kindness, let me. I needed to be as near to Dan as I could.

We'd had our brush with losing a child, so that should have been it for us – we'd had our turn. When Jacob had been a tiny baby he got sepsis; we never knew quite how, and we spent two days in baby intensive care, the doctors not knowing if he'd make it. My midwife had told me, in those earliest days back home with my brand new baby, that touch and talk helped premature babies to thrive and survive like nothing else could, so that's what I did with my poorly baby. I stroked his tiny head all the time I could (till the oxygen machine beeped to tell me I needed to close the incubator up again), and talked and talked to him. Jacob, in that miraculous way tiny babies often can, suddenly picked up and was back at home with us just a few days later. So now I stroked Dan's head, and talked and talked, as I had to baby Jacob 18 years before.

I thought too of all those stories of people who'd been deeply unconscious, and hovered on the edge of death, who'd heard the voice of someone they loved calling to them, and had chosen to come back to consciousness, and back to life. I thought, he needs to hear my voice, then maybe he'll come back. So, I talked, lots. Lots of nonsense. Lots of anything I could think of, just to keep talking. Lots of telling him how precious he was, how much I loved him, how much we all loved him. Telling him he was doing so well, he could fight this, we could fight it together.

I remembered Dan's last words to me. He'd told me he loved me, and he'd promised he wouldn't die. I told him, you promised, Dan.

I couldn't eat because I felt so sick. I could drink tea with lots of sugar, but that's all. I hadn't slept since I woke to find Dan not home in the early hours of Saturday morning. I didn't want to sleep, I just wanted to be with Dan, but by the afternoon of the second day I was so tired that at one point I dozed off, my head next to Dan's on his pillow. I only knew I was asleep when our vicar, who'd come to pray with Dan and with us, woke me to tell me she was leaving. People came and went, bringing us food and drink, sitting with us, waiting. Others were sending messages, reading my texts to them, praying and hoping for us and for Dan. Jenna's mum brought me a change of clothes and some things to have a bit of a wash. A friend took Tim and Jacob home to get showers and catch some sleep, and brought them back again. Jacob, the big brother, being so strong for his mum and dad, holding it together when we were unable to, hoping if he did then it would all be alright for Dan, for us all. But it was all so wrong. So wrong for him to feel that weight of responsibility, to have to watch his parents falling to pieces, to have to watch his brother dying.

By that last night I was still trying to talk and talk to Dan but I was so tired I dozed off a few more times for a few more moments with my head next to Dan's on his pillow, and I felt so sick I had to keep leaving his room and rush to the toilets, all those miles away back by the main entrance. I just wanted to be with Dan, but my stomach was all in a muddle, just like my head and my world. The very kind junior doctor on duty said it was because of not eating and sleeping and all the anxiety and stress, and when she went on her break she brought me back a bar of chocolate and a bottle of Lucozade. I tried to eat it but then I was actually sick, outside the unit, on my next rush to the far away toilets. There were warning signs all around the hospital about norovirus, a sickness bug which was a big concern at the time, and I thought, now they won't let me back in, and then what? But they did.

Everyone worked so hard to try to save Dan. Nurses, doctors, changing shifts, handing over, coming back. But there were so many things that were going and already had gone so badly wrong for Dan. One of the big problems they had was that he was bleeding so much, and his blood was clotting so abnormally. The wounds on his legs from the surgery wouldn't heal and he was losing blood as fast as they could replace it. He lost 17 litres of blood that second day. And his heart was so badly damaged and his circulation so poor. They had the vascular surgeons in, considering amputating his legs, but too much was too badly wrong for it to make the difference it would need to make.

Losing a child to drugs doesn't just involve hospitals, it also involves police. They appeared at Hillingdon hospital before we'd even seen the consultant, or really knew what was happening to Dan. They were trying to piece together what had happened before Dan got to the hospital, before he got to the rave, before he took the MDMA, and everything since. They'd got hold of his phone, and they needed to contact everyone else who had taken MDMA with Dan because they needed to get to a hospital to get themselves checked over. The police needed to know if this was a dodgy batch of drugs, in which case they needed to put out a warning. But they couldn't get into Dan's phone because he had a PIN. We had no idea what this would be, but Jenna knew. It was their first date.

Then it was our Family Liaison Officer, Steve, a big, tall Liverpudlian, who was to become a strong, safe presence in our broken lives, but who was introduced to us, as I remember, just as we were walking alongside our unconscious Dan as he was being wheeled through the ward with all the machinery keeping him alive, out of intensive care to the ambulance to take him to Kings, if he made it. And then at Kings on that first night, the officers doing the investigation into the dealer were back, giving us an update. The police were all so kind to us from beginning to end. Over the next two days at Kings, Steve kept appearing, telling us what they'd been doing, where they'd got to with the investigation. We really appreciated them wanting to keep us updated, and that they were working so hard to try to find the person who sold the drugs that were doing this to Dan – we later learned that people had come off leave and worked double shifts to try to make arrests – but it was very hard to be at all focused on anything they said, or to make it matter, when all our focus was on Dan, dying or not dying. Which was it to be?

In all the ups and downs of hopeful and hopeless, all the comings and goings of family and friends, all the being with Dan then having to wait outside, all the doctors saying things I don't remember – the first night, the second day, the second night, the last morning – there were the police.

And then it was Monday morning. At 5 pm the previous day the consultant had told us they had one last drug they could try, the last chance Dan had, and the next 12 hours would be critical. I thought, if he can just get through the next 12 hours, then maybe he could make it. All that night I'd watched the numbers going up and down, willing them up, willing him through every minute of every hour, and he got there, he was still with us 12 hours later. I knew that only really meant we still had him with us, nothing more, but we did still have him and what a blessing and gift that was, and maybe just maybe he'd make it.

That last morning the 8 am handover, which usually took half an hour, went on and on. We waited in our little waiting room. Family came and friends came, got Tim and Jacob some breakfast, got me some tea with lots of sugar, and waited with us. Then, finally, the consultant came. He sat down and looked at us, and he told us there was nothing more they could do. The side effects of this last drug were incredibly strong and had reduced the size of Dan's capillaries so much that his arms and legs had died. The surgeons had been back in to see whether amputation could keep him alive, but it was too late by then for Dan. He would die that morning.

How blessed we were to have those days with him. He could have been dead by the time we knew there was never a party in Clapham. How blessed we were to be able to be with him as he died. Us and all our families. My parents had chanced upon an earlier train from Dorset, not knowing they were coming to see Dan die. Everyone was there, holding onto each other; Jacob's big cousin holding him, while I was holding Dan. Everyone standing around his bed as the nurses gently and quietly turned everything off that had been keeping him alive. And somehow, in those most awful of all awful moments, there was an incredible sense of peace, like nothing else.

I held Dan's face. There were too many tubes and wires and machines to hold any more of him, so I held his beautiful face in my hands, put my face next to his face and listened to the beeps on the machine get slower and slower while I told him how much I loved him. I told him he needed to go now. Then there was just one long beep that didn't stop. Then someone turned it off and it was quiet. Then it was just Tim, and me, and Dan, and the very kindest of nurses. I couldn't let go of Dan's face. I knew when I did it would go cold and then it would never be warm ever again. How could I possibly let it go? But I had to, and we had to leave him, and go back to our home where there was no longer Dan.

4

I wish I'd known about the teenage brain

Choices, friends and managing risk

When it comes to making decisions about drugs and alcohol as a teenager, and making those decisions as safely as possible, it's vital not only to have sufficient knowledge and understanding of the risks at hand, but also to understand what makes the safe navigation of these risks more complicated than at any other time of life, and the skills to be able to take control. The most highly intelligent, well informed and sensible people can make the most terrible decisions and take the most ill-judged risks, and never more so than in their adolescence. Most of us will have at least one eye-watering, toe-curling, hair-raising memory from our own younger years. The business of this chapter is unpacking a bit of this in the context of drugs and alcohol.

Understanding what makes the adolescent brain unique, and different from the adult brain, or the child's for that matter, is incredibly helpful for parents trying to make sense of some of the mysteries of their teenagers' words and actions. It is also essential for teenagers to have a good understanding of what's at work in the dynamic of their decision-making so that they can make sense, take control, manage risks and stay safe. It increases the potential for both parents and teens to work with, rather than battle against, what's going on in their heads and translating itself into what they do and say, and when and how they do and say it. And it's important not just for teens but for pre-teens and those in their 20s, too, because this is a process that begins at around the age of ten, and takes until your mid-twenties to end.

When Dan died I knew a bit (not anywhere near enough) about drugs, but nothing at all about the adolescent brain. Understanding the complex processes at work has been a great help in understanding the decisions Dan and his friends made, and making sense of some, at least, of the madness, but it was a long and bumpy journey, and a journey that will, of course, never end with a clear conclusion about what was going on for Dan. I wish I'd known more about all this before he set off that night.

Dan's story: the decision

Losing a child ranks high on the list of the most awful things that can happen to someone, and one of the many complications tangled up in losing a child to drugs is the fact – and it's unavoidably a cold, hard, solid fact – that somewhere along the way to their death your child made a decision that could have been different. A different decision could have had a different ending. There may have been no ending at all. They could have come home, gone to bed and got up the next day. Life could have gone on. You may never have known that drugs had been involved in their decision-making the night before.

The decision they made hadn't ever been to die. It was probably the very same decision that was being made at the very same time by one or more of the people around them. It probably seemed like a very small decision at the time. But the outcome for them, from that one particular decision, cost them their life. No opportunity to learn from a mistake, take a different path or make a different choice next time. No opportunity to hide from your mum and dad (and in Dan's case, any member of the general public who read papers or watched the news) the fact that you'd been taking drugs.

I don't want to make excuses for Dan. I did at first, I have to confess. I didn't want anyone, anywhere, to judge Dan. I knew people would, and I'm sure people did, but I wanted to say to the world, 'He wasn't like that, he was like this. He wasn't that sort of boy.' But in making those excuses I'm complicit in judgement. There are many reasons why people might choose to use drugs, and there is no sort of boy, or girl, who deserves to die from drugs, or come to any sort of harm, for that matter. There should be no judgement. So, I tried not to make excuses, but I did try very hard to understand. *Why did he do it?*

As the policeman was telling us about the ecstasy, as we were racing to the hospital, waiting outside his room, waiting by his bed, watching him dying, we were having to process the fact that Dan had chosen to do this. Dan was a boy who had chosen to take a drug that may kill him, was killing him, had killed him. We thought we knew Dan. We didn't know this Dan. Who was the Dan who went to a rave, who chose to take drugs, who wasn't here any more to ask? Had I misunderstood Dan all this time? I'd thought he was the lovely boy who sat on the side of the bath while I put on my makeup in the morning so he could carry on chatting about this and that and everything, who slopped around in his baggy tracksuit bottoms after school leaving a trail of chocolate biscuit crumbs behind him, who stuck his always smelly feet, in their always odd socks, underneath your nose if you sat near to him on the sofa to make you moan and groan and laugh.

There was this Dan, and there was Dan who took drugs and died. Which was the right Dan? We lost our Dan forever, here and now and with us, but we also lost the Dan we thought we knew, just for a little while, before we realized of course this was all Dan. Kind, funny, chatty, bright and big-hearted boys can, and do, also take drugs.

But it was a puzzle, this last decision Dan made. Nothing quite made sense, and we couldn't ask Dan.

Dan was curious, adventurous, embraced new experiences, lived life large. Little Dan would put snails in the garden in his mouth, just to see what they were like. Bigger Dan would always pick the weirdest item on a café menu, just to see. When a food outlet at Victoria Station started selling grass juice, freshly blended from punnets growing on the counter, he persuaded us all to try it – at great expense, I might add. New experiences, but always with the right degree of caution, even if he hid this caution well. Little Dan was climbing before he could walk, and he never stopped – up the back of the furniture, the bannisters, a tree, a lamppost – anything and everything clamber-able, and he never once had an accident. He was always a good judge of what was and wasn't safe. And he had a mum who was as vigilant as she could be over a small scrambling boy ending up somewhere precarious.

But that didn't quite make sense of this. When Dan was 13 we'd had a holiday in Bude in Cornwall, where there's a canal that goes out to the sea, and at certain times of certain days, when the tide is high enough for the water to be really deep, but low enough for there to be a decent drop down, teenagers jump from the side, down with a splash, and it looks like great fun. That's what Dan thought anyway. We'd seen them the evening before, and Dan had been really keen to go back the next evening and have a go himself. Dan could get his mind fixed on something. So off we set, Dan in his wetsuit (Jacob was always more cautious), and there the teenagers were, jumping off the side, down with a drop and a splash into the water, climbing out and jumping again. We could see the water was deep enough to be safe, we'd seen it at low tide to know there weren't hidden hazards, and were happy enough, in our worried parents' way, for Dan to join in, and he was happy, too, but also characteristically cautious.

We stood and watched by the side, while he stood on the edge, ready to jump, but watching the other teenagers, gauging how safe it would be for him. We stood and watched, and he stood and watched, for ages. And ages. From time to time I'd remind him he didn't have to jump if he didn't feel safe, it was fine just to go home (looking at my watch as time ticked on), but in the end he did. He jumped, he climbed out, he jumped again. It was great fun. But he'd needed to know it was safe. That was Dan. Adventurous but cautious. Needing to know he'd be safe. So that didn't quite make sense of this big, last decision.

When Dan died people talked about peer pressure, and bad influences, but that didn't make sense either, at least not in the simplistic, stereotypical peer pressure of teen movies. Dan didn't need to do things he didn't want to so people would like him and be his friend, or think he was cool. Everyone liked Dan, you couldn't help yourself. Dan was cool without trying, which is what made him cool, or so I'm told. He did like people to be happy, though, and he did like people to be having fun, and to feel cared for. He was a people-pleaser in the generous sense of someone who wanted the people around him to be happy and enjoying life. And that can sometimes mean you make decisions you wouldn't otherwise make. But that didn't really make sense of it.

The Dan we knew had always been vocally anti-drugs, even anti-smoking. His friend Hope had taken up cigarettes in year 11 and she said he gave her such a hard time for smoking, telling her how disgusting it was, saying she might as well be doing drugs, that in the end she gave it up just to get some peace from Dan. As a family we had watched at close hand the devastation drug addiction can cause for an individual, and their family. We had done all we could, over several years, to support someone we loved in the midst and out of the chaos of it all. Another story, and a long and hard one, but suffice to say that Dan had good reason to see drugs as something to treat with caution. But of course, crack and heroin are a different kettle of fish, as it were, to a little bag of MDMA with a bunch of boys on a Friday night.

We knew nothing more about any of any of Dan's decisions about drugs for the next six months. Six months of trying to figure it out, make it make sense, reconfigure, reclaim Dan. In the meantime, Dan's friends had been spending time at our house, which was a great source of comfort to us, and probably also to them. Especially Dan's friend Alice. Alice, it turned out, hadn't been at the rave at all. Dan had told me she was because he knew I always thought he was safe if Alice was there. He knew I'd be more likely to relent, to overcome my worries, to agree he could go to this fictional party, if he said that Alice would be there too. She'd look out for him and make sure he got home in one piece.

Dan's list of friends was a very long list, but Alice and Dan had been friends since year 7, exploring the woods and climbing trees, then later the parties and gigs, with a lift home from her dad. The only time Dan had got roaringly drunk at a party it was Alice he threw up over, and Alice's dad who brought him home early. I was mortified. And furious. He sat on the toilet floor with his head over the bowl for the rest of the night, being told off by me, as he moaned and heaved and told me I shouldn't be cross, I should be grateful, because he'd never, ever do anything that made him feel so ill ever, ever again.

When the police had got Dan's PIN from Jenna and could get into his phone, while Dan was still in the hospital they started making calls, knocking on doors, visiting Dan's friends and asking them questions, and the person who was given the most grief of all was Alice. They questioned her hard, stripped the sheets off her bed, tipped out her drawers, turned her room upside down and inside out, and I could only think this was because I'd told them she was there at the rave. I apologized to Alice for six months for unintentionally causing her this grief, to add to the unintentional grief her great friend Dan had caused by choosing to take drugs and ending up dead.

In the meantime we'd also started a drugs education charity, and commissioned a play that tells Dan's story. This is another long story, and part of that story is a play, another long story in itself, but I need to tell a little of this story to explain how we came to know more about Dan's decision. In the story of the play there is an incredible playwright, Mark Wheeller. The play is a verbatim play, which, I learned, means all the words in the play are real words spoken by the real people in the story. So six months after Dan died Mark came to Croydon and recorded hours and hours of interviews with me, Tim, Jacob, Jenna and her mum and brother Archie, and a bunch of Dan's friends, and transformed these thousands and thousands of words into a beautiful verbatim play, *I Love You, Mum – I Promise I Won't Die*.

The first round of interviews was not long after the trial of the two young men charged with supplying the drugs that killed Dan. The second round of interviews was not long after the sentencing. This is significant because, as we were driven home from the court – after I'd stood in the witness box and read out my trembly victim impact statement to a courtroom packed with the family and friends of the supplier, assorted legal professionals, police people and reporters; after we'd walked out of the court into a wall of heat, and reporters, and cameras and film crews – after this big, long day, our Family Liaison Officer, Steve, handed us Dan's phone.

I hadn't forgotten about Dan's phone, but I hadn't thought about the police giving it back and when that might happen, or how it might feel. It felt big. Too big to do anything but leave it on one side in its police evidence bag until we felt ready.

When Mark Wheeller came back the following Monday to interview Dan's friends, some of them had decided this was the time that the true story had to be told. If someone was going to come and write down what happened, then what they wrote down needed to be what had *really* happened. When Mark came and told us what they'd said, we got Dan's phone out of its evidence bag. We looked at his texts, from that night and from the months leading up to it, from when he'd got his new phone the September before, and there we found a lot of the lost pieces of the puzzle of Dan's story, including the story of the decision he made that night.

This was when we learned that this wasn't Dan's first time with MDMA, as we'd thought. This was his third (and last) time. That was hard. There was a journey we had no idea about. But what was harder was that this was the point we also learned that what had really happened involved Alice, and it involved her a lot. We dropped through a hole right back to the beginning with our reconfiguring. We weren't just missing pieces, we had a different puzzle altogether, a different picture, a different story.

Alice was the girl in the boys' group, chivvying them along, getting them organized, keeping an eye out for them, keeping them safe, and also, it turned out, getting them drugs. Not big time stuff, not even little time, just a bit of social supply, sorting out your friends, possibly only a recent venture. The reason the police had given Alice so much grief was because they'd seen the texts. They'd seen she'd supplied Dan with MDMA both the first and second times. They'd seen she'd offered to supply him that last night. The only reason she hadn't was because she'd forgotten her keys and was locked out of her house, but when the police were turning her bedroom upside down and inside out they were looking for more of the drugs that they thought, not without reason, had killed Dan.

The first time Alice had given Dan MDMA was at a gig they'd been to with some other friends that October. It sounded as though she shared hers with him. It was good. It made his Shredded Wheat taste really nice the next morning apparently. The next time was at another gig a month later. This second time hadn't been good, for Dan or for Alice. Piecing it all together, reading these texts, I remembered him spending a few days in bed with a temperature. I just thought he must have picked up a bug at the gig. Probably not the most hygienic of places, and easy to do. I hadn't realized people took drugs at gigs. I thought they listened to music and maybe danced a bit. I have added this insight to the very long list of things I've learned since Dan died. Things I wish I'd known.

The third time was the rave. In between times two and three came a few other parties or gatherings or events where drugs would have been involved, and each time Dan had made up excuses, different family events I knew weren't true. Then it was New Year's Eve, and Alice had been taking MDMA with her boyfriend for 16 hours, apparently.

'Good god, you guys should try this.' Dan's response? 'Well, I actually want to live past the age of 25…xx'.

And then, 17 days later, there's the rave, and we saw his decision-making played out in a long, circular string of excuses over a 33-minute rapid exchange of texts – *I'm really tired* (probably true), *I have no money* (not true, he'd just been paid), *it'd ruin George's party the next evening* (probably true), *I have to visit my grandpa in hospital* (totally made up), *I don't want to go if you're not going* (true, I'm sure). Over and over, Alice comes back with an answer. To all of Dan's 'but…'s she has a rebuttal.

This was very, very hard. We now understood his reluctance to take the MDMA that night, and we now saw his reluctance to go in the first place, and this was the hardest of blows. If he'd been left alone, if instead of rebutting there'd been relenting, then perhaps, just perhaps, that decision wouldn't have been his last.

It would be very easy and very unfair to blame Alice. Dan was more than capable of sticking to his guns, of saying 'no', of deciding not to go out, to stay at home, under his duvet, watching some nonsense on TV, getting up with his alarm the next morning to deliver papers to his little old ladies, coming home for breakfast, making me coffee.

And Alice wasn't the only person persuading Dan to go. Alice had more influence over Dan than many other friends, but his friend George told me everyone had been on at Dan to go. Why did everyone push him to go when he clearly wasn't keen? George replied that if he was ever doing anything, he'd always want Dan to be there, because everything was more fun when Dan was there. Which it was.

And, of course, Alice hadn't meant Dan to come to harm. She cared about him, they'd been friends for years, she looked out for him and kept him safe; she was devastated when he died. Of course.

It would be very easy to blame Alice, but it would be very unfair, because it's just as easy to be the Alice as the Dan in the story.

Why take drugs?

When reports of a young person's death from drugs gets into the online press or onto social media there are always those who feel the need to say something along the lines of, 'If you choose to do something so stupid you deserve to die', with a throwaway sense of the evolutionary fitness of this particular outcome for that particular decision. For the grieving parents, the painful awareness that there had been a choice in all this is more likely to be framed as an agonized, 'Why did they do it?' With drugs, and with alcohol, there's always a choice. That's an important fact, and it might seem an obvious one, but it isn't always something people making those choices are particularly conscious of. It's an important but very hard fact for anyone who cares for someone whose choices about drugs or alcohol have led to harm, as it was for us when we lost Dan, but holding on to the fact there's always a choice has the potential to lead to empowerment, independence, confidence, good risk management, and getting to go home. That said, choices can be complicated, and never more so than in your adolescence.

With drugs and alcohol there is rarely just one choice to be made. More often one choice leads to another, and off you go into a sequence of choices, which can sometimes seem a lot smaller and more insignificant than they turn out to be, when they get added into the mix of all the other choices being made. The first choice could be as simple as agreeing to meet up, or meet up at that particular place, or with those particular people. Each one of these is almost always complicated by factors relating to the wider or more immediate social context, and to all sorts of things going on in the head and heart and life of the individual making the decision. And of course there will be all the same layers of complexity at work in the choices being made by the people around them, and that social dynamic is a powerful thing in your teens, as we'll see – and as you'll no doubt remember from your own experience.

Behind each choice, somewhere or other, there is a reason. There may be more than one, and none of them may be very good ones, but they'll be there somewhere. Digging them out can take a bit of work, and a lot of self-awareness and reflection – again, a challenge in your teens. We make decisions all the time, throughout our lives, often without really reflecting on why we did or said what we did or said. Indeed, it can take years of professional digging and expensive therapy to unravel the whys and wherefores of our words and actions, but there'll be a reason in there somewhere.

A good starting point for parents helping children navigate their decision-making safely is to hold on to the fact there's always a choice, and always a reason, and that choice is always theirs, even if it doesn't feel like it at the time. That's also an important fact – the choice is theirs, and not ours, and when they make this choice we're very unlikely as their parents to be there to help them through it, and of course it's only right that we're not, especially as they get older. Our scary, important job as parents is, of course, to prepare our children to set off on their own and manage the world of choices safely all by themselves as they gradually step into independence. The more everyone involved understands how those choices are being made, the better it is all round.

The motivation behind the decision

Behind every decision there's a reason, sometimes clear and other times murky, and there are lots of reasons why young people smoke, drink or take drugs. In the Public Health England school survey that I keep coming back to, 11- to 15-year-old students who had taken drugs (not alcohol, smoking or vaping) were asked why they took them at first and on the most recent occasions they took them.[1] The options given were:

- I wanted to see what it was like.
- I wanted to get high or feel good.
- Because my friends were doing it.
- I had nothing better to do.
- I wanted to forget my problems.
- Just because I was offered.
- It was a dare.
- Because it's cool.
- Other.

---

[1] NHS Digital (2019) *Smoking, Drinking and Drug Use Among Young People in England 2018 [NS]* [online]. *NHS Digital.* Available from: <digital.nhs.uk/data-and-information/publications/statistical/smoking-drinking-and-drug-use-among-young-people-in-england/2018> (accessed November 2020)

Unsurprisingly, the biggest reason by far, across all age groups and both sexes, is curiosity. What's it like, what does it do, how does it feel? Girls were more driven by curiosity than boys. They were also more likely than boys to do it because their friends were. Boys were more likely than girls to take something for the effect it can have, or to do it for a dare. Otherwise the data is pretty similar between boys and girls.

There are fewer variations according to age. The main age-related difference is that for 11-year-olds the next biggest motivator after curiosity is boredom, whereas from 12 years upwards what comes next is the urge to get high or feel good. It'll be no surprise that what came next as the reason pupils said they'd taken drugs was because their friends were (the survey doesn't ask specifically about peer pressure). What may be a surprise, however, is to learn that just as many were taking drugs for the first time to forget their problems.

Drugs and mental health

This is a worrying trend. As a reason for taking drugs it has grown over the last ten years or so, from 9 per cent of 11- to 15-year-olds in 2007 to 16 per cent in 2018, the highest level on record. Of course, adults have turned to drugs and alcohol as a coping mechanism from time immemorial, taken to numb, distract or help manage things that are painful or difficult, but it is a concern that even at the age of 12, one in five (19 per cent) said this was the reason they took drugs for the first time.[2]

---

[2]   NHS Digital (2019) *Smoking, Drinking and Drug Use Among Young People in England 2018 [NS]* [online]. *NHS Digital.* Available from: <digital.nhs.uk/data-and-information/ publications/statistical/smoking-drinking-and-drug-use-among-young-people-in-england/2018> (accessed November 2020)

This can be seen across older teens and people in their 20s too. In the same year, the NUS and Release published a survey of university students which found that although by far the biggest reason for taking drugs was for recreational purposes (80 per cent) or to enhance their social interactions (39 per cent), around one in three who had used drugs said they did so to help them deal with stress, and one in five used drugs to self-medicate for an existing mental illness.[3] And many young people are now living with mental ill health.

A recent major national survey of the mental health of 5- to 19-year-olds commissioned by the Department of Health and Social Care (DHSC)[4] found that one in eight children and young people had a mental health disorder, and this grew to around one in six 17- to 19-year-oldsolds. In this older age group girls were more than twice as likely as boys to have a disorder of some sort. In a YouGov survey of university students this figure came out even higher, with more than one in four reporting having a mental health problem of one sort or another – again, more girls than boys. In all cases these figures are dramatically higher for LGBT+ young people. The DHSC survey also found that one in five of those with a disorder reported they were waiting more than six months for contact with a mental health specialist. With drugs more easily available to young people than ever before – and support becoming less and less available over the past ten years[5] – it is hardly surprising that some are turning to substances to help them cope.

---

[3] Release and National Union of Students (2018) *Taking the Hit: Student Drug Use and How Institutions Respond* [online] *NUS*. Available from: <www.release.org.uk/ sites/default/files/pdf/publications/Taking%20the%20Hit%20-%20Student%20 drug%20use%20and%20how%20institutions%20respond%20-.pdf> (accessed November 2020)

[4] NHS Digital (2018) *Mental Health of Children and Young People in England 2017* [online]. *NHS Digital*. Available from: <digital.nhs.uk/data-and-information/ publications/statistical/mental-health-of-children-and-young-people-in-eng- land/2017/2017> (accessed November 2020)

[5] Neufeld, S.A.S., Jones, P.B., Goodyer, I.M. (2017) Child and adolescent mental health services: longitudinal data sheds light on current policy for psychological interventions in the community [online]. *Journal of Public Mental Health*, 16(3), 96–99. Available from: DOI: 10.1108/JPMH-03-2017-0013

In the context of stress, study and students, it's worth mentioning nootropics or 'smart drugs', about which there have been growing concerns in universities across Europe in recent years.[6] Fear of failure, rising levels of stress and anxiety, and pressure to achieve loaded on to them by heavy debt, have led to reports of increasing numbers of students using these performance-enhancing drugs to get that essay finished, cram in some extra revision and get better results. Available online, the most commonly used ones are Modafinil, Ritalin and Adderall, which are normally used to treat disorders such as narcolepsy and ADHD. There has been little research done into the risks posed to people without these conditions self-medicating with them, but what research has been done into their benefits seems to show that although they can keep you awake and working for days and nights on end, the quality of what you produce isn't generally improved by staying awake for unnaturally long periods of time. What works much better, of course, is good food, good sleep and plenty of exercise.

Supporting children with mental health issues can be incredibly challenging for parents, and is the topic of many another book and way beyond the scope of this one, but in the context of drugs and alcohol it is important, if you have concerns about your child's mental health, or they have a diagnosis of a mental health condition, that you include the risks specific to drugs and alcohol in your conversations with them. They may be more vulnerable to using substances as a coping mechanism, and using drugs can in turn exacerbate their mental health problems. If they are on medication there may also be substances that would be particularly risky for them to take, and this is worth discussing with your GP. We will go on to look at the complicated relationship between mental health, drugs and addiction in Chapter 9.

---

[6] The Guardian (2017) Universities must do more to tackle use of smart drugs, say experts [online]. *The Guardian*. Available from: <www.theguardian.com/education/2017/may/10/universities-do-more-tackle-smart-drugs-say-experts-uk-exams> (accessed November 2020)

Talking point

A conversation about motivation to use substances, whether drugs or alcohol, could be in response to something watched together on television or seen in the news. It is important children and young people become self-aware and self-conscious in decision-making situations so they can weigh up their own motivation in a situation involving risk, and also that of the people around them.

If you are aware your child has taken drugs, finding out their motivation is important, if you can, in helping both you and them understand the factors at work, and beginning to find a safe and healthier way forward. Advice on going about these sorts of conversations, and how to tackle issues if there are any, will come along in Chapter 9.

If you have a child at university, a conversation about 'smart drugs' would be good. Are they aware of other students using these? What do they think?

The amazing adolescent brain

In Chapter 2 we looked at the complex, intricate, super-efficient super-highways of communication that whizz messages around our brain, making everything we do, think, say or feel happen – the busy business of neurons and neurotransmitters, communicating across synapses from axon to dendrite. From before we are born, and on through our childhood, teens, adulthood and old age, our brain is constantly changing, referred to as 'plasticity' by neuroscientists. However, there are certain critical periods in the brain's development, one of which is adolescence. This process lasts 15 long years, and there are many, very important, changes taking place during this time. This is all relatively recent knowledge, only possible since technology has developed to enable neuroscientists to examine healthy living brains at work, and there is much more yet to be discovered. For the purposes of this book we'll be focusing on what these changes mean for making safer choices about drugs and alcohol. It's all a delicate balance of self-regulation, sensation-seeking and social sensitivity.

Talking point

There are three books that have helped me get where I have in understanding the adolescent brain, to which I owe a huge debt, and each one of which I'd thoroughly recommend for any parents of pre-teens and teens.

- Sarah-Jayne Blakemore, *Inventing Ourselves: The Secret Life of the Teenage Brain* (Doubleday, 2018).
- Frances E. Jensen, *The Teenage Brain: A Neuroscientist's Survival Guide to Raising Adolescents and Young Adults* (HarperCollins, 2015)
- Nicola Morgan, *Blame My Brain: The Amazing Teenage Brain Revealed* – written for a teenage reader, it also makes for a clear and accessible read for parents (Walker Books, 2012)

Taking a risk

Much as we want to protect our children from risk, because of course everything in the very core of our being as parents wants to protect them from harm of any sort, taking risks is important for many reasons. It's a part of how we learn. Taking the risk that the question you're burning to ask may be searing and incisive, or may be so stupid and obvious that you'll never hold your head up high in public again. Taking the risk of being shockingly bad at painting in the hope that a few weeks, months or years of practice will lead to praise and perfection.

It's also part of our evolutionary development. If we hadn't set foot outside the cave we'd have lived a short, dark life and left no ancestors to populate the planet: 'The willingness to take risks, even life-threatening risks, might well have proved advantageous to our ancestors when refusing to incur such risk was in fact even more dangerous to survival or reproduction. However chancy running through a burning savannah or attempting to cross a swollen stream might have been, not doing so might have been even more risky.'[7]

---

[7] Steinberg L. & Belsky J. (1996) An evolutionary perspective on psychopathology in adolescence. In: Cicchetti D. and Toth S., editors. *Rochester Symposium on Developmental Psychopathology*. Vol. 7 Rochester, NY: University of Rochester Press

It's important, too, because it's only in taking risks that our children will learn to manage them, and whether we like it or not, their lives will be full of hazards they'll need to be able to weigh and measure and make their way around, through or away from, mostly without our help as they move into adulthood. Adolescence is a time of more than regular risk-taking, however, for reasons we'll explore. Not all these risks end well, and as we've seen, risks relating to drugs and alcohol are complex. The more parents and teens can both understand the dynamics at work, the fewer sticky endings there are likely to be.

Research shows, and we all know from experience, that risk-taking increases from childhood to adolescence, then decreases into adulthood, peaking around mid-adolescence. The optimum age for risk-taking seems to be between 13 and 16, and this seems to be consistent the world over, regardless of cultural context. How this manifests itself in different parts of the world may be different, but the patterns of behaviour are the same.[8] The 15th birthday party may be one to face with extra special caution.

Research also seems to show that a lot of the common beliefs about teenagers and risk are in fact myths. In tests, teenagers showed that in the cold light of the social psychology research project, they're just as good at weighing up the riskiness of a situation as adults. They're no more likely to think they're invulnerable and immortal, nor to embrace risk for risk's sake, than those whose brains have passed through adolescence and out the other side. It turns out that teenagers are generally just as logical and accurate in the ways in which they perceive and judge risky activity as their parents.[9] But there are dynamics at work in adolescence that can, and all too often do, trump all the sense of the most sensible teenager faced with a risky decision. This is why knowledge and understanding can only get you so far when it comes to decisions about drugs and alcohol, and don't always get you to the other side of the decision safely.

---

[8]   Duell, N., Steinberg, L., Icenogle, G. et al. (2018) Age patterns in risk taking across the world [online]. *Journal of Youth and Adolescence.* 47, 1052–1072 (2018). Available from: DOI: 10.1007/s10964-017-0752-y

[9]   Steinberg, L. (2008) A social neuroscience perspective on adolescent risk taking [online]. *Developmental Review.* Available from: DOI: 10.1016/j. dr.2007.08.002

It's all to do with the shifting balance between the brain's development of its socio-emotional system, the bit that leads to increased reward-seeking, and its cognitive control centre, the bit that helps us self-regulate. It's primarily the limbic system that's responsible for the former, and the pre-frontal cortex for the latter. In the developing brain, one of these is racing ahead, the other lagging behind. You can probably guess which is doing which.

Getting wired up

Put very simply, our brains are divided into different regions, which serve different functions, and need to be able to communicate with each other efficiently in order for us to do most of the things we do – and think, and say, and so on. We're born with brains crammed full of neurons but not the connections we need, which is why, despite all those brain cells, we're still helpless as babies. The process of wiring these areas of our brain takes place throughout childhood and adolescence, and happens from the back of our brains to the front. The significance of the order in which this happens in relation to making decisions about drugs and alcohol is that the brain area that's the very last to fully connect is the sensible bit, our pre-frontal cortex. This part of our brain, just behind our forehead, is responsible for all our executive functions. It's the area we need to access for all our higher-level cognitive processes, things like planning, decision-making, problem solving, self-regulation, and acting with consequences in mind. It's also responsible for moderating social behaviour, social interactions and self-awareness. It's just that bit harder to access all of this during adolescence, and it takes us up to our mid-twenties for this process of connection to be completed.

Talking point

Explain to your teenager why it can sometimes be a struggle to think through consequences, manage emotions and make decisions. Encourage them to try to give themselves time to think if they're making decisions involving risk – which decisions about drugs always do – so they can access that sensible part of their brain to help them make a decision that will be more likely to keep them safe. You could think about different stalling tactics together and talk through possible scenarios.

Rewards

The limbic system of the brain is stimulated by social and emotional variables, and develops both earlier and faster than the pre-frontal cortex. It has been described as the 'feeling and reacting brain' as opposed to the 'thinking brain'.[10] So, until sense can catch up with sensation, the desire for rewards and social pressures can all too easily override rational thinking. Dopamine plays a big part in this. Dopamine is a neurotransmitter that gives us a natural happy high, and this is very much associated with the limbic system and with reward. Scans have shown that the hit the teenage brain gets from reward is so much more intense than we ever experience again as adults, because not only is the release of dopamine enhanced but so is the brain's response to it.

Risk and reward are inextricably linked in the structure of the brain, and in your teens this intense sense of reward gets some of its biggest hits in response to risk. Frances E. Jensen refers to a Stanford University study which examined brain activity when participants took risks related to decisions about fake stocks. The highest rewards required the riskiest decisions. Scientists found, interestingly, that the reward centre of participants, the part of our brain associated with release of dopamine, lit right up just in anticipation of taking a risk, not from the reward of the fake money itself. They found that heightened positive emotions are indicators of a likeliness to engage in risk-taking behaviour.[11] When emotions are running high, that's when risks often get taken – and these were sensible, highly intelligent Stanford doctoral students taking part in the study. The average 15-year-old out at a party would be experiencing emotions at a much higher level of intensity. And with teenagers, the more immediate the risk, the bigger the hit. Delayed gratification is something that has to wait a while.

---

[10] Swenson, R. (2006) *Review of Clinical and Functional Neuroscience* [online]. Chapter 9. *Dartmouth Medical School*. Available from: <www.dartmouth.edu/~r-swenson/NeuroSci/chapter_9.html> (accessed November 2020)

[11] Trei, L. (2005) Areas of brain linked to risky, risk-averse financial choices, researchers find [online]. *Stanford News*. Available from: <news.stanford.edu/news/2005/september28/neuron-092805.html> (accessed November 2020)

Talking point

Talk to your teens about situations when their emotions may be running high – what is it that gives them a real buzz? Being aware that in such situations their likelihood of taking a risk will be increased can help them manage those decisions more safely.

They're also more likely in adolescence to take risks if emotions are running high because they're feeling under pressure. Talk about the situations, individuals or groups that might make them feel pressured, and work through scenarios to manage – or avoid – the sorts of pressure they feel might make them more vulnerable to taking a risky decision.

Learning a lesson

It's a truth often told that we learn from our mistakes. Indeed, taking the risk of making a mistake is an important element in all sorts of learning. Mistakes made when taking risks with drugs and alcohol can be so serious there's no option to learn for the next time, as we know. However, I've also been at some pains to reassure my readers that mostly this isn't the case, and usually teenagers do get the chance to do things differently another time. They might get the chance, but they can't always make the most of it, however, and this is because of their developing brain again. The part of our brain that stores negative information, all those decisions that went badly wrong, is the pre-frontal cortex, which means learning from mistakes during adolescence is harder to do than at any other time of life. The knowledge that we messed up last time when we made that exact same decision is tucked away in that part of our brain it's hardest to get into quickly and easily to bring it to bear the next time. On the other hand, there are more areas, and more accessible areas, of the brain that store positive information, so it's much easier to learn that a risk that paid off and made you feel amazing from the taking of it is worth doing again, than to learn you should never do certain things again, or at least not like that.

The role peers play

As I said in my story, when Dan died lots of people talked about peer pressure – the kind attempts of my own peers to try to reassure me it wasn't Dan's fault, it was all those bad peers, pressuring him to do bad stuff. It was genuinely good-hearted to try to deflect blame from Dan. After all, he'd paid the heaviest of prices for the decision he made that night, without having to bear the blame for it, too. But as with all these things it's a whole lot more complicated than it might seem. And in any case, blame gets you nowhere very useful most of the time, and rarely anywhere very positive, unless it helps you understand and change your choices for the next time.

Peer pressure is definitely a very real and powerful force in adolescence, and there are reasons for that we'll come on to, but it's worth remembering that we can all tend to follow the crowd, and shape our behaviour to please our peers, to greater or lesser extents throughout our lives, and for good evolutionary reasons. As early humans we survived because of our ability to band together. Promoting social harmony and avoiding dissent was vital, because falling out with the group, and falling outside its protection, could mean death. The world is also a complicated place, and we just don't have the time we'd need to research and reflect on all the decisions that fly our way continually to be able to reach our own independent conclusions. Following the crowd can be cognitively efficient, and we can use the decisions of others as shortcuts. As philosopher and mathematician Alfred North Whitehead apparently said, 'Civilization advances by extending the number of operations we can perform without thinking about them.'[12]

When it comes to adolescence, there are extra special, extra-ordinary factors at work in addition to all of this. One of these is the need to gain independence; the social imperative that drives adolescents to forge some degree of separation from their childhood family unit in order to be able to function successfully as an adult. As a newborn our survival is dependent on having at least one good and reliable adult in the role of a parent looking out for us. As a teenager our survival is dependent on being socially accepted by our peers, at a deeply unconscious but visceral level. Sarah-Jayne Blakemore describes the 'social risk' factor at work in adolescent decision-making.[13] This is where intelligence, encyclopaedic knowledge of the risks and a naturally cautious frame of mind can fall by the wayside when it comes to decisions about drugs and alcohol. The social risk of being rejected by your friendship group may outweigh the known risk of taking that pill, or having another drink when you know you're already well over your personal sensible limit.

This is one of the reasons why teenagers are more likely to take risks when they're with their friends. Another reason was demonstrated by a couple of neuroscientists at Temple University, who set a group of teenagers and adults going on a driving game, with their brains wired to a functional magnetic resonance imaging (fMRI) machine.[14] The goal was to get to the end of the game as quickly as possible, with various risks along the way that could get you there faster, and speed was linked to the size of financial reward. On their own in the virtual car, all the participants, whether adult or teen, had roughly the same rate of risk-taking. However, when they played the

---

[12]   Henderson, R. (2017) The Science Behind Why People Follow the Crowd [online]. *Psychology Today*. Available from: <www.psychologytoday.com/gb/blog/after-service/201705/the-science-behind-why-people-follow-the-crowd> (accessed November 2020)

[13]   Blakemore, S-J. (2018) Avoiding social risk in adolescence [online]. *Current Directions in Psychological Science*. Available from: DOI: 10.1177%2F0963721417-738144

[14]   Nauert, R. (2011) Friends Drive Friends to Take Risks. *Live Science*. Available from: <www.livescience.com/11668-friends-drive-friends-risks.html>

game with their peers watching, the levels of risk the teenagers took shot up, and the fMRI machine showed the hit they got from a sense of reward shot up too. The scientists already knew that the reward people experience is much greater when they're already glowing from another reward. They hadn't seen this quite so powerfully at work in teens, however. They concluded that because adolescents have such a heightened sensitivity to social reward, being with their friends 'primes the reward system and makes teens pay more attention to the potential payoffs of a risky decision'.

Talking point

Talk to your teenager about the driving game experiment. Have they seen a similar dynamic at work, where someone who is usually sensible has made a risky decision because their friends were there? Encourage them to take a moment if they're making decisions about drugs or alcohol and to ask themselves, 'Would I do this if I was on my own?'

Using your powers for good

In the same way many drugs can be of huge benefit medicinally as well as cause harm when used recreationally, so peer influence is also a powerful force that can be brought to bear for good or ill. It can often take just one person in a social group to express a little doubt that this really is such a good idea for others to feel released to do likewise. There can often be an 'Emperor's new clothes' factor at work with teenagers. They might all assume everyone else thinks this is going to be a great experience, and they're all totally up for it, when actually all their respective boots are being quaked in. It's likely that the part of their brains that knows this is risky is already weighing this known risk up against the potential but more potent risk of jeopardizing their social acceptance and status. The power of one. Easier said than done, of course, but worth pointing out to your teenagers.

Talking point: Matt's story

One morning towards the end of January a few years ago I spoke to a hall full of year 12s, and as usual, told Dan's story. A few weeks later we held a workshop for parents at the school, and a couple came and spoke to me afterwards, and told me their son's story. Matt had been in the audience that morning in January when I spoke, and unknown to me was still suffering the after-effects of having taken MDMA on New Year's Eve with a group of his friends. He'd taken it before, but for whatever reason this time had left him experiencing such high levels of anxiety and paranoia that his mum was having to sleep in his room at night all these weeks later.

His mum told me that he'd come home from school on the day I'd spoken and told her about Dan. He said it made him realize how close he'd come to this himself. Sitting there and looking at me, he'd been thinking not only that it could have been him, but also that it could have been his mum standing up there talking to a hall full of year 12s about her lovely boy who didn't come home.

Matt told his mum he knew he had to speak to his friends and tell them he wasn't going to do MDMA any more, but he wasn't sure what the impact would be on their friendship and shared social lives. Hard though it was, he did it, not at all sure what their reaction would be.

His mum told me he'd come home, however, and said, really surprised, 'You know what, Mum, I think they were all relieved'. Perhaps they'd also been shaken by Matt's reaction on New Year's Eve. Perhaps they were also sitting in the hall that January morning. It's a powerful illustration that appearances can be deceptive at the best of times, and especially in our teens.

It's worth remembering, when you're feeling unsure of yourself as a teenager, that you're surrounded by other teenagers also needing to know they're accepted by their peer group, also getting a bigger buzz than at any other time of life from risk and reward, and also needing a bit of help to access that sensible bit of their brains that might give them pause for thought about whether this really is such a good idea after all.

Jack's advice about making decisions

The night of the rave, as I mentioned, the boys had all made up stories for their parents about why they wouldn't be home that night, most of them saying they'd be sleeping over at a friend's house, including Jack. His mum had dropped him and his overnight bag off at this friend's house, not knowing the plan was to head straight out to meet up with the others, to pick up drugs, to find a rave.

When Dan died, of course Jack's parents knew that he was distraught – after all, his best friend had died so suddenly, and in such an awful way. What they didn't know was that Jack had been at the rave, too. They didn't know he'd shared Dan's last hours, and witnessed the disturbing effects of the MDMA on his soon-to-be-unconscious friend, a traumatizing sight for poor Jack. The longer Jack left it, the harder it was to tell them, and the worse he felt, because he's really close to his family. Eventually, some long weeks after Dan died, he and his mum were up at Dan's grave and he told her. Of course, she was just so disappointed he hadn't told her sooner, told his dad, and so on.

When we started doing all we could through the Foundation to support other young people to make safer choices, we asked Dan's friends what their advice would be to other young people. We were keen to harness the power of peer influence, and the passion they shared with us to make the difference to others they couldn't make for Dan. What Jack said was this: if it's something you can't tell your mum, then it's probably not a good idea.

Easier said than done, as Jack of all people knows, but it's another useful gauge for your own children to keep in their heads when they're making decisions about drugs and alcohol.

If it's something you can't tell the person who loves you best in the world, then it's probably worth a second thought.

And some very last words from Alice

I sent Dan's friend Alice the bit of his story that involves her, because although I knew it would be an incredibly hard read, I didn't want to include it without her knowing it was there, and somehow being at peace with that – a big ask, because of the inevitable pain of it all. I wanted her to know that in order to unpick this part of the story for Dan I'd gone back to all the texts between them both again after all these years, and what I'd written is based on what's there. I wanted her to know my intention was to be honest but also fair, and to illustrate in this chapter how easy it is in your adolescence to make decisions you might come to regret not just for yourself, but also through influencing the decisions of a friend – and thereby, through it all, to help other parents help their children. But I knew how much courage it would take for her, and I wanted the last words of this important chapter about decision-making to be hers.

A letter from Alice

I read over the chapter of your book that you sent me. It took a few attempts to get to the end as it was very hard to read. I can't imagine how difficult it was for you to write. It's hard to say that I have no problem with you using the texts that I sent to Dan all those years ago because they evoke such feelings of guilt, regret and shame. To be perfectly honest I wish I could erase them from the face of the earth. I do however understand the importance they hold in Dan's story, and if you using them in this book prevents even one person from suffering like Dan did then the discomfort they cause me is irrelevant.

It would be nice to think that although your book will be about helping parents to keep their kids safe from drugs, perhaps it may also prevent their children from making the same mistakes I did. I wish I could go back and tell myself all the things I know now. Hopefully your book will allow parents to impart what we have learned onto their children without them having to suffer the loss of someone so close to them.

I remember taking the photo that was used to make the logo for the Foundation. It was in the music room at school after he had been playing guitar. He had those braces on that he had started wearing to school, looking dapper as ever. He always used to get annoyed at me taking pictures and videoing him playing guitar and doing the usual crazy Dan stuff but now I am so glad that I did. And it's nice to still see Dan's face brought to life by all the work you do.

I still think about Dan all the time. He gives me the motivation to try my best with everything. I feel like I need to make up for what he has missed. I feel so guilty about everything that happened and the role I unfortunately played. I can't go back and change what happened, but hopefully I can try and make the most of every opportunity that comes my way, just as I know he would.

I also hope that people can learn from the mistakes I made and that the Foundation, play and now book may save some lives along the way. If using the messages I sent to Dan, and telling other people about all that happened, prevents someone else from repeating it all, then of course please share it, painful though it is.

5

I wish I'd known the legal fallout

Drugs, alcohol and the law

When Dan died the only dealings with the police we had experienced as parents, or at all for that matter, were when Jacob had got mugged in year 8 by older kids from another school, twice in close succession (poor Jacob.) All we knew about judges, juries and the drama of court was what we'd seen on television or in films, where the public gallery was generally an actual, literal gallery, with wooden railings and plenty of space for interested parties to oversee proceedings, and not two rows of six plastic chairs all squashed up together at the side of a small hot courtroom. Of course I knew illegal drugs were illegal, but I had no idea quite how many pitfalls there were for young people, and along with many young people I hadn't thought through the fact that the legal consequences of a conviction for a drug-related offence can be even more damaging and lasting than many of the physical and mental health consequences of drug use, serious though those can of course also be.

Like most law-abiding adults, the majority of young people don't want to get on the wrong side of the law. However, their levels of exposure to illegal substances, and the illegal practices surrounding these substances, are so much greater than they ever were, and one of the effects of this can be to normalize not just drug use but also drug supply, and other criminal activity around drugs. Social media plays a role in this, as we saw in Chapter 2, and will explore in more detail later in this chapter. And the decisions they make in this drug-related arena are of course all made with those teenage brains we've just been reading about, which don't always help them out when it comes to thinking things through and managing risks, whether these risks are related to their physical or mental health or to the law of the land. Much as all parents hope their child will never end up in court on a drug-related charge, and most of them won't, these risks do exist. As with many other drug-related risks, they can be avoided with some knowledge and understanding of what the risks might look like, and where they might be found.

Even while the battle for Dan's life was being fought fiercely in the hospital, our learning curve about drugs and the law had already started, and there was a very steep climb still to come.

Dan's story: the trial, the sentencing, the aftermath

Evening Standard, 21 January 2014, Daniel Spargo-Mabbs: two men charged with supplying drugs after teenager who 'took ecstasy' at west London rave dies

The day after we packed up our little waiting room in the liver intensive care unit at Kings and set off home without Dan, the police arrested and charged two local men for supplying the drugs that killed him. Nicqueel Pitrora was accused of having taken the calls from the boy in the group with Dan, and of organizing the drugs and the drop-off. Ryan Kirk was accused of having delivered them. They appeared in court the following day, and both pleaded not guilty to being concerned in the supply of Class A drugs (the drugs that killed Dan) on the night of 17 January. They were both denied bail and sent to HMP Wormwood Scrubs where they spent the next six months awaiting trial. The trial was set for 14 July. Nicqueel was 18, Ryan was 20. Ryan was to have his 21st birthday in prison.

The media found this all very interesting, which was surprising to us at first, but of course, surely the whole world must be reeling at the loss of Dan? Surely the equilibrium of the universe itself must have been knocked out of kilter by the reality of Dan being there, and then not being there? Being here, and then not here. With us, then not with us.

In between the bail hearing and the trial there were four Plea Case Management Hearings. I'd never heard of a Plea Case Management Hearing before. It wasn't something that had cropped up in any of the courtroom dramas I'd seen on television. Apparently, they need to review the charges and timescales and various things like that, and it was all made more complicated because the Crown Prosecution Service was looking to see whether a manslaughter charge could be brought. This was serious stuff.

I can't now remember when this bigger charge came into the picture, but early on, I had no idea whether I had a right to feel any of this was anything to do with me, or anything I was allowed to be affected by, interested in, involved in. I did feel affected, interested and involved, but was I supposed to? I didn't know what the rules were about these things. They'd been asked to supply some drugs and they'd done as they were asked (or so the charges alleged). Dan had taken said drugs of his own free will. They had nothing to do with Dan other than being (allegedly) concerned in the supply of the Class A drugs that killed him. He had nothing to do with them other than taking the drugs they (allegedly) supplied. They had never even met. And at every Plea Case Management Hearing they said they didn't do it, it wasn't them, they were Not Guilty.

It was a week before the trial that we finally heard the decision about the manslaughter charge. It had been dropped. It had been referred higher and higher, right up to a leading specialist prosecution barrister, but it wouldn't have stuck, so it had to go. Back to supply. If it had been manslaughter, our Family Liaison Officer Steve had said the trial would almost certainly have to be postponed so the defence would have time to gather enough evidence, and by this stage I just wanted it to stop being there, hanging there over our heads. So, we knew the date, just seven days to wait, and then it would all be over and done with.

I thought I'd be relieved, and I was at first, but relief unexpectedly turned quickly into total devastation. Where would Dan be in this now? It would just be about whether they did or didn't supply Class A drugs on the night of 17 January 2014. Dan would be invisible. It wouldn't matter that the Class A drugs they did or didn't supply had caused my son to die. Dan wouldn't matter, his death wouldn't matter.

MyLondon, 18 July 2014, Drug dealer pleads guilty to supplying ecstasy which killed Daniel Spargo-Mabbs

But it turned out it did matter. The whole trial seemed to be driven by the fact that Dan had died. His name was in the air every day at some point or other. *Daniel Spargo-Mabbs. This terrible tragedy. Daniel Spargo-Mabbs. A boy lost his life. Daniel Spargo-Mabbs.* Dan was there, and he mattered, and it mattered in the court that his life had been lost because of the drugs supplied that night in January.

On Day One, Nicqueel Pitrora pleaded guilty. Steve had said he would. He'd said there was so much phone evidence making it clear he'd been supplying the boy in the group who'd made the call for at least a year before, and others as well, that they'd stopped looking any further back.

But Ryan Kirk pleaded not guilty, so off we set into the trial that was to last the next five days, in a hot little courtroom on the other side of London. Steve picked us up first thing every day, we sat in traffic across London for a couple of hours there, then again for a couple more hours back home, on the hottest week that summer.

I hadn't sat through a trial before, and despite watching the cleverness of barristers argue their way in, around and through their cases on those television dramas, I had forgotten that of course it isn't about truth, it's about evidence, which should be the same thing but isn't. We wanted truth, but we realized on Day One that wasn't what we were necessarily going to get, at least not in any pure sense of who actually did this thing. It was about the quality of the evidence, and it turned out the quality of the evidence that Ryan Kirk had or hadn't done this was flawed, because of something to do with how or when it had been taken in the initial stages. He may have done it, he may not have done it, and we knew the verdict may not be the right one in that pure sense of truth and of right.

When we arrived at the court on that first day, all 12 of the plastic seats in the public gallery were full of the family and friends of the defendants. We were a party of six that hadn't really thought about there not being any room for us. Tim, Jacob, me, Tim's brother, his sister, our big nephew. We went in that first morning, looked for a seat, saw there weren't any, and had to come out again. Steve sorted it out. Steve sorted things out. We loved Steve for sorting things out. He organized it so that they had the front six seats and we had the back six, and that's how we spent the next five days, sitting squashed up behind the family and friends of the defendant. Nicqueel Pitrora's mum sat in the row in front of us that first day, shoulders shaking, weeping. I really felt for her. She'd lost her son too, in a way. There he was behind the glass and not with her. But then, on the other hand, he'd be back, he'd be with her again, and Dan wouldn't, not ever. I lent her a tissue.

It was the strangest of social dynamics. Although we bore them no ill-will – why would we? – nor they us, it appeared, nevertheless we were on different sides in this. Not that there were really sides as such, or shouldn't be if it was all about truth and justice and if that was what mattered, but we were both emotionally invested in the outcome for our son/brother/cousin/nephew/friend, and they wanted him to be cleared, and we wanted to know if he was guilty, and if he was, then we wanted him to be found guilty. And in that strange social mix there was also a group of reporters, and we became three bubbles for that week, inhabiting the same space in that little hot courtroom, and outside it, most of the time pretending the others weren't there, even though there they were, every day, for five days. The reporters' bubble diminished as the trial began to seem less interesting, but one or two stuck it out to the end. Steve sorted it out for us to have a little private room to wait in so it felt less uncomfortable sitting alongside the other bubbles eating our sandwiches at lunchtime, or waiting out another legal discussion we weren't allowed to witness, but it didn't have any windows or any air and in that hottest of weeks we could only manage so much privacy before we had to break out for oxygen and a bit of a breeze.

So, what was hardest about that week? Apart from the strange social dynamic, the squashed-up seats, the hot little room, the hot long journeys? It was hard hearing the defence barrister trying to get the case thrown out because of a legal technicality over the process of gathering evidence (the only day I sat and cried, silently, the clerk handing me tissues). It was hard hearing the witness's testimony. The defendant's defence. It was hard hearing the story of that last night of Dan's replayed in court. It was hard hearing Dan's name on everyone's lips but feeling so numb and disconnected. I held onto his Travelcard all the time, looking at the photo I'd taken for him, wearing his favourite sloppy yellow t-shirt. The t-shirt we'd given the funeral directors for him to wear in his coffin.

It was hard that we were totally, utterly invisible in that courtroom where all this was happening. To hear Dan's name on the lips of the judge and the barristers, this terrible tragedy of our son's death referred to continually, without any acknowledgement that the mum and dad and big brother of the boy who'd lost his life in this terrible tragedy were sitting there listening to it all. The dynamic of the courtroom all takes place between the judge, legal teams, witnesses, defendants and jury. Nobody else. Not us.

Jacob is a leg-jiggler, and there was a lot to jiggle about that week, and all those 12 plastic chairs were soldered together so that when one person jiggled everyone did.

And then it came to the verdict. The jury went out on Thursday afternoon, and we waited, but they couldn't decide. They came back into court, and we did, too, to see again all the faces that had and hadn't been identified by the one witness, the boy in the group who'd made the call and sorted the deal and gathered the cash and collected the drugs and shared them out that night back in January. But they still couldn't decide. So, we were back on Friday, waiting again.

I had spoken to our little party of six and said whatever the verdict, we don't react in court. We can have our reactions later, but not in that public space, because whatever our reactions are, they could be hard for Ryan's family and friends, and that wouldn't be fair. If he's found guilty and we're visibly happy that would be hard for them. If he's found not guilty and we're visibly sad that would also be hard, though they probably wouldn't notice because they'd be so happy, but nevertheless we needed to respect them and bide our time and respond off radar. We would be dignified, and respectful.

BBC News, 18 July 2014, Daniel Spargo-Mabbs death – Ryan Kirk cleared of drug supply

Finally that Friday we were called back into court, to hear Ryan Kirk being found not guilty. His family had clearly not had the conversation about saving their reaction, because they were over the moon, metaphorical hats thrown in the air, happy as they could be, and not remotely mindful of the fact that just behind them, squashed up in those six seats, was the family of the boy who had died as a result of the drugs that were dropped off that night, whether by their son or not. Of course they were happy, and of course they needed to express that, but their jubilation was to such a degree that the defence barrister was asked by the judge to tell them to tone it down after we'd all left the courtroom and it continued unabated outside.

Of course we knew whatever the verdict it would never bring Dan back, and of course we knew the person who dropped off those drugs on his bike was the tiniest of players in the process that ended up with Dan getting a fatally strong bag of MDMA, and as I said we never wanted an innocent person to be found guilty. But this was hard. Because, we were told, a different jury, a different day, a different verdict, perhaps. It wasn't about truth it was about evidence. And what was the truth?

Daily Mail, **1 August 2014, 'We would willingly have given our lives in place of his': Mother of schoolboy who died after taking ecstasy reduces courtroom to tears with emotional speech as dealer who supplied drugs to her son is jailed**

And so, to the sentencing. I had written a victim impact statement. I wanted to have a voice in that courtroom. I wanted to be visible in that place where we had spent an invisible week. I wanted to let Nicqueel Pitrora, and his family and friends, know that his decision to supply drugs had consequences, and that for us and for Dan, those had been significant. I wanted him to make those connections, so he'd stop selling drugs and find something better to do with his life. He was just 18. He had the whole of the rest of this life ahead of him. He'd already had more life than Dan had managed, and statistically he had a lot of years to go, even if he'd chosen a career path with a shorter than usual life-expectancy. He could do good things with those years, and that life. Dan would have done good things with his life, if he'd still had it. He had a great big heart, an acute conscience, he cared about right and wrong, about people being treated fairly and being happy. Nicqueel Pitrora couldn't give us Dan back, but he could live the good life Dan would have lived, if he'd been able to stick around. That would be the best – the only – restitution he could make for a good life lost. Dan's life.

But over the days before the sentencing, I wavered. Up until that very last day I didn't know I could do it. I'd written it before the trial, and now I knew who'd be listening I was increasingly sure I didn't want to read it out to them. My bared soul, my poured-out heart. It would be in the *Daily Mail* the next day. Did I really want my bared soul and my broken heart in the pages of people's Saturday papers?

I had bought a dress. My second clothing purchase that year. A funeral dress, a sentencing dress. Hard to find the right clothing for these wrong occasions, but it was important to me on this important occasion to do my best to look dignified and undefeated. I'd rejected five I'd ordered online – too short, too shiny, too frilly, not quite right – and found something on a dash into Croydon that was the closest I could find, as someone with little patience for shopping at the best of times, let alone these worst of times.

The court was packed, with family and friends, reporters, legal people, senior police, others. And it was all about Dan dying, from start to finish. The defence barrister, doing his job, tried to minimize Nicqueel Pitrora's role and maximize his potential as a reformed citizen. *Working hard at college, trying to get qualifications, a troubled home, sorry for what he did, never do it again, wanted to work with young people and warn them about the risks of drugs.* That would be good.

Then I stood in the witness box and read out my victim impact statement. I nearly didn't make it through to the end, my voice all a wobble, shaking from head to toe, almost giving out when I got to the bit in the story where Dan died. Tim stood with me in case I didn't make it, but I did. Apparently, I made people cry – journalists, court officials, Pitrora's prison guard who had to leave her post behind the glass screen and be replaced. And Pitrora's mum. Perhaps she knew it could make things worse for her son? Perhaps she knew the love a mother has for her son, and how broken his loss might leave her? Perhaps she felt partly responsible for what her son had done? Like I felt responsible for what Dan had done, for being a mum who made a boy who said 'yes' and not 'no' that night in January.

Pitrora was jailed for five years for being concerned with the supply of MDMA, and two years and four months to be served concurrently for the supply of cannabis. No penalty was added for a count of simple possession. He had three previous convictions for which he had youth rehabilitation orders – for supply, for carrying an offensive weapon, for assaulting a policeman. These were revoked.

This is what Judge Martin Edmunds QC said:

> 'I keep well in mind that you are being sentenced for being concerned in supply and not for manslaughter. But there can be no question that you bear a heavy weight of responsibility for the death of Daniel.
>
> That said, no sentence I can pass can in any way equate to the depth of grief felt by those that loved him, nor the value of that young life lost.'

As he stood, and the court stood with him, he turned towards Tim and me, looked at us, and bowed his head.

And so we walked out of court into the sunshine, we three remaining Spargo-Mabbses, hand in hand, to face the wall of reporters, cameras and film crews, and do our best to talk to the press as the low-flying planes roared repeatedly over our heads to land nearby at Heathrow.

'Fiona, in court you said losing a son was like having a limb ripped off without an anaesthetic. Could you tell us a bit more about that...?'

Drugs and the law – a starting point

The primary legal framework which governs current charging and sentencing relating to drugs today is the Misuse of Drugs Act, passed in 1971. There had been various laws put in place since the turn of the century, but until this point drugs laws in the UK were considered relatively liberal. This Act significantly extended the range of prohibited substances and divided them into classifications dependent on their perceived risks, which related in turn to sentencing guidelines. It also added to the existing categories of possession, supply, possession with intent to supply, import and export, including allowing your home, or premises you own, to be used for the production or supply of controlled drugs.

The three classes of controlled drugs

Controlled drugs are put into three categories based on the level of harm: Class A (most harmful), Class B and Class C.[1]

Class A: Crack cocaine, cocaine, ecstasy (MDMA), heroin, LSD, magic mushrooms (psilocybin), methadone, methamphetamine (crystal meth)	Possession: Up to seven years in prison, an unlimited fine or both	Supply and production: Up to life in prison, an unlimited fine or both

---

[1] Gov.uk (2020) Drugs penalties [online]. *Gov.uk*. Available from: <www.gov.uk/penalties-drug-possession-dealing> (accessed November 2020)

Class B: Cannabis, ketamine, codeine, amphetamines, Ritalin, synthetic cannabinoids ('Spice'), mephedrone	Possession: Up to five years in prison, an unlimited fine or both	Supply and production: Up to 14 years in prison, an unlimited fine or both
Class C: Anabolic steroids, benzodiazepines (including Xanax), tramadol, GHB, khat	Possession: Up to two years in prison, an unlimited fine or both (except anabolic steroids which are legal to possess for personal use)	Supply and production: Up to 14 years in prison, an unlimited fine or both

No longer 'legal highs'

In 2016 the Psychoactive Substances Act was passed.[2] This prohibited the import, export, production and supply (but not the possession) of any psychoactive substance, which the legislation defined as 'a substance (which) produces a psychoactive effect in a person if, by stimulating or depressing the person's central nervous system, it affects the person's mental functioning or emotional state'. Until then there had been a rapidly growing range of (mainly) synthetic substances widely referred to as 'legal highs' which, although never legal for human consumption, were nevertheless being openly sold on high streets, in corner shops, tattoo studios, garages and so-called 'head shops' across the land. These were causing damage to the mental and physical health of the people who used them, they were responsible for a number of fatalities, and many young people were confused by their apparent legal status and assumed they must be safe.

The change to the law was the result of years of campaigning. Head shops disappeared, and many of the substances they'd been selling went along with them, or moved into the illegal market. People who were using them generally went back to the original substances these had often been manufactured to imitate, or onto others. One substance from that era that stubbornly remained is synthetic cannabinoids, now referred to generically by one of its old brand names, Spice.

---

[2] Legislation.gov.uk (2016) Psychoactive Substances Act 2016 [online]. *National Archives*. Available from: <www.legislation.gov.uk/ukpga/2016/2/contents/enacted> (accessed November 2020)

Thankfully this is rarely a drug of choice for young people, but it remains a cause of serious harm and havoc among vulnerable homeless and prison populations.

One substance covered by this Act with which young people may currently cross the legal threshold is nitrous oxide. This is a substance made more complicated in terms of its legal status because it also has legitimate uses, primarily in cooking – it's what puts the whip in whipped cream, for example. This in turn means it's widely and openly available in regular, legitimate online marketplaces, without purchasers ever having to risk the dark net or dealers. It's also available in many a corner shop. It is legal to possess, but not to supply for psychoactive purposes, and having bought a box or two online as easily as ordering your biology revision book it can be easy to forget that sharing your purchases with your friends at a party is illegal under the Psychoactive Substances Act and wouldn't be granted the same status in the eyes of the law as, for example, sharing a few packets of crisps. See below for more on supply.

What's the deal with drugs?

As we've seen, there are several offences relating to drugs classified under the 1971 Misuse of Drugs Act – possession, possession with intent to supply, supply (or offer to supply), import, export and production. There's also allowing your home to be used for the production, use or supply of drugs, which is a potential pitfall for parents we'll come back to.

Neither the import nor export of drugs has historically been a particularly common pastime for young people, and this remains largely the case. However, the increasing ease of access to online routes for both buying in bulk from anywhere on the planet, and selling substances on either locally or further afield, means this is something to watch, because if someone orders a drug online and it is delivered from overseas, they are technically importing a drug. Young people also need to be very careful when travelling abroad – more on that below. Production is also an activity less frequently engaged in by young people, but one that's worth highlighting for any young chemists considering getting hold of a recipe and component parts online, or a budding botanist who fancies trying their hand at growing a few cannabis plants somewhere unobtrusive. If this is happening in your home, then you could also be held liable legally.

The two prime legal pitfalls for young people to be aware of are possession and supply, and both have complexities as well as consequences.

Possession

Not all young people are aware that possession of drugs is a criminal offence, especially if drug use is commonplace in their friendship group. Those that are may not, however, be fully aware of the ramifications of this. And although this might seem like an obvious one, it may not be so obvious to young people that drugs don't have to be physically in their possession at the time they get found for this to count. They could be in a blazer pocket hung on a hook, or a school bag or locker, or back in their bedroom at home, and still be legally in their possession.

Possession of cannabis

Cannabis is the most complicated substance in relation to possession, which is a nuisance with it being the controlled substance most likely of all to be found in the possession of a youngster. There's a colourful patchwork of various approaches and responses adopted by police forces across the country that make it difficult to give definitive guidance, and a range of possible options for under- and over-18s.

For over-18s there's a wide spectrum of options. Someone caught with a small amount of cannabis could be given a caution, a Cannabis Warning, a Penalty Notice of Disorder, a Conditional Caution, a Community Resolution, or they could be arrested and charged. The ins and outs of how these all work, which do and don't give you a criminal record, which will and won't show up on which sort of Disclosure Barring Service check, and which will and won't bar you from travel to the USA among other places, would take up several pages of this book, and so I'm just going to focus on the under-18s, which is still not totally straightforward.

A child under ten found by police in possession of cannabis is immediately considered to be 'at risk' and a referral would be made through local child protection processes. From ten to 17 there is usually an escalating response by police, with a reprimand for a first offence and a phone call to parents. If it happens again, they are likely to be referred to the Youth Offending Team to work through a community resolution of some sort. Arrest is generally a very last option, and usually only happens if someone has been stopped several times before.

Community Resolutions can be used in response to crimes considered relatively low-level for people of all ages, including possession of Class B and C drugs. They avoid giving someone a criminal record and wouldn't show on a standard DBS check, though they may on an enhanced one in the 'relevant information' section. Generally speaking, a Community Resolution will only be applied if the individual concerned accepts full responsibility, has no prior convictions, cautions, Penalty Notice of Disorders, Cannabis Warnings or Community Resolutions, and offers or agrees an 'act of reparation'. What form that might take is very variable in different parts of the country, but for cannabis it will often involve a commitment to engage with some sort of programme of drugs education and/or treatment for a specified period of time. For under-18s these are generally much more tightly managed and scrutinized than for over-18s, involving the Youth Offending Team and local young people's services.

A 2018 report showed that prosecutions and convictions for possession of cannabis for both under- and over-18s had fallen in a five-year period to 2017.[3] However, young people caught with a bit of cannabis need to know they can't rely on having a blind eye turned on them, or no action being taken. It's still a Class B drug, and possession is still a criminal offence under UK law. And even if no legal action is taken, that doesn't necessarily mean no action will be taken at all for that young person. Even at the bottom end of the spectrum of police responses their parents will be told, and that might mean trouble with parents if not with police, depending on the views on such matters held in the family home.

Possession of cannabis in Scotland

In Scotland changes were made to the law in 2016 which enabled police to issue a Recorded Police Warning to anyone aged 16 or over caught in possession of cannabis, as part of a range of options to be

---

[3] McCulloch, L., Matharu, H., North, P. (2018) *The Children's Inquiry* [online]. *Volteface.* Available from: <volteface.me/app/uploads/2018/09/The-Childrens-Inquiry-Full-Report-2.pdf> (accessed November 2020)

used at their individual discretion. A recorded warning is the lowest level option and is used for first-time, minor possession cases. This would not give the individual concerned a criminal record. If officers felt a charge was the best option, this of course would happen. Children under 16 will be referred to the Children's Reporter. Their parents or carers would be contacted so, as in the rest of the UK, that could spell trouble at home, if not with the law.

Talking point

If you have a child aged 14 or over, or even younger, it is very likely they will know someone who uses cannabis. A conversation about the legal risks from cannabis, as well as the risks to adolescent mental health, can be one with a real context for them within their wider peer group. Many young people perceive cannabis as a substance about which police aren't bothered, so this is an important conversation to have. As always, talking in terms of their friends or peers is a useful sideways route into making sure they have the information themselves.

- Do they know anyone who's been stopped by the police for cannabis? If so do they know what happened?
- Do they think young people their age are generally aware of the possible legal consequences?
- What do they think should happen legally when it comes to cannabis? The law has changed in some parts of the world, debates are going on in others, and this can be an interesting discussion as well as a useful way of reinforcing what may happen if police get involved in the UK.

Supply

This is probably the biggest risk for young people, and has the bigger penalties. It's something they're often unaware they're doing, but it can carry serious sentences, which in turn can have devastating consequences. 'Possession' can become 'possession with intent to supply' as soon as the amount someone has on them when they get caught is considered too great for their personal use, and this then takes them into a much more serious range of potential consequences.

'Social supply'

This is something I had no idea about before we found ourselves in the legal fallout after Dan died. The boy in the group that night, who'd called his dealer, arranged the drop off, and had taken their collective cash to hand it over to the lad on the bike with the drugs, was the key witness in the trial. He was the one with at least a year's worth of calls on his phone to the dealer. He was the one who'd seen the lad on the bike in the hoodie who brought the drugs to the drop off, the same lad who'd done the same thing from the same house on several previous occasions. He was the one who therefore had to stand up in the witness box, in that courtroom in West London, and testify in front of the judge and jury, the defendant and his family and friends, and the family of the boy who died. This was the only reason, we were told by the prosecution barrister, that this year 11 boy from a very nice school wasn't charged with supply himself. He hadn't made a penny on the transaction, he was basically the errand boy on that occasion, but what he was doing was a criminal offence, and a serious one at that. He had supplied Class A drugs to four other teenagers, one of whom died soon after.

Other young people aren't so lucky. Christian Pay died the summer after Dan, at Kendal Calling Festival. He was 18 and was there with a group of friends. They'd all decided they'd take some ecstasy. One of the friends, Simon, still had a dealer's number from the previous year's festival. So it was Simon who organized getting the drugs, and Simon who collected their money, went off to pick up the pills, brought them back and shared them out. Chris was pronounced dead in the early hours of the next morning, and two months later Simon was arrested for conspiracy to supply Class A drugs. He wasn't a professional drug dealer, he had never profited from drugs in his life, including that night at the festival, but in the eyes of the law he'd supplied controlled drugs, and was sentenced accordingly. He spent six months in prison for supplying the drugs that killed his friend. There are other, similar stories.

Is it normal?

Just as drug use has to some extent become normalized among young people, so has drug supply. Indeed, social supply has been described in research on the subject as 'the "other side" of the history of normalisation'.[4] This research found that the social supply of recreational drugs has become accepted 'as something closer to gift-giving or friendship exchange dynamics within social networks rather than dealing proper', and that this supply relationship was viewed on both sides as distinct from one with a 'real' dealer, 'in order to reinforce their preconceptions of themselves as relatively non-deviant'.

Talking point

You can see an eight-part mini-documentary series that retells the story of Christian Pay on YouTube, 'One Night of Ecstasy', originally on BBC3. Depending on the age of your child, you might want to watch this with them.

When Simon was arrested and then sentenced (Episode 7), different opinions were held by some of the people involved:

- The police said: 'His actions were drug supply ... Christian Pay passed away because of his actions ...'
- Jordan, another friend who was there and who also ended up in hospital, said: 'It could have been me ... It could have been any of us...'
- The judge said: 'He had every intention of giving drugs out ... He knew exactly what he was doing ...'
- Christian's mum Debbie said: 'I think it's wrong he got arrested ... In my eyes he's not a criminal...'

What does your child think? What do you think?

Getting down to business

Whereas some young people are crossing a legal line in ignorance, others are consciously supplying drugs for financial gain. It can, however, be very easy to take tiny steps into supply without setting out to be a dealer. It can start with perhaps sharing some of your own with your friends, or getting involved in a bit of social supply, then

---

4   Coomber, R., Moyle, L., South, N. (2015) The normalisation of drug supply: The social *supply* of drugs as the 'other side' of the history of normalisation [online]. *Drugs: Education, Prevention and Policy*. Volume 23, issue 2, pages 255–263. Available from: DOI: 10.3109/09687637.2015.1110565

friends asking you to get some for their friends, and their wider social networks, and so on. It can, equally, be a conscious step, and there can be various motivating factors behind this. Just as for adults this could be for the money or status drug supply can bring, or to fund their own drug use, which can get very expensive if it gets to significant levels.

Talking point

Possible signs to look out for with a child getting involved in supplying drugs can include:

- More money than usual and/or nice new things like expensive clothes or gadgets
- Multiple phones
- Changes to their phone-related behaviours, for example, frequent short phone-calls or messaging followed by popping out of the house briefly
- Changes to friendships; perhaps dropping old friends for ones that may provide a customer base
- Keeping odd hours, staying out late or leaving the house without saying where they are going.

There could be other reasons for all these things, and the last ones could just be normal teenage behaviour, but each would be worth keeping an eye on or having a chat about, and together they may be an indication that concern is warranted. Before jumping in with accusations, though, check your information, and plan your approach. Have a look at Chapter 7 for suggestions for tackling these trickier conversations.

Social media and drug supply

Social media has altered the landscape of drug supply in recent years. It provides easy, ready-made, open routes into the business, often reached through a process of drift similar to that seen in the offline world. Young people who use drugs can easily become 'casual sellers' through offering any surplus supplies they have for sale through their social media networks. With special offers and incentives to buy in bulk, this can not only reduce the cost of their original planned purchase but bring in some extra cash to boot. For some young people it's more of a deliberate choice than a drift, however, and the displays of money and associated lifestyle arrayed on dealers' social media feeds are designed to be a great temptation.

This sort of solo operation within their broader peer group is seen by young people as quite distinct from 'real' drug dealing, and in fact many would prefer to go to someone in their social network who they know uses drugs than to find a 'professional'.[5] But even the traditional drugs trade has lost its somewhat seedy edge with the move online, thanks to the normalizing effect of the heightened levels and frequency of exposure to drugs, the marketing tools employed, and the familiarity and sense of security this particular social environment provides. Dealers may post not just pictures of their wares but also of their dog or their dinner, and so shift their identity from the illicit into that familiar friendship space.

However, just as there are opportunities unique to social media when it comes to selling drugs, there is also a unique set of risks for young people. One is the ease with which 'casual selling' can escalate to more serious supply without necessarily intending it to do so, with all the risks not just legally but from the criminal world with which it is then necessary to engage at a more committed level. Another is the visibility of every post young people make, and the digital footprint each one leaves. When an individual does get caught, there may be much more evidence to bring to bear in a criminal investigation than there ever would from transactions made offline. And the pace at which social media operates means this can all get out of hand both easily and quickly:

> 'It was quite a frightening experience for this particular young person. They said that, actually, they suddenly felt that instantly they were in over their head. They were getting requests from everywhere, from people they didn't know. Their account and subsequent contact details were being circulated without them really having any control over that. And all of a sudden, it felt like, you know, they're...what had been for this young person, a quite casual and social dealing – you know, amongst peers, picking up a couple of ten bags for people – all of a sudden, he felt like he was placed in a position where he didn't want to say no to people, but

---

[5] McCulloch, L. & Furlong, S. (2019) DM for Details: Selling Drugs in an Age of Social Media [online]. *Volteface*. Available from: <volteface.me/app/uploads/2020/08/Volteface-_-Social-Media-report-DM-for-Details.pdf> (accessed November 2020)

then he was getting requests and hit up from people he didn't even know. So, he suddenly felt really out of control with it.'[6]

Grooming, exploitation and 'county lines'

On top of the unintentional drift into dealing, and the more deliberate career moves, there have long been serious risks of exploitation of children and young people by older dealers into drug supply, often using the same grooming methods as for sexual exploitation. These continue to operate offline, but social media has provided a new playing field not only to engage and recruit but also to manipulate and control. The Children's Commissioner for England has recently estimated that 46,000 children and young people in England are involved in gang activity, and 4000 teenagers in London alone are being exploited through what has become known as 'county lines' drug dealing.[7] 'County lines' is so-called because it's typically set up around a network of phone lines across the country, often linking major cities with more rural areas, and marking routes of supply. The supply is most often of crack cocaine and heroin to vulnerable drug dependent users, and the drugs are transported from place to place by equally vulnerable youngsters.

Although the children and young people who may find themselves targeted are often vulnerable, in care, not in school, disengaged and disadvantaged – eager for a place to belong and be valued – there is also a tendency to pick out youngsters not known to the police or children's services, who are less likely to be on any official radar. These are known as 'clean skins' and can come from any family. The process typically involves picking out a teen or pre-teen, enticing and manipulating them through kindness and generosity, and then controlling them through fear and violence, to force them to travel with drugs and return with cash, often spending weeks at a time holed up in the home of a person vulnerable through their addiction or through learning disabilities. When dealers take over the over the home of a vulnerable person to use

---

[6] Drug and alcohol practitioner, DM for Details: Selling Drugs in an Age of Social Media, *Volteface*

[7] Children's Society. County lines and child criminal exploitation [online]. *Children's Society.* Available from: <www.childrenssociety.org.uk/what-we-do/our-work/child-criminal-exploitation-and-county-lines> (accessed November 2020)

it as a base for their drug dealing operation it is known as 'cuckooing'. It could, however, be in an Airbnb or budget hotel. It could mean long train journeys or a minicab. The exact shape this takes is continually modulating and evolving all the time, but the basic business model is the same. Find a child, make friends, make them sell your drugs.

What are the signs of criminal exploitation and county lines?

- Unexplained absences from school, work or home
- Returning home late, staying out all night or going missing
- Being found in areas where they have no obvious connections
- Increasing drug use, or being found with large quantities of drugs
- Growing isolated or being secretive about where they are going and who they are with
- Suddenly acquiring money, phone(s), clothes or jewellery that cannot be explained
- Uncharacteristic disruptive or aggressive behaviour, including new use of sexual, drug-related or violent language
- Unexplained injuries or looking particularly dishevelled
- Having hotel cards or keys to unknown places.

For more information about gangs and criminal exploitation of children see the NSPCC website.

If you have concerns about your child there is information for parents on the Children's Society website.

Talking point

Talk to your children about how the grooming process can work and what to look out for, for themselves or for a friend.

Talk through what they would do if they were worried for themselves or about someone they knew being exploited. Would they feel they could speak to an adult, at home or at school? If not, would they know where to go to get help?

- **Childline** is a good place to find help and advice for children and young people – they can look on the website or call 0800 1111.
- **The Mix** has a useful guide for teenagers concerned a friend is getting involved in a gang in their crime and safety pages.

- **Fearless** is the youth service of Crimestoppers. If your child is aware that a crime has taken place, or is underway, they can report this totally anonymously online on the Fearless website.

What about parents?

Parents can also fall foul of the laws about drugs if they're not careful. The pitfalls may seem obvious in the cold light of day, but an instinctive protectiveness can send the most sensible parent a little legally adrift if they know their child is using drugs. For example, after a workshop a parent told me about the dad of her son's friend, who was supplying his child and their friends with ecstasy in pills he'd broken into quarters, so he knew they wouldn't be taking too much at a time thus reducing their risk of overdosing. Another parent after another workshop asked me about growing their own less potent strains of cannabis at home to avoid their child's mental health being harmed by the high levels of THC in most of the cannabis sold illegally in the UK, something I'd just been talking about. Despite the logic in operation, and their clear motivation to reduce the harm to the children they love, this is supply of Class A drugs, and to minors, in example one, and production of Class B drugs, in the other.

Perhaps less obvious but still a breach of legal boundaries is the fact that if you know that drugs are being taken or shared in your house or garden you are guilty of allowing premises you own, or for which you are responsible, being used for the use and supply of drugs. You may feel if it's under your roof, and under your scrutiny, it's better than them doing it out and about where if something went wrong you wouldn't be on hand to help, and again that protective logic is at work.

Also, if you find drugs on your child – in their bedroom, in their trouser pocket when you're doing the laundry, you need to do something with those drugs quick sharp because all the time you have them you're in possession of controlled drugs. Whether you take them to the police station, find a local amnesty box (some local drugs treatment services will offer these) or destroy them in some way, it's a choice for you to make.

Foreign trips, drugs and alcohol

As older teens start having holidays abroad with their friends or heading off travelling, it's important they're aware of local laws about drug and alcohol use. The consequences can be complicated at best and severe at worst, and not something anyone wants to have to cope with a long way from home in the middle of a time that was meant to be about relaxing and having fun, or new experiences and adventures. Turkey, for example, a popular holiday destination, has strict laws against the use, possession or trafficking of controlled drugs. Anyone convicted of any of these offences can expect to receive a heavy fine or a prison sentence of 4 to 24 years.[8] Greece also has serious custodial sentences for drugs offences, including for possession, and authorities have recently been clamping down heavily on the sale of nitrous oxide.

At the most extreme end of criminal consequences, there are 35 countries and states around the world that hand down death sentences and executions for drug offences, and although only four of these reported having carried out executions in 2019 (China, Saudi Arabia, Singapore and Iran), that's more than enough to worry about. Many of these are popular destinations for gap year or 20s travellers, such as Thailand, Indonesia and South Korea. Check out Harm Reduction International's most recent report, The Death Penalty for Drug Offences: Global Overview 2019 (pub. March 2020) for more detailed information about where to be aware of.[9]

Talking point

If you have a child heading off on a foreign holiday or going travelling overseas, look together at the laws in the country relating to drugs and alcohol. Information about European countries can be found on the EMCDDA website – search for 'Drug law penalties at a glance'. Some

---

[8]   Gov.uk. Foreign travel advice: Turkey [online]. *Gov.uk*. Available from: <www.gov.uk/foreign-travel-advice/turkey/local-laws-and-customs#:~:text=Turkey%20has%20strict%20laws%20against,of%204%20to%2024%20years> (accessed November 2020)

[9]   Harm Reduction International (2019) The Death Penalty for Drug Offences: Global Overview 2019 [online]. *Harm Reduction International*. Available from: <www.hri.global/files/2020/02/28/HRI_DeathPenaltyReport2019.pdf> (accessed November 2020)

other parts of the world can be found on the gov.uk website searching by country.

If they have medication they need to take with them make sure you check how they can travel legally with this. See the gov.uk website and search for 'travelling with controlled drugs', or speak to your pharmacist.

Advice on how to avoid becoming a victim of drugs abroad

- Pack all luggage yourself and make sure it's securely fastened
- Keep your luggage with you at airports and other departure points to avoid the possibility of having drugs planted in it
- Be aware of approaches from people at airports – even seemingly innocent requests to look after someone's belongings can lead to problems
- Don't carry anything through customs for someone else – if drugs are found, you will be held responsible
- For similar reasons, don't cross borders with people you don't know or drive across borders with unknown companions
- Carry a doctor's prescription for any medication you may need to avoid unnecessary delays at customs and immigration checks
- Be very cautious when accepting gifts from people abroad – it's easy to hide drugs in items such as trainers, cosmetics and children's toys.

From NI Direct Government Services: Arrest and prison abroad: <www.nidirect.gov.uk/articles/arrest-and-prison-abroad>

Drugs, alcohol and sexual consent

According to the Crown Prosecution Service, 'When there is an allegation of rape or sexual assault, prosecutors will consider … whether the complainant had the capacity to choose whether or not to take part in sexual activity, for example whether the use of drugs or alcohol may have affected their ability to consent'.[10] The law also requires that the person performing the act needs to have 'reasonable belief' that consent was given by the other person, and if the person holding that belief wasn't in a fit state of mind themselves because of drink or drugs, their testimony may be invalidated in court.

---

[10] CPS. Sexual offences. Available from: <www.cps.gov.uk/crime-info/sexual-offences> (accessed November 2020)

Certain drugs can alter people's feelings about sex. MDMA can create a strong sense of emotional connection, cocaine can make people feel sexually confident and aggressive and a moderate amount of alcohol can reduce inhibitions, increase libido and lead to people taking more risks sexually. Factoring in the effect a substance might have on attitudes towards sex and sexual behaviour in any encounter or relationship is very important. Communication is key when it comes to consent, whatever the state of mind. However, a lot of communication is non-verbal, and this is harder to gauge accurately when either person is intoxicated.

If being absolutely, totally clear on mutual agreement is impossible then sex should be avoided, for so many reasons. In terms of the legal ones, if someone is found guilty of a sexual offence they risk not only a criminal record and possible prison sentence but also having their name put on the sex offenders' register, which can of course have devastating consequences.

Talking point

Sex, when either of the people involved is under the influence of alcohol or drugs, should always be avoided, because consent on either side risks being unclear legally if anything was to come to court, and of course can be a dubious choice morally as well.

Although the effects of drink or drugs may be evident in another person – slurred speech, drowsiness, lack of coordination and so on – they may not be, and especially if the person making that judgement call is also not thinking clearly or seeing things straight.

Have a look at the information about consent on The Mix website for more advice, and their article 'Too wasted for sex?'

Drugs, alcohol and violent crime

The links between alcohol and violence are well established, though inevitably complex. According to the Crime Survey of England and Wales one in five assaults recorded by the police in 2018 were alcohol-related, and 15 per cent of all manslaughters; 39 per cent of victims of violence believed the person who hurt them was under the influence of alcohol; and 21 per cent thought they were under the influence of drugs.[11]

Alcohol and certain drugs make changes to the way the brain is functioning that can lead people to act angrily and aggressively, in a way that is often totally out of character. Alcohol lowers inhibitions and affects our ability to think clearly, focus our attention, and process information, all of which can lead to people missing, or misinterpreting, important social cues and responding inappropriately. Cocaine can make people feel anxious or impulsive, and with the boost to confidence and energy levels it can also result in an aggressive response in situations that would not, with a clear head, warrant it. On the comedown people can feel very gloomy and paranoid, as the body restores the natural balance of neurotransmitters knocked out of kilter by the high, and this can also change people's behaviour for the worse. And, perhaps surprisingly, cannabis, the classic chill-out drug, has also been linked to violent crime, especially for users of high potency cannabis who have developed cannabis-induced paranoia and psychosis.[12]

'Five minutes of madness'

Ray and Vi's story

Ray and Vi's son Chris was 18 when he died. Walking home from his big sister's house one Friday night around midnight with his brother Phil and a friend, they reached the brow of a hill and saw a big group of 14 teenagers coming in the opposite direction, walking towards them. This group had, it turned out, spent the day together drinking and taking various drugs. Apparently they'd been kicked out by one of their aunts earlier on for getting rowdy and had been causing a nuisance locally all day since.

The teenagers parted to let the boys through, but as Phil led the way one of the younger ones decided to punch him in the face, knocking his nose right out of joint. Instinctively Phil grabbed his nose and pushed it back into place but the pain of this made him collapse. With Phil on

[11] Office for National Statistics (2019) The nature of violent crime in England and Wales: year ending March 2018 [online]. *ONS*. Available from: <www.ons.gov.uk/peoplepopulationandcommunity/crimeandjustice/articles/thenatureofviolent-crimeinenglandandwales/yearendingmarch2018> (accessed November 2020)

[12] Miller N.S., Ipeku R., Oberbarnscheidt T. (2020) A review of cases of marijuana and violence [online]. *International Journal of Environmental Research and Public Health*. 17(5):1578. Available from: DOI: 10.3390/ijerph17051578

the ground, two of the boys started stamping on his head. Chris of course jumped in to protect his brother, and they then set on him. Ray said, 'They backed him into the main road as they were fighting, another one got behind him, they got him on the floor, took penalty shots to his face and head, and then they were stamping on his head. In fact, in court there was a witness and the judge said, "Can you describe it?" and he said, "I can't describe it. I'll have to show you it." And he came out of the dock and stood in the well of the court and brought his leg up so high, and the force of it coming down, the whole court rang with the noise. As I'm talking, I can still hear it. In fact, the jury shook – jumped – with the noise.'

With Chris now on the ground in the middle of the dual carriageway, someone got wind the police were coming and a girl in the group ran into the road to get Chris back on the pavement, but one of the boys shouted to leave him there, and so they all ran off and left him. The first car coming over the hill saw him just in time and managed to swerve and avoid him, but the second just behind him didn't get chance to react quickly enough and ran right over him. Chris' belt caught in the exhaust pipe and he was dragged 40 metres down the road under her car. He died in hospital hours later.

Four teenage boys were arrested and charged.

It took 16 weeks till the body was released for his parents to bury him because the coroner and legal teams needed all the evidence they could get to make the decision about whether it was the beating or the car that had killed him. The family was strongly advised against having an open coffin when they finally got him back. In the meantime, one of the boys had pleaded guilty to assault and got a fine, but the other three were charged with murder. One was 15, one was 16 and one 19. It took six weeks of trial at the Old Bailey for the jury to reach the decision these three teenagers were guilty of the murder of Chris Donovan.

Would they have done this without the alcohol and drugs? Peer influence, the adolescent brain and all sorts of other factors would have played their part, but the boys all felt their actions that night would have been very different if their heads had been clear, and Chris would still be alive and well.

Chris Donovan, with permission from Ray Donovan

To watch the documentary that tells Ray and Vi's story, or to find out more about the Chris Donovan Trust, see

Drink and drug driving

In the UK it is illegal to drive, to attempt to drive or to be in charge of a motor vehicle on a road or in a public place if your ability to drive safely has been impaired by the consumption of alcohol or drugs, and also if you have alcohol or drugs in your system over legal limits.[13] With certain drugs, including prescription and over-the-counter medicines as well as illegal drugs, they just have to be in your system for it to be illegal to get behind the wheel, even if your abilities are unaffected. And it's not just on the way home after a night out. Almost a fifth of drink driving convictions, and a third of all breath tests, were for people stopped by police between 7 am and 1 pm,

---

[13] Crown Prosecution Service (2019) Road Traffic – Drink and Drug Driving [online]. *CPS*. Available from: <www.cps.gov.uk/legal-guidance/road-traffic-drink-and-drug-driving> (accessed November 2020)

before the driver's body had managed to get to the end of processing whatever substances had been taken.[14]

If the police have pulled someone over because they think they're driving under the influence of alcohol or drugs they can perform a roadside test, using a breathalyser for alcohol, or taking a sample of sweat or saliva to test for cannabis or cocaine. If this test is positive the driver will be arrested and taken to the police station for a blood test which would then be used as evidence if charges are brought. Because roadside tests are currently limited to just these two drugs, police can also ask a driver to do a 'field impairment assessment', which is a series of tests of their reaction times, coordination and judgement, such as walking in a straight line. If they judge from this that they're unfit to drive because of having taken drugs they will arrest them and make them take a blood or urine test at a police station, so they can identify any other substances that might be in their system. The results would be used in evidence if charges are brought.[15]

In England and Wales, convictions for drug driving have risen sharply since 2015 when it became a specific criminal offence. In 2019 the *Daily Mail* reported the results of a Freedom of Information request they'd made to the DVLA, which found that the numbers of people being convicted of driving under the influence of drugs had almost quadrupled over a four-year period, with just short of 20,000 being banned from driving in the previous year. Of these, 95 per cent were male, and most were in their 20s, though it also included 200 newly qualified 17-year-olds.[16] This increase may of course just reflect an increase in detection rates and improvements in roadside testing

---

[14]   Auto Express (2019) A fifth of drink-driving arrests are made the morning after [online]. *Auto Express*. Available from: <www.autoexpress.co.uk/car-news/107003/a-fifth-of-drink-driving-arrests-are-made-the-morning-after> (accessed November 2020)

[15]   Gov.uk. Drugs and driving: the law [online]. *Gov.uk*. Available from: <www.gov.uk/drug-driving-law> (accessed November 2020)

[16]   Camber, R. (2019) Britain's drug-driving epidemic: How more than 60 motorists are banned from the roads each day as convictions triple in two years [online]. *Daily Mail*. Available from: <www.dailymail.co.uk/news/article-7615445/Britains-drug-driving-epidemic-60-motorists-banned-roads-day.html> (accessed November 2020)

rather than a rise in drug driving itself, but whatever the reason the fact remains that more people are being stopped, tested, charged and convicted every year, and most of these are young, and mostly male.

In Scotland new drug driving laws were added to the Road Traffic Act in 2019. The updates brought Scotland into line with England and Wales, allow for the roadside drug testing of cannabis and cocaine and provide legal upper limits for the detection of drugs in the body.[17]

Talking point

If your children are drivers, remind them that although they may feel fine after a few drinks (or taking drugs) this doesn't mean they're safe behind the wheel of a car. It also doesn't mean the police would consider them fine if they pulled them over. Legal blood-alcohol levels don't correspond neatly to the numbers of units of alcohol consumed, and it's safest not to drink at all if you're driving. Many drugs, including cannabis, can be also detected in the body for some days after use.

Remind young drivers in your family, too, about the amount of time their liver will need to process any alcohol consumed the night before, because they could still have excess amounts in their system if they're planning on heading out in the car the following morning. It takes an hour to process each unit (if awake – it happens more slowly during sleep), and the first hour doesn't count. The Drinkaware website has a unit calculator which is useful, if they can remember what, when and how much they consumed.

Do remind them also of the legal penalties and other possible consequences they may not have been aware of, for example, their car insurance costs will increase significantly, and if they drive for work, their employer will see a conviction on their licence.

Alcohol and the law: when does legal become illegal?

Although alcohol is legal to buy and sell in the UK, there are limits to this and lines that can be crossed which can result in trouble for young people. As this is one of the psychoactive substances most

---

[17]   Gov.scot (2019) New drug driving laws to be introduced [online]. *Scottish Government*. Available from: <www.gov.scot/news/new-drug-driving-laws-to-be-introduced/> (accessed November 2020)

commonly used by people young and old, it's important both parents and their children are aware of where these lines fall.

Under-18s and alcohol:

- Under-18s drinking alcohol in public can have their drink confiscated, and they can be fined or arrested by police.[18]
- Under-18s buying, or trying to buy, alcohol can be fined.

Over-18s and alcohol:

- Police have the power to charge those over 18 who knowingly buy alcohol for anyone under the legal drinking age (buying by proxy). A conviction could lead to a fine and a criminal record.
- Police can confiscate alcohol from adults if they believe it's to be drunk by someone underage.[19]

Spiking:

- Spiking someone's drink by adding another substance without them knowing, including alcohol, is a criminal offence. A conviction can result in a prison sentence, whether any further harm was done to the recipient or not, but if assault, robbery or sexual assault has taken place as a result that will obviously carry a more significant sentence.[20]

It is legal for adults:

- To provide alcohol at home for children from the age of five (but remember the Chief Medical Officer's advice in Chapter 2 which recommended avoiding alcohol under the age of 15)
- To purchase beer, cider or wine in licensed premises for 16- and 17-year-olds to drink with a table meal, if the premises permits this.

---

[18] Gov.uk. Alcohol and young people [online]. *Gov.uk*. Available from: <www.gov.uk/alcohol-young-people-law> (accessed November 2020)

[19] Drinkaware. The law on alcohol and displayed as 'under 18s' on website [online]. *Drinkaware*. Available from: <www.drinkaware.co.uk/facts/alcohol-and-the-law/the-law-on-alcohol-and-under-18s> (accessed November 2020)

[20] Devon and Cornwall Police. Drink spiking – the law [online]. *Devon and Cornwall Police*. Available from: <www.devon-cornwall.police.uk/advice/your-community/drugs-and-alcohol/alcohol/drink-spiking/> (accessed November 2020)

Drug and alcohol policies: school, college, university and work

As well as the law of the land, there are local policies and practices that can result in consequences that can have a damaging impact on young people's future outcomes and opportunities, even if not criminal convictions. All schools, colleges and universities will have drugs and alcohol policies that are worth reading to check where the local lines are drawn and what sanctions may be imposed if they are crossed. These will be many and varied, depending on the individual institution and the offence. And then there's the workplace.

Schools must weigh their pastoral and safeguarding responsibilities for the wellbeing of individual students whose drug use has come to light against their responsibilities for the school community as a whole. This can be a tricky balance for them to find, and their responses are enormously varied, initially depending on what the trigger has been. A student may have admitted using drugs outside school, they may have been caught with drugs inside school, they may have been selling drugs to other pupils – either inside or outside the school grounds. Some schools routinely bring in sniffer dogs, others will do random urine testing. Some will do targeted testing of students who have come on to the drugs radar, others will have testing as part of an agreement made with students and their parents, if a drug-related school rule has been broken. For something like possession or use, many schools will refer students for counselling, or for support within existing school structures. Some schools will permanently exclude pupils if they admit to having smoked cannabis at a party at the weekend, however, while others would do so only for a serious offence on school premises, such as supplying drugs to other students.

School exclusions for drugs and alcohol have been on the rise in recent years. In the academic year 2018–19 more than 12,000 pupils in England were excluded either temporarily or permanently in relation to drugs or alcohol.[21] Many parents would want their child's school to exercise a 'zero tolerance' response to drug use, because

---

[21] Explore Education Statistics (2021) Permanent and fixed-perioed exclusions in England. Available from: <explore-education-statistics.service.gov.uk/find-statistics/permanent-and-fixed-period-exclusions-in-england> (Accessed February 2021)

of course drugs are a threat to our children's safety and wellbeing. However, most of these parents, if pushed, would acknowledge individual circumstances can make a blanket response unduly harsh at times. And if it turns out the drugs in question were being used by their own child this is definitely a less appealing approach. The most punitive responses also don't necessarily translate into lower levels of use, but will often just lead to higher levels of deceptive behaviour by students, and those who do need help are unlikely to ask for it – or, importantly, to get it.

When it comes to **universities** the policy landscape is equally variable. In 2018 the National Union of Students and drugs advocacy charity Release published research they had jointly undertaken into student drug use and universities' responses to this.[22] When it came to the possession of drugs, a range of different disciplinary outcomes were seen across different educational institutions, from a formal warning, temporary exclusion or referral to fitness to practice procedures (which ensure a student has the skills, knowledge, health and character to carry out the profession for which their course is preparing them safely and effectively), right up to permanent exclusions. One in four such incidents were reported to the police. In addition to this, students can find themselves being disciplined by their accommodation provider for drug-related behaviour that doesn't break the law, and can even end up being evicted because of a breach of their licence agreement relating to drug use.

Most **employers** will also have drugs and alcohol policies, and as teenagers move into the workplace, whether in part-time jobs alongside their studies, as apprentices or as fully paid up employees, it's important they know this is the case, because a breach of the policy could cost them a job and a good reference. Some employers will require pre-employment drug testing. Some will test employees after an incident which causes an injury or damage, or which comes close to doing so. Some workplaces

---

[22] Release and NUS (2019) Taking the Hit: student drug use and how institutions respond [online] *Release and NUS*. Available from: <www.release.org.uk/sites/default/files/pdf/publications/Taking%20the%20Hit%20-%20Student%20drug%20use%20and%20how%20institutions%20respond%20-.pdf> (accessed November 2020)

will routinely and randomly drug test their staff, especially in industries where safety is paramount such as construction.[23]

Consequences

The consequences of getting a criminal record for a drug-related offence can be far-reaching and long-lasting, and limit opportunities for young people in ways most will never have envisaged. Those hoping to go to university need to know that any criminal convictions have to be declared on their UCAS form. Those hoping to work in a profession that requires a Disclosure Barring Service (DBS) check need to know their entry may be blocked and their career choices more limited. Those hoping to travel need to know there are countries that will never allow them to cross their borders, including America[24] and Australia,[25] and others where entry will be dependent on the decision of a visa department. It's also worth knowing that even police-administered drug cautions will make a person ineligible for entry to the US via the Electronic System for Travel Authorisation (ESTA), and may stop them getting in altogether.

Legal risks and consequences are among the many that young people need to be able to navigate safely, in this world in which the presentation of the positive so often trumps the negative when it comes to drugs and alcohol. A good grounding of knowledge can go a long way in helping them stay safe.

---

[23] TUC (2019) Drug testing in the workplace: Guidance for workplace representatives [online]. *TUC*. Available from: <www.tuc.org.uk/resource/drug-testing-workplace> (accessed November 2020)

[24] U.S. Embassy and Consulates in the United Kingdom. Criminal records and Ineligibilities [online]. *U.S. Embassy and Consulates in the United Kingdom*. Available from: <uk.usembassy.gov/visas/visa-waiver-program/additional-requirements/> (accessed November 2020)

[25] Australian Government Department of Home Affairs. Enerting Australia [online]. *Australian Government*. Available from: <immi.homeaffairs.gov.au/entering-and-leaving-australia/entering-australia/can-i-go-to-australia#:~:text=Enter%20Australia%20with%20a%20criminal%20record&text=You%20may%20need%20to%20provide,a%20visa%20to%20enter%20Australia> (accessed November 2020)

6

I wish I'd known how to talk about it better

Conversations about drugs

In the 1990s BBC comedy series *Harry Enfield and Chums* we see one of the recurrent characters from his previous series, an energetically annoying little brother called Kevin, turning into a teenager. As midnight strikes the night before his birthday we witness an excitable, exuberant 12-year-old bouncing around the room and counting down to the big moment amidst breakneck chatter to his parents, immediately transformed on the final chime into a hostile, emotional, irrational and inarticulate being who hates those same parents and everything they say and do. The humour comes from the exaggeration, of course, but the stereotype of the moody, inaccessible, uncommunicative teenager is one that is deeply embedded in our cultural expectations.

Some families will glide gently through their children's teenage years, but for others this simplistic 'Kevin' stereotype is their reality, and it's certainly no joke, either for parents or teens. For most there will be a bit of both. There will be moments, or spells, or longer phases when communication is challenging. Equally there will be moments, spells or longer phases when their teenagers really want and need to talk, when they're receptive to what their parents have to say, and conversations can be had about all sorts of important issues they face, including drugs and alcohol.

Sometimes, after I've delivered a workshop to parents, someone will come up and tell me about how close they are to their teenagers, about the open and honest conversations they have about everything that matters, including drugs. How they're sure, because of this, they'd know if their child ever did have any involvement with drugs (but because of this openness and honesty they're reasonably confident their child would never consider such a thing). I want to say that I had just this with Dan. We talked, we listened, we ranged across vast expanses of conversational topics both heavy and lightweight. But I don't say this, because I know they want to feel safe, and feel that their child is safe, and it sounds as though they're doing lots of good things which will of course help. And saying *but that's just what I had with Dan*, when it so singularly and publicly failed to keep him safe, feels like condemning their child to the death that found Dan.

Good conversations about drugs are no more a failsafe, sure-fire, cast-iron guaranteed way to stop your child coming to harm from drugs than anything else, but they have the potential to be a powerful protective factor, and are a vital element in our work as parents to prepare our children to manage that world of decisions safely. They can be awkward, they can go horribly haywire, but they are always important, and the more that can be done to make them an easy, comfortable place to come back to, the better for all concerned.

Dan's story: Talking to Dan

Dan liked to talk. He used to follow me around chatting if I was busy. He used to sit and chat in the bathroom while I did my makeup in the morning, telling me about something that had happened in school the previous day, playing absently with my blusher or brushes. *Mum, girls are so complicated! If she broke up with him why did it matter if he started going out with her friend? If she still liked him why did she break up with him in the first place? You'll never believe what Miss so-and-so...* And so on.

He also liked to listen. He liked to hear what you thought about something – an issue, an idea, a situation. *So mum, what do you think about...?* Sometimes very concrete, political, moral. Sometimes less so. *So mum, would you rather be eaten by a shark or by a bear?* Discuss. He was working out what he thought about the world himself as he grew through his teenage years. He also found a mischievous enjoyment from setting someone off into a conversational, logical, ethical tangle, but with genuine interest in what they had to say behind the amusement. *But mum, surely feminism is redundant in the twenty-first century?* Discuss. His head of sixth form, who was teaching him English literature A level, wrote in the tribute book his school gave us shortly after he died, 'It is your incredible wit and charm that I will remember always – and the way in which you would combine the two to raise the most 'left field' questions in lessons, then watch us all tie ourselves in knots trying to respond.'

In all the terrible decisions you have to make when a child dies, and so early on, we were spared the one about burial or cremation because it turned out that not only did Jenna know his views on the subject, she also knew how strongly he held them. Apparently they had had a discussion not long before he died about the respective merits of the two, and Jenna said he was so adamant that burial was better that she ended up having to concede, and pretend she agreed even though she didn't, just to shut him up on the topic. I can just imagine how it started, *So Jenna, burial or cremation?* Discuss.

In the film *Shrek* when Donkey first greets Princess Fiona, she's understandably amazed: 'It talks!' Shrek's response is, 'Yeah, but it's getting him to shut up that's the trick.' All the stereotypes of teenage boys grunting monosyllables from behind a locked bedroom door, emerging only for food before disappearing back into the silent pit of unwashed clothes and headphones, didn't work for Dan. Dan was like Donkey in *Shrek*. A teenage boy who talks? But what for Shrek was a problem, for us was a gift. It was precious. What Dan was saying in his endless chat was often nothing of life-changing gravity, but it was almost always interesting, engaging, amusing, endearing, and although I never realized it was time-limited by shortness of life, I always knew it would be limited by the normal natural moving on and moving away as he grew into adulthood. That's not to say there weren't grumpy moments, crossness responded to with crossness, defensiveness, closed doors. And of course, I was never under any illusions he told me everything. That would have been unnatural, and not to be expected, not least because a lot of the things I'd have found really interesting in his life were to him humdrum, routine, and had not even registered in his conversational reference library.

And it wasn't just us. His conversational skills were a big factor in his popularity at school. Not just interesting to listen to – even, perhaps especially, in his most random rambles – but an interested listener. He really wanted to know, he really cared, he really wanted to make things better if they needed making better. He wanted everyone to be happy, and everything to be alright. A couple of years and many hours of watching *Jeremy Kyle* later and the boy who was bewildered by the mysteries of the female mind was the boy to whom the girls used to tell all their relationship problems. He really wanted to know, he really cared, he really wanted to make things better.

I know drugs entered our family conversations at a much younger age for Dan than they might ordinarily have done. I mentioned earlier someone we loved very much who had struggled with addiction for many years, who we'd tried our best as a family to support, to stand with, to help through the devastation they were causing to her life and to those around her. Bright, curious little boys wanted to understand the what and why and how of it all, but accepted explanations hooked around stories of illness and bad backs. Bright and curious somewhat bigger boys were no longer satisfied with these stories, and needed more honest information about what was happening to these people we loved very much, so they could make sense of it all. So Dan was aware, much younger than he might otherwise be, of the damage and destruction drugs can do, because of these events. As a consequence, he had always been very much opposed to anything drug-related, including smoking as I've said, right into year 11.

I wish I could remember the conversations I did have with Dan about drugs, when they became something on his own social radar. We always knew they would, and of the two boys, we always knew Dan, despite all this damaging drug stuff in the first part of his life, would be the one who might be curious. Cautious curiosity, adventurous wariness, always conscious of being safe, but with that zest for life we knew may sometimes get the better of him. Jacob was always more steadily on the side of caution, wariness and safety, always my little shadow as a small boy, always there by my side, often holding on to my leg, but Dan was off on an adventure, exploring new worlds and experiences beyond the confines of his buggy or his parents' safe hands. I was forever running after him, or stopping to wait while a little Dan, absorbed in a puddle or ants' nest, was ready to move on to the next great discovery. I knew of the two it might end up being Dan, but never really thought it would, or if it did that it might be the end.

I knew a fair amount about the messier end of drug addiction, thanks to what we'd witnessed earlier. And Tim and I had done a six-week course for parents about young people and drugs when the boys were a bit younger, perhaps 11 and 13. I can't now remember what we learned. I felt I knew about signs of drug use, paths to addiction, the price of a joint of cannabis, but whatever I knew it wasn't anywhere near enough, and wasn't what I needed to have known to be able to save Dan.

So, what did we talk about?

I remember when Dan came back from a party where there was cannabis for the first time, I think perhaps at the start of year 10. He told me all about it. I can't remember now the details of what he said but I do remember how new and surprising it all was to him. I don't remember what I said either, but I do remember saying how much I felt for the parents of the lad whose party it was: it was Halloween and I imagined this good Christian family letting their son have a party in place of trick or treating, which they perhaps viewed with suspicion, and there they were with their house full of kids smoking weed instead. Whether it was this time, or another – this wasn't the last of the cannabis stories over the next couple of years – my cannabis conversations went along these lines: it can seem like no big deal but: a) it's illegal so you can get in trouble with the police; b) because it's illegal you have to be in touch with a dealer, who may want to sell you other stuff too (*yeah mum, gateway drug, I know*); c) because it's illegal you never know exactly what you're getting, even with weed; d) it can trigger serious mental health problems. I worked with someone whose daughter had smoked cannabis at university and it had triggered psychosis, and several years on her mum had only just been able to get back to work, and could still only work part-time because her daughter was still unable to cope independently. I told that story.

There were other incidents and other conversations. A party where a girl in his year had taken something and collapsed and an ambulance had been called. A time after school (I think this was year 12) when a couple of the boys he was with were smoking weed and were stopped by police *and* – this is what made it a tale that was amusing to tell – *get this, it turned out one of the policemen had been bullied at school by the dad of one of the boys smoking weed*. I wish I could remember how these went, and where I went wrong, because I feel I must have done somewhere. Was I too lax or too lecturing?

Too liberal and understanding, too hesitant to face tricky issues head on? Did I shut the door to future meaningful conversations by being too predictably panicky? I just can't remember. It could have been any of those things.

But I know that 11 months before Dan went to a rave and died from drugs, we had a conversation about raves and the risks therein, and drugs and the risks thereof. In those days, drugs came into dramas with so much less carelessness or frequency than they do now, but when they did, we could talk about it. Did we always? I don't remember. But I do remember an episode of *My Mad Fat Diary*, a drama that came out in 2013 that Dan and I used to love, and sat and watched together every week. Sixteen-year-old Rae had been recently released from four months in a psychiatric hospital following a suicide attempt, and struggled with her mental health and identity. It was funny, quirky and touching, and explored lots of teenage issues.

In an episode aired on 11 February 2013, a year to the day before we buried Dan, the characters in the story went to a rave. They piled in a car, ended up in a field in the middle of nowhere, music booming out of an empty country house, teens gathering from all directions. Inside the rave, in the midst of the music and lights, fallen out with her mum, in love with Finn, Rae took a pill. She danced. Then the dealer who'd sold them the first ones popped another in her mouth. She danced some more. Then she did some shots. And finally she passed out, and woke up in the early hours on her face in a field on her own.

Lots to talk about there. *You don't know what you're getting, you don't know how it's going to affect you, how easy it is to lose track of the people you're with at that sort of thing if you're off your head on something, how vulnerable it can make you, she could have got assaulted* (the dealer was having a go), *she could have got left behind* (she didn't but she could have), *she could have ended up in hospital* (she didn't...), and so on. From memory it really wasn't a lecture, it was genuine gobsmacked commentary as it went along on the risks to which this character we'd come to love was exposing herself.

And then there was Reading Festival. Pick up your GCSE results, head off to Reading. Perfect timing for one of the few festivals that lets in 16-year-olds, and consequently it's full of the youngsters of the south of England, a mass exodus, a rite of passage, fresh from the highs or lows of whatever that brown envelope held for them, away from home on their own with friends for the first time, in a tent alongside tens of thousands of others. Alice, Jack and a couple of the others were going, he'd saved up his paper round money, he'd studied the line-up, he was desperate to go, and I let him. We had another drugs conversation – I did know festivals had drugs, though no idea of the extent at that stage – but to be perfectly honest I was more concerned about him eating properly while he was away without a responsible adult to get him three square meals.

When he'd come back, safe and sound and nourished well-enough, he told me about the headline acts, the terrible toilets, the dodgy older cousin of a friend he was with who bought them all beer from Tesco's until he disappeared. He told me about his conversion to rap thanks to Jack who made him watch Eminem (*It's just like Shakespeare mum! Look at these lyrics…*) and throwing his old Toms up on the stage. And he told me about the people he'd seen who'd taken ecstasy. It was the first time he'd witnessed this. *You should have seen them mum, they were so funny!* They were doing this, saying that, so funny.

So, less than five months before Dan died, we had a conversation about ecstasy. I didn't know enough, and neither did he. What I did know was that you don't know what's in it, you don't know how strong it is, and you don't know how it's going to affect you. All of that's true, so well done, me. I told him about Leah Betts, how one pill can kill. That's also true, but not true for most people most of the time, and now I know those scare tactics aren't always the best (even though they seem to make so much sense), and now I know, too, it wasn't the pill it was all the water poor Leah drank.

Yeah mum but it's one in (however many) million. Not quite true, not such a high number, but I got the point. It's not very likely. Dan was to become, of course, that one-in-however-many-it-was back in January 2014.

You're more likely to die making toast. Probably statistically true, but not true for Dan, who had made lots of toast in his 16 years and lived to make some more another day.

I didn't know all the other useful things I now know about how to reduce the risks if someone does take ecstasy, and if I had, and if I'd said them, then perhaps he'd have known enough five months later to keep himself safe. But I didn't, and he didn't. And he didn't tell me about the first time he tried MDMA, or the second time, and he couldn't tell me about the third, or anything else by that stage, for that matter. We both needed to have known more, and to have talked more about it. It may have made no difference, but it would have been worth a few awkward conversations just in case.

Why do conversations matter?

It surprises many parents to learn that the first place most teenagers turn for helpful information about drug use is to their parents, and the same goes for alcohol. In the government's 'Smoking, Drinking and Drug Use' survey, just over three-quarters of 11- to 15-year-olds said they would ask their parents if they wanted to learn more about alcohol, and just under three-quarters said the same about drugs. Parents come out well ahead of their friends, the internet and any of the others places those same parents generally expect their children to think are more useful.[1] You may not feel like a valuable resource in your family when it comes to drugs, but statistics show that your children think you are. Their friends are becoming increasingly important during their adolescence for reasons we've explored, but their parents are the ones they continue to need for the big, important stuff of life.

Conversations about drugs can feel very daunting, though. What on earth do you know about drugs these days? Why on earth would they listen to you when they know so much more themselves? Will they roll their eyes, switch off, get angry or defensive? Will you make things worse? But remember, your teenager may feel just as worried about broaching the subject as you. Will they make you worry? Will they disappoint you? Will you jump to conclusions? Will you panic and never let them leave the house again?

---

[1] NHS Digital (2019) Smoking, Drinking and Drug Use Among Young People in England 2018 [online]. *NHS Digital*. Available from: <digital.nhs.uk/data-and-information/publications/statistical/smoking-drinking-and-drug-use-among-young-people-in-england/2018> (accessed November 2020)

What makes for a good drugs conversation?

There is good evidence to show that conversations between parents and adolescents about drugs and alcohol can and do make a difference to the choices they make. A recent literature review examined 42 studies which had researched the role parent-child connectedness, and parent-child communication, played in adolescent substance use, and what sort of conversations had that vital protective factor.[2] Parent–child connectedness is defined in various ways, but the one I like best is 'feelings of closeness, warmth, love and satisfaction a child has with their parent'. Parent–child communication is to do with how comfortable both feel talking to each other about a range of topics, including sensitive areas like drugs and alcohol.

It's perhaps unsurprising that the effectiveness of communication depends heavily on the quality of connectedness, and the quality of connectedness is equally dependent on the effectiveness of communication. It also makes sense that where parents and adolescents felt strongly connected, and were able to communicate well, the conversations they had about drugs and alcohol could make a big difference in the decisions those teenagers made. When parent–child connectedness is high, communication about drugs is more comfortable, and more likely to be protective, but when this is low then communication can feel stilted, is more likely to be one-way, and can sometimes end up doing more harm than good.

The importance of clear messages and open communication was emphasized by both parents and teenagers. The study refers to 'harder' communication, which focused on rules and boundaries, and 'softer' communication which explored possible risks, potential consequences and the importance of decision-making. It found a blend of both is what works best, not necessarily at the same time but within ongoing conversations. In fact, when parents just emphasized the rules without explaining the risks and consequences this was actually damaging and led to higher reported levels of substance use.

---

2 Carver, H. et. al. (2016) Parent–child connectedness and communication in relation to alcohol, tobacco and drug use in adolescence: An integrative review of the literature [online]. *Drugs: Education, Prevention and Policy.* 24(2). Available from: DOI: 10.1080/09687637.2016.1221060

Lecturing can do the same. Those on the receiving end of a one-sided conversation of the lecturing variety tended to be unreceptive – now there's a surprise – and those messages were less likely to be assimilated and lodged in the young head on the receiving end, to retrieve when they needed them. The most effective conversations were those which were constructive, in which both parents and teens participated equally, and the views of both were heard and respected (even if not absolutely agreed with). So how does one go about this?

The art of communication

Before we consider conversations about drugs, we need to begin with conversations about anything at all, and what's going on, and sometimes going wrong, in conversations with teenagers specifically.

The *Oxford English Dictionary* defines communication as 'the imparting or exchanging of information by speaking, writing or some other medium'. It continues with more nuance: 'the successful conveying or sharing of ideas and feelings'. Our focus in this chapter is on the speaking side of communication, and it's well established that there are many dimensions to this, above and beyond the mere stringing together of sentences. All those non-verbal messages and cues we send and receive without any words even leaving our lips: body language, gesturing, facial cues, intonation and so on, as well as the context itself. Until recently it was a widely accepted belief that 93 per cent of our communication was nonverbal,[3] and although the accuracy of this analysis has been questioned,[4] all agree that the balance comes out significantly on the side of the unspoken.

There are, of course, at least two people involved in any form of communication, the 'sender' and 'recipient'. The sender encodes a message – frames all the verbal and non-verbal elements as best they can into what they hope will be received. The recipient decodes it all, as best they can in turn, and interprets it into the message they hear.

---

[3] Mehrabian, A. (1971) *Silent Messages: Implicit communication of emotions and attitudes*, Wadsworth Publishing Company.

[4] Strain, K. (2020) How much of communication is really nonverbal? [online]. *Premier Global Services*. Available from: <uk.pgi.com/blog/2020/03/how-much-of-communication-is-really-nonverbal/> (accessed November 2020)

This all takes place within a broad, as well as very specific, social context. Altogether it's not surprising that miscommunication can happen en route between the encoding and the decoding, and only surprising it doesn't happen more often. Throw into that what we've learned about adolescence, and it's easy to see why misunderstandings can happen in communication between parents and teenagers, but the more this can be understood, the better it can be overcome, or at least managed, or borne with.

Talking with teenagers: what can make it (sometimes) tricky?

A couple of the developmental changes associated with adolescence that we've already looked at are also relevant to communication during this period of change, and what can make it smooth or rocky. That deep-seated need adolescents have to carve out a different order of relationship with their parents as they journey from their childhood into independent adult lives includes shifting the way communication takes place within that family space. You may be saying just the same things you have many times before, encoding your message in just the same way, but what they hear is something quite different because its decoding is now framed in the context of needing to know they can survive outside the safety and security of the family nest. The most innocuous comment might be received as a threat to their vital steps into independence. The imbalanced rates of development of the racing ahead (emotional) limbic system and the lagging behind (sensible) prefrontal cortex are another factor, and mean that a highly charged, high velocity leap to a (possibly false) conclusion might beat a more rational and reflective (and possibly more accurate) interpretation hands down.

There are a couple of other developmental factors that can affect how well those conversations turn out. Our ability to communicate effectively, whether as sender or receiver of the message, relies heavily on our ability to understand each other. Our capacity to appreciate that someone else's perspective, opinion and worldview may be different from our own is referred to by psychologists as 'mentalizing'. We start being able to do this at around 18 months old, but it's still developing between late adolescence and adulthood. It's a time when it's just that bit harder to step into someone else's shoes, let's say those of their parents, and to understand that their words may come from a perspective that has validity, is based on many years of experience and is borne of love and concern.

That brings us on to the second important factor at work in teenage conversations relating to the mutual understanding that underpins its success. Essential to decoding what someone says is the ability to interpret facial expressions accurately. Think of how many different facial expressions could be used when just the single word 'Really?' is spoken, with exactly the same intonation, that would alter its meaning entirely. Various studies have explored how this works, and when it doesn't, and how it changes during childhood and adolescence. One element in this is the part of our brain we use. Scans of the brains of adults, pre-teens and teens looking at images of faces which display a range of emotions show that whereas adults use their pre-frontal cortex, which enables them to exercise judgement and regulate their response, in childhood and adolescence it's the amygdala that does the work, the bit of our brain linked to gut reaction and raw emotion. A quick and heated reaction may therefore trump a more measured and reflective response in teenagers, based on a possibly misconstrued facial expression.

Which brings us on to hormones, which are indeed raging during adolescence. The hormones responsible for menstruation, hairy legs, deepening male voices and all those familiar physical changes, also play a role in emotional regulation. Testosterone, oestrogen and progesterone have been around since childhood, but never before at these levels. Oestrogen and progesterone are both linked to mood, and their fluctuation during girls' menstrual cycle is responsible for those unpredictable swings from flights of joy to pits of despair. Testosterone is a hormone most active in the amygdala, where our fight-flight response sits, so a harmless comment to your teenage son may elicit an unexpectedly aggressive response. It's important to remember the effect all this can have on our child is just as new to them as it is to those witnessing it at work, and can be just as bewildering. The teenage brain needs a bit of time to adjust to this influx of powerful chemicals at such increased volume, and to work out how to regulate their effects. In the meantime, the fallout may affect the quality of communication between parents and teens.

Knowing what lies behind the heat of the moment won't necessarily make that moment less intense, painful or confusing to the average parent, but if you're able to manage your own emotions in the face of the unexpected, and to take a pause, a deep breath or a step aside, this will help you both – your relationship, your conversation and your conversations to come.

Talking point

Some tips for soothing closed the storms if they come:

- Try to stay calm and not get angry or defensive yourself, and be aware of your non-verbal communication in case this sends a different message.
- Don't try to argue or reason when emotions are running high.
- Let them finish what they're saying and listen without interrupting, interpreting or interfering (see below for more advice on listening).
- Try to separate the words or actions from the child you know and love.
- Try to focus on the problem they're airing, empathize and show you're on the same side.
- Reframe things from negative to positive if you can.
- Try to use 'and' and avoid 'but', for example, 'I can see what you're saying, and I can also see the need for...'
- Look for things you can praise your teenager for – they're likely to be feeling very vulnerable, even if it doesn't show.
- Give your teen choices, for example if they want to come back to this later.

The art of listening

Listening is an art. It is also a gift. We all know how important it is to feel someone has really listened to what we've had to say. Conversely, we know how bad it can feel when they haven't, especially when what we said mattered to us. There are many verbal and non-verbal signals that betray the lack of attention our audience is paying to our words, and just as we can pick this up easily, so can our teenagers when we do this to them, which we all will have done at some time or other. They will do it to us too, but it matters more from our side, because we're the grown-ups. We're also modelling our behaviour to them – more on this below – and we can surely help them to learn to be good listeners. If we give them our full listening attention, they're also more likely to give us theirs in turn. Quid pro quo. Those equally balanced, two-way conversations, with as much listening as talking on both sides, are what all the research shows are most effective in preparing our children to make safe choices about drugs and alcohol.

Much has been written about how to listen well, and there are some general principles that are good to keep in mind. They are also good to practice, because not only is listening an art and a gift, but also a skill, and skills can always be improved.

- **Stop**: if your child wants to talk, stop what you're doing and listen if you possibly can. This might be a unique opportunity for openness when their situation, thoughts, mood and emotions are in alignment, and you are the person they need to share this with. It may have taken a lot of courage to approach you if the topic is as tricky as things to do with drugs and alcohol can be. Of course it won't always be possible for you to drop everything you're doing at that moment, and sometimes our children have a knack for choosing the worst moments of all, but if this is the case suggest another time, and try to make sure it's not too far off.

- **Open and closed questions**: asking open questions is a lot harder than it seems, but a question that requires more than a monosyllabic answer gives the other person scope to share their knowledge, thoughts or feelings in some detail. That said, it's perfectly possible to answer a vast array of carefully crafted open questions with 'S'alright' or 'Dunno'. *How was your day? What did you think about...? How do you feel about...?* With teenagers, asking the right questions, in the right way, at the right moment, really is an art, in which luck plays a big hand too. It's also a balancing act. It's important to be sensitive to where the tipping point might lie between healthy interest and unhealthy nosiness. Although showing an active curiosity about their life is important, it can easily morph into something experienced as intrusive and invasive, even if this is another of those teenage misinterpretations of your best of intentions.

- **Are you listening or just waiting to talk?**: This is something many of us are guilty of. While the other person is talking to us our mind is busy framing our response, and we're no longer paying proper attention, really just waiting for a pause so we can get in there with our own thoughts or experiences. It's good to think through what you might want to say, but better to concentrate on what's being said to you.

- **Acknowledge their feelings**: you may not agree with what they are saying, or feel their reaction is appropriate or proportionate, but it's important for them to know their emotions have validity. As we've seen, these emotions can be very powerful in adolescence, even if sometimes irrational, and although they may well pass, they need to be acknowledged and accepted for what they are.

- **Don't make assumptions**: it can be easy to jump to the wrong conclusion when we're listening to our children, and especially in conversations that can be more loaded like ones about drugs or alcohol. Your child may be telling you about something involving drugs that sets off all your protectiveness radars, but you may not have got it quite right. It's useful to go back over what you think they've said, not just for checking you've understood it correctly, but also for your child to sense-check and further process what it is they're trying to say. The added bonus of this is that it gives you a bit of extra processing time if you need it, while you work out how best to respond.

- **Don't panic**: if your assumptions turn out to have been correct, and your radar was right, try not to let your (totally understandable) reaction close that conversation down for both now and the future. That said, your child knows you well, and may have entered the conversation totally expecting you to panic, but if you do let it out, try to reign it back in as soon as you can, and get back to listening, and identifying what positive steps forward can be made.

> ## Talking (listening) points
>
> Be honest with your children about wanting to improve your listening skills, if you feel you do. How would they rate you? When do you listen best? And worst? What do they think would help? Even if they think you're terrible at listening, the fact you want to get better, and have listened to their views on your listening, will help make amends if amends are needed.
>
> An obvious point, but try to put your phone aside when your child is talking to you. We can be just as bad as teenagers at prioritizing the conversation on the phone over the one in the room without realizing we are, or intending to do so.

Opportunistic or planned?

There are two basic orders of communication parents have with their children about drugs and alcohol. Both are important, both can make a difference, and a blend of both is what works best. One is reactive: the taking of an opportunity, the seizing of the moment – something in the news, or on television, or that's come up at school. The other is proactive: a more deliberate and planned conversation, perhaps on a specific topic or in preparation for a specific event, or just because you felt it was needed. Either way, there need to be spaces in which these conversations can happen.

Making spaces

When your children are small you do everything with them. Outside of school, and all the parties and play dates and extracurricular busyness, spending time together is a given. As they grow older, though, and begin to forge that necessary independence from their caregivers, these times can be harder to find. However, it's so important parents do what they can to make them keep happening. It's important not just in order to create the opportunities for useful conversations about things like drugs and alcohol, but because they are the foundations of those positive parent–child relationships, which in turn make those conversations work better. And as we've seen, those strong bonds of connectedness, and open and effective channels of communication, have been shown to be some of the most protective factors when it comes to teenagers and risky behaviours around drugs and alcohol. As with most aspects of parenting, it doesn't have to be perfect, and it doesn't take much for it to be good enough to make a difference.

Family mealtimes are a simple example of setting up that conversational space. Several studies have found that something as simple as eating together can do lots of good and lasting work in protecting teenagers from taking risks with alcohol and other substances.[5] Whatever you do to make time to be together, though, it doesn't have to be for long, it doesn't have to be a special occasion, and it certainly doesn't have to be expensive. In fact, just doing something quite ordinary alongside each other can make for a more relaxed conversational space for you both – even sitting in the car from A to B and back again, yet again, as their taxi for the night. Knowing they have a parent to themselves, however briefly, can be very important for teenagers, even if not a word is said.

Talking point

Try to make the most of any chance to spend time together you can, especially as they get older, and create opportunities when you can, even if it feels like a bit of a nuisance in a busy life. Little things can make a big difference, and these opportunities won't come along forever.

If you don't already have regular family mealtimes, think about how you might start to re-introduce them. It might just be one evening a week, or a Sunday lunch, and if you can get your children on board in the planning and execution, so much the better. And no phones!

When and how to start the drugs conversation

If it's not too late then it's good to start talking about drugs before your children come across them, to set that comfortable conversation

5   Harrison, M.E. et al. (2015) Systematic review of the effects of family meal frequency on psychosocial outcomes in youth [online]. *Canadian Family Physician.* Feb; 61(2): e96–e106. Available from: <www.ncbi.nlm.nih.gov/pmc/articles/PMC4325878/#:~:text=Overall%2C%20results%20show%20that%20frequent,-self%2Desteem%20and%20school%20success> (accessed November 2020)

in place so it can be revisited as and when it's needed, and ready for the days when drugs and alcohol begin to become part of their social environment. There are no definitive rules to how, what and when you do this because every child is unique, will mature at their own rate, and will be inhabiting a different set of circumstances to those of other children, even within one family. That said, there are some basic guidelines as to what to talk about when, and whatever age they are, a key component of managing risk is building their inner strength and resilience, and their confidence in their own views and values within their peer group.

From pre-school to around 8 or 9 years:

- Conversations about healthy choices generally, and looking after their wellbeing, both physically and mentally, can start from a very early age.
- There are opportunities to introduce the risks of drugs by talking about medicines, perhaps looking at instructions and talking about why it's important to follow them.
- There are likely to be other substances around them that can provide opportunities to introduce the concept of risk and harm, and how risk needs to be managed: coffee, smoking, vaping or alcohol.

Pre- and early secondary school (10–12 years)

- Your children are likely to become more aware of specific substances, and to be curious about the effects they can have, as they get towards the end of primary school. As they move to secondary school they will be around older students, and may see and hear things that are new to them. They may also find themselves beginning to be presented with choices.
- As well as all the above, you could begin to have more focused conversations about smoking, vaping and alcohol, as well as cannabis if this is on their radar.

13–15 years:

- Opportunities for unplanned conversations are likely to arise more frequently, for example as their exposure across various media changes and their awareness of relevant issues increases.

- Planned conversations begin to become more important (see the checklist below) as their independence increases, the range of social activities and events expands, and their exposure to substances may begin or increase.
- It's around 13–14 years that teenagers often settle into their friendship groups, parties begin to start, and alcohol starts to appear, so conversations about the risks of alcohol at this age are important, and being clear about your own family boundaries relative to 'everyone else's parents'.
- They may begin to be around cannabis, and possibly other drugs such as nitrous oxide and MDMA at this stage, so these are substances to be aware of yourself, to bring into conversations.

16–18 years:

- Drugs are likely to be increasingly part of their social environment online and offline, and a wider range of drugs than before. Find out more about substances like ketamine, cocaine, LSD, magic mushrooms, benzodiazepines and anything else that may be on their radar. Listening is more important than ever at this stage. Clear boundaries are also still important, though continually needing to be renegotiated and redrawn as they reach adulthood. Try to remain open, calm and non-judgemental, and keep those conversations open.

The drug conversation: a checklist for planning ahead

1. What would a good time and place look like? When will they feel relaxed and receptive? When is a good time for you? What would be best to avoid?
2. What are your own views and values? Sometimes these aren't as clear as we think without taking time to reflect and examine them.
3. What are your family boundaries? Are you open to renegotiating them? If so, how far might you be prepared to go?
4. Are you prepared to hear things you might not want to? How will you react if you do? (Try not to panic.)
5. Do you know where to go if help or support is needed, for you or for them? (See the back of the book.)

---

6. Are there any tricky questions for which you might need to prepare answers? 'So, mum/dad, did you ever...?'
7. What will you do if it all goes horribly wrong? Try to keep your own emotions in check, hard though that can be if things fly your way at high intensity. See tips above.

The drug conversation: what to avoid

When you're involved in a good conversation with your child about drugs, what you're doing is basically informal drugs education. These conversations will be all the better if you know what works and what doesn't, and thankfully there's a solid international evidence-base of good practice when it comes to drugs and alcohol education. Some of the things that research has demonstrated don't work can seem counter-intuitive, however.

Surely they just need to be told to say no? Saying no to drugs will indeed always be their safest option, and is an option they need to know is always open to them, especially if they're feeling pressured to do something they don't want to. But as a solo strategy the evidence shows it isn't so simple. Anyone old enough may remember Nancy Reagan's 'Just say no' campaign of the 1980s (and *Grange Hill*'s take on this). This was delivered to elementary aged children in schools across the US, and still is in many places. The 'just say no' approach was evaluated extensively, however, and was found to be ineffective. Thirty-five years later and sadly the US has drug-related death rates which are off the scale, which could be seen as proof in itself that it hadn't worked.

Surely scaring them witless with a shocking image of the impact drugs can have will make them think twice? A teenager on life support after experimenting with MDMA, a nose without a middle after years of snorting cocaine, a body emaciated by years of smoking crack. For some this will work, but for the majority it apparently doesn't, and for some it will be traumatizing.

Surely they just need to know the facts? Sadly it's not as simple as that either. As we've seen, all the knowledge in the world doesn't necessarily help you when you're making decisions in your teens because there are other, more powerful, forces at work.

So what does work?

The European Centre for Monitoring of Drugs and Drug Addiction (EMCDDA) is the authority on all things evidence-based across Europe in relation to drugs and drug-related issues, pulling together current data and research to inform professionals in the field. This includes, very usefully, a Drug Prevention Curriculum which provides a very clear framework for what works in drugs education. Useful for practitioners and policy-makers, and also for parents – in summary form at least.[6]

Up-to-date, accurate, relevant information that is age-appropriate and evidence-based. You don't need to know everything, and you couldn't possibly learn all you'd need to know about young people, drugs and decisions and also fulfil your many other responsibilities as a parent, so knowing where reliable information can be found is essential. Your teenager may also not know as much as they think, they may well have picked up a number of myths and misconceptions, and their own sources of information and advice may not be so robust. And you can always find out together.

A lifeskills approach that enables young people to develop the tools they need to be able to navigate those decision-making situations safely. Help your children understand all we explored in Chapter 4 about the adolescent brain, the role of their friends and managing risk.

An interactive approach that doesn't lecture but allows time and space for discussion, reflection and further exploration. Active and mutual engagement with all these matters makes for the most effective learning, as we've already seen.

Challenging social norms that reinforce young people's perceptions of the extent to which their peers are taking drugs or drinking to excess. These perceptions are always, on average, much higher in their heads than they are in reality, for all sorts of reasons, and this risks affecting their own decision-making. As we've seen, the more normal we think something is the more likely we are to do it ourselves, even if we know we shouldn't.

---

[6] EMCDDA (2019) *European Drug Prevention Curriculum: a handbook for decision-makers, opinion-makers and policy makers in science-based prevention of substance use* [online]. *EMCDDA*. Available from: <www.emcdda.europa.eu/publications/manuals/european-prevention-curriculum_en> (accessed November 2020)

Talking point

Reinforce the fact to your children that the majority of young people, at any age, are neither taking drugs nor drinking too much. Nowhere is this normal across their wider peer group, even if it's become so within a smaller friendship group.

This is also the moment to mention the need to exercise caution in talking about your own substance use, if you have experiences in your past with either alcohol or drugs. While honesty is important, evidence shows that a parent's own previous issues with drugs or alcohol, even if told as a salutary tale, can normalize use to a teenager and give tacit permission to go and do likewise.

Laying out the boundaries

One of the many stereotypes about teenagers is that they rail against any boundaries put in their way, and there is a natural instinct to do just that at this age. But although they may question, challenge and chafe at the bit, they need to know there are clear lines in the sand and where these lie, in order to feel safe, loved and cared for. It's also important because it's a stage of life when setting their own boundaries is difficult because it's their pre-frontal cortex, that part of the brain that's the last to connect up, that does all the organizing and planning and goal-setting they need for knowing where those lines should lie.

Clear expectations for behaviour and boundaries have been shown to be another strong protective factor against risk taking, substance use and negative peer influence.[7] Boundaries set the limits on what is and isn't acceptable for your child, in your family, at this stage of their life. They do of course need to shift as they grow older but, once agreed, they need to be clear, consistently applied, and any consequences that were part of the package need to be followed through. Easier said than done in the face of that natural teenage instinct to kick over the traces, but holding onto the knowledge they need this even if they don't think they do can help you to hang on in there.

---

[7] Youth.gov <youth.gov/youth-topics/risk-and-protective-factors>

Where the boundaries lie in your family are for you to decide, ideally following discussion, negotiation and the agreement of all parties concerned – and they will inevitably be different from those of their friends, because of course 'everyone else's parents' are always a whole lot more lenient than their own.

Talking point

Boundaries work best if they are agreed. Some families will do this in the form of a simple written contract, some will find this too formal, but however you go about it, it's important to make sure there's just as much listening as speaking all round. Showing your teenager how to negotiate, present their point of view respectfully and come to an agreement is also giving them a valuable life skill.

Once agreed, if there's more than one of you parenting it really helps to have a **united and consistent front** to reinforce messages, and especially if these boundaries are breached or challenged.

Positive messages are also very important at this stage of life when confidence can often take a knock. Praise when the rules are respected, and recognition of anything unexpected done above and beyond (in a good way), will do lots of good.

Parental monitoring

Parental monitoring is something that tends to decrease during adolescence, as teenagers spend more time with friends and less with family. Those parental reigns do have to slacken to enable them to achieve the independence they ultimately need as adults, and the ongoing adjustments and judgements can be hard to call and the best balance tricky to find. An interesting recent study from the US explored the links between the alcohol and cannabis use of 13- to 15-year-olds, and the extent to which their parents monitored what they did, where they did it and with whom it was done.[8] The focus was on how young these teenagers were when they started drinking

---

[8] Rusby, J.C. et al. (2018) Influence of parent-youth relationships, parental monitoring and parent substance use on adolescent substance use onset [online]. *Journal of Family Psychology.* 32(3), 310–320. Available from: DOI: 10.1037/ fam0000350

or smoking cannabis, if they did, because early onset of substance use is linked to a whole host of negative substance-related outcomes for young people, including use of other substances, use of stronger substances and use that continues into late teens and 20s, and develops into addiction.

The results showed that parental monitoring was a strong protective factor, and just as we might expect, key to this being effective was the quality of that parent-child relationship, and key to the quality of the relationship was frequent and honest communication. Conversely, coercive communication patterns, involving a pattern of conflict and withdrawal behind closed doors, literal or metaphorical, reduced the protective impact parental monitoring could have. This style of parenting can be perceived by teens as controlling and a threat to their independence, rather than concern that provided boundaries within which they could learn to make their own choices safely. Parents can feel uncomfortable keeping too close an eye on their older teens, but creating an expectation that states you want to know where they are and when and who they'll be with, because you need to know they're safe, can help as you flex this age-appropriately as they move towards independence. And let's face it, we still generally want to know when the adults around us are planning to get home.

Saying it again and again, and again

Saying the same or similar things more than once, and in more than one way, does also help when it comes to making conversations about drugs and alcohol make a difference, even if it elicits some rolling of the eyes. One of the functions of that pre-frontal cortex to which we keep returning is something called prospective memory. This is our ability to hold in our mind the intention to perform a certain action at a future time. This ability stops developing in early adolescence, around the ages of 10–14, and only really picks up in our mid-twenties. A pre-teen or teen may fully intend in that particular moment to do, or not to do, something in particular in the future, but when that future moment comes their access to this intention may not be as quick or easy as they need it to be. The repetition and reinforcement of an important point by their parents, even if it seems to have reached impermeable ears, may be the very thing they need to know in the moment in which they later find themselves.

Modelling

As parents we are role models to our children, whether we or they like to admit it, and this continues into their teens despite all appearances to the contrary. From the swear word that slipped out that finds itself in our innocent toddler's mouth, to how we cope in a crisis, relate to the people around us or consume alcohol, our children are watching and learning. Some of the most powerful non-verbal messages are those we communicate through what we do, and we can make an enormous difference for good or ill. Which brings us back full circle to the quality of parent-child connectedness, because all our communication, whether what we say or what we do, will have so much more lasting value to our teenagers, and so much more protective value when it comes to drugs and alcohol, if this most important of relationships within which it all takes place is strong.

Talking point: the drugs conversation – ten top tips

1. Do what you can to strengthen your connectedness to your child.
2. Take and make opportunities for conversations generally, and for conversations about drugs and alcohol specifically.
3. Don't feel you have to be an expert in young people, drugs and alcohol before you can have a conversation, but do keep your knowledge as up to date as you can.
4. Listen as much (if not more) than you talk and try to avoid lecturing.
5. Emphasize social norms around drugs and alcohol – most young people aren't taking risks.
6. Try not to make assumptions, pass judgements or jump to conclusions.
7. Make sure your family boundaries are clear, reviewed and agreed.
8. Remember some degree of parental monitoring, as appropriate to your family and child's age, which will help to keep them safe.
9. Repetition and reinforcement helps important messages to stick.
10. If it all goes haywire, don't give up. Take time out, come back to it when the dust has settled, and have another go. It's too important to be deterred or to let that conversation get shut down.

Talking point

And finally, what advice would a teenager give to a parent?

- Pick your moment.
- Make sure you do your research before starting the conversation. If the school offers an information evening then GO!!
- Think about getting older siblings involved.
- Be careful with your tone. Don't make it too formal. Be friendly and casual and use small talk to ease nerves. But also get to the point!
- Don't talk about the topic like you're trying to control your child, or come off as aggressive and pressurizing, implementing strict rules from the get-go. It may have an adverse effect and cause more trouble later.
- It is important to talk about and build trust. Don't get angry, judge or accuse, but instead listen and try to understand the situation. If they have taken drugs, then try to see the reasons why.
- Don't force someone to talk or share if they are not ready yet. They will come to you when they are.

With thanks to DSM Foundation year 12 Youth Ambassadors.

I wish I'd known we needed to talk about drugs

By Sharon Crossley, mum of Jack (18)

We're incredibly close as a family. Jack and his big sister Mollie have eight cousins, mostly of similar ages, and all his socializing was done with this big bunch of ten, as well as a small group of close friends he'd kept since primary school. Jack's dad died from cancer when he was nine, which might be why he stuck so close to his family. It was also why he'd always been so anti-smoking, and because of this I'd never really been concerned about him taking drugs, and I didn't know much about them anyway. I wish I'd known more, because then we'd have talked, like we did about everything else.

At 18, Jack had everything to look forward to. That summer he'd just passed his two-year college course and was busy looking for an apprenticeship to qualify as an electrician, while working at our local pet shop at weekends. Jack loved sport – he was a massive Chelsea fan, and he'd played football for the same team from the age of seven at our local sports and social club. He played cricket there too in the summer, and a bit of darts and pool in the club house. Jack got on with people of all ages, and everyone loved Jack. He was a big, friendly, gentle giant.

Jack never really ventured too far until that April, a few months after he'd turned 18, when he and a friend went for the first time to a club up in London where they played the sort of music he liked. That first trip was a new experience for me too. I lay awake all night, texting the mum of the friend he went with from the early hours till 7 am when he finally called. The club hadn't shut till 6 am, he said. They were just grabbing a McDonald's breakfast, and then he'd be home.

In June they went back again for a second time, and this time they knew the type of culture the club had to offer, and this included MDMA. That very same night an 18-year-old boy died from taking drugs there. I wish I'd known, and I wish we'd talked about it, because Jack went for a third time on Friday 5 August, and that was his last. Unfortunately, Jack and his friends had smuggled in some MDMA. During the early hours he was approached by a man in the club asking if they wanted to buy more, and they did. The overdose that killed my boy cost him £10.

At his inquest I had to sit and listen to the horrific, traumatic ordeal that Jack's body went through that morning. It will haunt me forever. No mother needs to hear this, but she does need to hear about the dangers out there, so she can have the conversation I never got to have. I wish I had known.

Jack Crossley, with permission from Sharon Crossley

7

I wish I'd known how to make things safer

Harm reduction and staying safe

It was some point after Dan died that I first came across the phrase 'harm reduction'. Reeling after the death of my son to drugs, and desperate to warn every other parent and teenager on the planet about the risks, the news that a set of advice existed that told people how to do drugs more safely was such a surprise, and I have to confess it was one that was anathema to me. Drugs had taken my son and destroyed our lives. Surely the best thing was to steer as well clear as you possibly could? Dan had fallen in a hole from which there was no return. We just wanted to tell everyone else to be careful. There's a hole over there, don't let yourself fall in it too, you might not make it out again. As a mum, and a mum deep in shock, trauma and grief, the simple solution was safest. Just don't do it. Just don't. Definitely don't start telling people it'll make it safer to do it if...

The safest option with drugs will indeed always be not to take them. This is the only way to reduce your risk to zero. As we've seen, risk is complicated when it comes to drugs. However, like it or not, as parents we have to accept that people do take drugs. Dan was a boy who did, in the company of other boys who did, in a world in which young people choose to take drugs every day and night of the week somewhere or other, whether their parents like it, or know about it, or not. As a mum, still reeling from the loss of my boy all these years later in a world that still doesn't quite make sense, my number one preference by a million, billion miles would always be that he'd said *no* and not *yes*, that he hadn't even gone to that stupid rotten rave in the first place, that he'd stayed safe at home with us. But as a mum, with a boy who did go, and did say *yes*, and didn't come home, I wish with all my heart both he and I had known what measures he could have used to limit the damage those drugs did to his happy, healthy, strapping young life. It broke my heart he didn't, and I didn't, and it broke it some more to learn how much he could have done, if only we'd both known.

What is harm reduction?

We're all fans of harm reduction, and we practise it every day. If you think about our behaviour on the road, we wear seat belts, we stick to speed limits (on the whole), we wear helmets on our bikes (or we should). When it comes to drugs, harm reduction began to be talked about as a specific approach in the 1980s. Rising levels of HIV infection among injecting drug users, who were sharing and re-using needles, led to the introduction of needle and syringe exchange schemes, which still operate in many local pharmacies. The term 'harm reduction' has come to encompass a raft of services, strategies and approaches, from safe consumption sites, to drug testing at festivals, and education and advice for young people. More broadly it also ranges across issues relating to human rights and social justice. It seeks to be pragmatic and non-judgemental, but also doesn't attempt to minimize or ignore the very real damage drugs can do.

Harm reduction in its pure sense will never escape controversy, because it will always seem to condone drug use, and if delivered without care it can do just that. Harm reduction messages for young people, then, have to be delivered with great caution. Most young people won't come to any lasting harm from drugs if they do say *yes*, but this is often more through luck than through the effective implementation of evidence-based harm reduction strategies. Some, however, will experience varying degrees of damage, and for all of them, having those strategies to pull out of their back pocket if they need them makes for less dependence on luck, and more on informed choice.

That said, there are plenty of general, practical principles and strategies around staying safe when you're out and about as a teenager that will never be controversial, and that's where we'll start. We'll save the tricky stuff till later, as we go into the next chapter.

Some phone-related safety strategies

Mobile phones are so deeply embedded in our lives it's easy to take them for granted and forget what an enormous asset they are when it comes to safety. There are many different ways a phone can be used to help our children keep themselves safe when they're out and about, in addition to the incredible gift of that basic bottom line of being able to make and receive messages and calls wherever they are.

- **Phone tip #1 – charge it up.** An obvious one, but get your children in the habit of making sure their phone is fully charged before they go out. If it's going to be a long day, night or weekend, then make sure they have a fully charged battery pack and lead with them, or a lead and plug if they'll definitely have access to power.
- **Phone tip #2 – ICE details.** Make sure they have In Case of Emergency details (in other words, your and/or another parent or carer's contact details) saved on their phone so they can still be accessed if their screen lock is on. This can be done on all makes and models of phones, and it just means if help is needed their parents or legal guardian can be contacted immediately, whether by one of their friends or by the emergency services. If you're not sure how to do this you can find instructions online.
- **Phone tip #3 – contact details.** A tricky one, but if you possibly can, try to get hold of one or two of their friends' numbers just in case you need them. Whether you can or not depends on many factors, and may be crossing a boundary that's important to your child, and if this is the case then try to persuade them to get your number on at least one of their friends' phones. This just means if there's an emergency you can be contacted straight away. Dan's friend Jack didn't have our number when the paramedics asked him, and he wishes he had. Of all the things to feel bad about if things are going wrong, not having your friend's parents' phone number is one that doesn't need to be on that list.
- **Phone tip #4 – maps.** Your children are probably more than adept at using all the apps on their phone, but if they don't already know how to use their phone map make sure they do. This is such a valuable resource, especially if they end up somewhere unexpected and unknown, and need to know where they are and

how to get home, whether on foot or public transport. Or if they need to tell a parent exactly where they are so they can come and pick them up.

- **Phone tip #5 – set up an escape plan.** When we realized Dan hadn't really been that keen to go to the rave, and that he'd been so wary of taking his MDMA, we also realized that the story he had made up for us would have meant he'd be back around 4.30 am at the latest, not sometime the following day after a fictional sleepover like everyone else in the group. And that made us wonder if he hadn't really meant to stay. Perhaps he'd meant to make his excuses, slip off and head home to bed, but that can be far easier in the planning than the execution. It can be awkward if you start to feel uncomfortable and just want to leave, but everyone else seems to be having a great time, you know they'll come back with lots of counter arguments to any excuses you make, and your excuses are likely to run out, and it'll all risk getting convoluted, confrontational and complicated. Easier just to go along with it. *But*, we thought, *if only we'd set up an excuse for him, an escape plan, a secret code, then perhaps he'd have been able to get away, and get home, and perhaps he'd still be here.*

Then I came across Bert Fulks and his 'x-plan'.[1] Bert works with teenagers in the US with drug addiction issues, and one day he asked them, 'How many of you have found yourself in situations where things started happening that you weren't comfortable with, but you stuck around, mainly because you felt like you didn't have a way out?' Every single one raised their hand. Bert, then, set up a system with his own children so they would always have a way out if they needed it. The plan was they would text him an 'x' – but it can be anything, as long as you both know that's what it means – and that would trigger an agreed response, which would give them the excuse they needed to escape. What Bert did was just to call them, not say anything much, so they didn't have to get involved in a convoluted reason or answer a lot of questions. They could just say that was their dad, they have no idea what's going on, but they need to get home now.

---

[1]   Fulks, B. (2019) *X-Plan Parenting*, Howard Books.

An essential element, and what makes it work, is that the parent has to promise if their child triggers the system, then no questions will be asked, and no judgements will be made. If your child thinks they'll be forced to undergo an inquisition from their mum or dad and risk being grounded for the rest of their lives, they're unlikely to send that secret code in the first place. The important thing is they get safe, and get home.

> ## Talking point
>
> There are just four simple steps to setting up your own escape plan with your child:
>
> 1. Decide the code.
> 2. Agree the response.
> 3. Plan the excuse.
> 4. Promise not to ask any questions.

- **Phone tip #6 – tracking.** Some families set up a tracking system on their child's phone so they can know where they are, when they're there, and when they're heading home. This is another tricky one. It works best, as with all these things, if there's agreement with your child, not least because if the system doesn't have their consent they may find ways to evade it, for example leaving their phone at a friend's house before heading out somewhere they'd rather their parents didn't know about, which leaves them even more vulnerable – out with no phone if they need it. It may cross an important boundary in their independence stakes, but this is where your own family boundaries come into play, and discussion is important. However, one of our year 12 Youth Ambassadors told us the fact her mum could track her phone made her feel safe, because she knew if anything went wrong for her when she was out, her mum would know exactly where she was.

Safer drinking: some general principles

Harm reduction relating to alcohol is much more familiar than anything to do with drugs because it's such a well-established substance in our social landscape. But it's also the substance that's most widely available to young people, most widely used, and across the population as a whole causes the most harm to health and to wider society, costing the NHS and criminal justice services more than either should need to be paying out for things that are preventable.

As we saw in Chapter 2, the UK Chief Medical Officer's guidelines recommend an alcohol-free childhood up to the age of 15, for the sake of those growing bodies, bones and brains. But remember, too, that research has shown the average age of having a first whole drink is 13, and the average age of first getting drunk is 14, so although in an ideal world they'd stay alcohol-free as advised, and most of them will, for those who do start drinking at a younger than ideal age, they need to know how to do this more safely, as do their older siblings.

Talking point: safer drinking – some tips for teens

1. **Eat before you drink (and during and after)**: It's not a myth that a drink on an empty stomach goes straight to your head. Any food in that stomach will get in the way of the alcohol as it makes its progress through the system, reducing the speed with which it reaches the small intestine which is where it's absorbed most quickly, and so the effects are felt less rapidly. Get your child to have a meal before heading out, or a quick starchy snack – anything that will stay around in the stomach for a while. Eating during and after drinking alcohol can also slow down the absorption of alcohol into the bloodstream. It doesn't prevent the effects taking hold if the alcohol keeps on coming of course, but it can slow down their progress slightly.

2. **Pace yourself**: Have a look back at Chapter 2 for some ideas and resources for understanding units. Drinkaware offers a free Track and Calculate Units app which can help people keep an eye on their drinking, in the course of an evening or over a week. Some good tips are to sip an alcoholic drink slowly, alternate alcohol with soft drinks or water, and avoid drinks that are very sweet, as well as salty snacks, because both these can increase thirst, and thus the risk of drinking more alcohol to quench it. Alcohol is dehydrating so the tendency to drink more is already there.

3. **Keep a clear-headed friend around**: This is essential advice, for any substance use. Someone who knows everyone in the group needs to stay sober, keep a close eye out and check in with them regularly, and get help if it's needed.

4. **Drink plenty of water**: As well as helping pace the consumption of alcohol, drinking plenty of water over the course of an evening can slow down its effects. Even small amounts of alcohol cause dehydration, which speeds up the impairment it can cause. Drinking water gives the liver a bit more time to metabolize the alcohol coming its way and can make the effects more manageable. Water can also help reduce the effects of a hangover, some of which are caused by dehydration.

5. **Beware of risks around you**: Under the influence of alcohol the busy road, the long drop, the open water, the people you don't entirely trust, the poorly lit deserted street, can all hold hazards they wouldn't when sober.

6. **Don't drink and drive**: Either home, or even the next morning, as well, depending on how many units have been consumed and how much time has passed since their consumption finished. See below for more on this.

7. **Beware of addiction**: As well as watching units over the course of an evening, it's good to keep an eye on how many are being consumed over the course of a week, and a month, and whether that's increasing. It's easy for this to happen without people realizing. A tolerance to alcohol can build up quickly, which means more has to be drunk to achieve the same effects, and this can lead to addiction for some. If anyone feels they need help with their drinking the NHS website has advice and can signpost people to support locally or online.

8. **Know it's OK to say no**: This is always so important for any substances, and, as we saw in Chapter 2, with alcohol it's something a growing number of young people are saying. If your child wants to say 'no', or to say 'no more', they're in good company. And even if they weren't, it would still be OK to say no.

Drinking at home – does it help or hinder?

There has long been a school of thought that introducing children to small amounts of alcohol in the safety of their own home, under close parental supervision and guidance, will reduce the likelihood these same children will turn into binge-drinking teens. An Australian academic study found the exact opposite was the case, however. Not only was there no evidence that children given alcohol at home by parents displayed responsible drinking habits as they grew older, but they were in fact more likely to binge drink and suffer from alcohol-related harms and alcohol use disorder symptoms than those who weren't.[2]

The notion that safe drinking at home leads to safe drinking outside the home has a lot of logic to it, but it comes originally from Europe, primarily from long-held British beliefs about the French. In France small children have traditionally been given diluted wine at meals from an early age, and generations of these children seem to have grown up into responsible drinkers, in stark contrast to what is perceived as the alcohol-fuelled rowdiness of UK youth. However, this appears to be a myth, or at least, it is now. In 2009 the French government passed various laws designed to restrict young people's access to alcohol as part of its battle with binge-drinking teenagers. The fact this is known as 'le binge drinking' should prevent the British attempting to claim any moral high ground, but what we can take away is the evidence that drinking at home, however safely it's done, is best avoided till they're at least 15, and even then handled with care.

Keeping your drink safe: spiking

How much does it happen? There are no official figures on the numbers of people reporting their drink being spiked, but a couple of recent Freedom of Information requests to police forces across the UK show it's on the rise. The most recent of these was made by the BBC in 2019, which found that reports from under-18s had more than doubled over three years, and were set that year to reach a five-year record. Although it's still more common for females, more than a quarter of victims were male. And as it's a hugely under-reported crime for all sorts of reasons – people may not remember anything about it, may feel embarrassed, may feel responsible, may feel they have insufficient evidence to prove anything anyway – there will be much more going on than the figures reveal.

---

[2] Mattick, R.P. et al. (2018) Association of parental supply of alcohol with adolescent drinking, alcohol related harms and alcohol use disorder symptoms: a prospective cohort study. *The Lancet* [online]. Available from: DOI: 10.1016/ S2468-2667(17)30240-2

What drugs are used? Drinks will most commonly be spiked with a drug that's in liquid or powder form because these will dissolve or dissipate most quickly, and so there will be no traces to spot it's been done. The drugs usually associated with drink spiking are the so-called 'date rape' drugs Rohypnol and GHB, but ketamine is also used, and other drugs like MDMA or cocaine. However, the most used drug is alcohol itself. A strong, clear spirit like vodka is easy to get hold of, colourless, odourless and pretty much flavourless, and a few units added to a drink won't increase the volume noticeably. Whatever it is, it's always risky, and it's always illegal, even if the substance used is itself legal.

What are the signs? There can be various signs and symptoms that someone has been the victim of spiking, depending on what substance has been used, and what other substances may also have been used that night, including how much alcohol has been consumed. Rohypnol and GHB can act within 5–30 minutes and their effects last for a few hours. GHB leaves the body quickly so there is often no trace in a urine test done the next day. Both are sedatives and slow down responses, and combined with alcohol their sedative effect gets an extra boost, which is why people can become drowsy, immobile and even unconscious. They can both also cause confusion and amnesia, so the person on the receiving end may remember nothing of what happened. As well as confusion, the signs of spiking can include loss of coordination, disorientation, drowsiness, nausea or feeling unwell or just strange. If someone thinks they may have had their drink spiked, it's very important they find someone they know and trust immediately.

What to do if someone's drink has been spiked? A good friend is often the best person to spot that someone's behaviour is out of the ordinary. If they think they're the victim of spiking, and especially if they seem to be losing consciousness, they need to get help either from an adult or member of staff on hand, or call emergency services. If they're losing consciousness or have passed out they need to be in the recovery position (see below). If this doesn't seem necessary, they need to make sure they get them home safely and stay with them until they know they're safe. The victim of spiking should never leave on their own, or with someone they don't know.

Talking point

Tips to avoid your drink being spiked:

- Never accept a drink from someone you don't know and trust.
- Always make sure you've seen every stage of your drink's journey from the bottle or tap to the glass in your hand.
- Keep a hand over a glass or a finger in a bottle top when you're not drinking it, especially in a busy place, or where you'll be easily distracted.
- Never leave drinks unattended for a moment.
- If something doesn't taste or smell right, don't drink it.

Some practical tips:

- Use drink stoppers for bottles which can be bought online.
- Keep hold of disposable drink lids from coffee shops or fast food outlets to cover the tops of cups or glasses.
- Testing kits are available online which can be dipped into a drink if someone has suspicions and can detect some of the drugs more commonly used for spiking drinks.
- While it's important to do what you can to prevent spiking, it's also important nobody feels it's their fault if it happens to them. The fault will always lie with the person who did it. In addition to having conversations about avoiding being the victim of spiking, it's also important to talk about not being the one who does the spiking. It's always risky and it's always illegal, even if it was only meant as a joke.

Staying safe on social media

We've looked already at the exposure young people are increasingly having to drugs through social media, and the many risks attached to this which are specific to the way social media operates and the way it's used by young people. Although a majority of young people surveyed hadn't seen drugs being sold on their social media feeds, a sizable minority from the ages of 13 to 24 had.

There are various ways your children can manage the risks of drugs on social media:

1. **By remembering statistically most young people aren't using drugs**, however much it might look like they are online.
2. **By reporting illegal activity**: their report will be anonymous and will ensure illegal activity is quickly acted upon.
3. **By blocking accounts that are engaging in illegal activity**, or making them feel uncomfortable.
4. **By keeping it between friends**: only accepting friend requests or messages from people they are actually friends with or know in real life.
5. **By checking their privacy settings**: do they know who can see their profile / send them messages / view their posts or stories?
6. **By choosing a strong password** and setting up two-factor authentication to make their profile more secure.
7. **By not sharing their contacts** with anyone, or they put their friends at risk too.
8. **By being aware of how algorithms can operate through their searches**: drug-related searches, even if done innocently, can lead dealers their way.
9. **By not trusting what they see**: the only way of knowing what the contents and strength of a substance are is by having it professionally tested.
10. **By remembering drug dealers aren't their friends**, however friendly they might seem. It is a business transaction motivated by making money.
11. **By not forgetting their digital footprint** leaves evidence that can stick around and limit future options.

Staying safe at parties

Teenage parties create a unique space in which a vast array of different families' – often very different – boundaries, rules and expectations all come together under one roof for the night. Nowhere is this more true than in two key components of the average teenage party: alcohol and adult supervision. Whether your teenager is host or guest, it's important you feel comfortable with whatever these are, and confident your child will be safe – as well as having a great time, of course. Keeping in mind all we've learned about that adolescent social sensitivity and quest for independence, it's also important the conversations about parties and expectations take on board all the best advice of the previous chapter, because they may not always run smoothly. Clarity, openness, and mutual agreement are key to peace of mind all round.

The teenage party guest

Whether your child thinks so or not, it's always acceptable to contact the parents of the hosting teenager, especially with younger teens. By doing this you can make sure you have the right number for them in case you need it, make sure they have your number in case they need it themselves, check the address and the start and finish times, and ask what the plans are for alcohol and adult supervision. In terms of your child, all the safety advice in the rest of this chapter holds true for teenagers heading off to parties as for any other night out: make sure their phone is charged, make sure they have a plan for getting home safely and agree when that will be, stick with their friends, be careful around alcohol, and so on.

The teenage party host

I'm someone who loves a plan and a list, and often has multiple lists and overlapping plans on the go, but whether you are too, or whether you're not, preparation is key to a happy, safe party. Working on plans with your child can be one of those lovely opportunities for spending time together, and despite perhaps feeling daunted, it can be lots of fun. It also gives your child a sense of responsibility and ownership. Of course, all the advice below is very dependent on the age of your child, and on your own family dynamics and boundaries, but there may be some useful suggestions you can take on board, adapt or ignore.

Talking point

Here are some questions you could work through together:

- **How many people will be invited and who will they be?** Are there people either of you would feel less comfortable being there?
- **How will they be invited?** Even if you try to avoid social media by using paper invitations it'll most likely end up there anyway, so make sure your child keeps invitations as closed and secure as they can.

- **When will it start, and when will it finish?** Be mindful of neighbours' ears, and parents' bedtimes.
- **Which rooms will be used?** Where will be out of bounds, and how will guests know this? It's good to limit the space if you can. It's also a good idea to remove anything from that space that might get damaged or go missing.
- **What food will you serve?** It's a good idea to plan a carb-heavy menu to line those stomachs, especially if there's going to be alcohol, and avoid salty snacks which can make people thirstier and wanting to drink more.
- **How many adults will you have there?** Who will they be, what will they be doing and where?
- **Will you have alcohol?** If you do, and the guests will be under 18, you need to contact their parents and check they are happy with this, and note their consent down. Explain what your plans are for what will be served, how much, and how it will be managed. It's a good idea to avoid a 'bring your own bottle' plan, even if you confine this to non-alcoholic drinks. If you have a 'no-bottles' rule, then a sneaky bit of vodka disguised as a bottle of water or hidden in a fizzy drink is less likely to find its way in, though there are many more sneaky ideas than that up teenagers' sleeves, and this is hard to avoid altogether.
- **What will you do about drugs?** It's important your child is aware that if drugs are shared and used on your premises then you are responsible legally, as well as having a moral responsibility for the welfare of young people in your home, especially if they are under 18. If you find someone smoking cannabis in the garden will you call their parents and send them home, or just tell them to stop? What about pills, cocaine or ketamine? If your child is clear what will happen, then they can tell their friends.

Hosting a safe party

- **Arrivals**: Try to have just one way in and out, and to have that supervised by one of your adults (depending on the age of your child). Even though they might not be keen on this idea, your child won't want gate-crashers any more than you do. Guests can be welcomed, and checked off the guest list if you have one, and this is an opportunity for you to collect parents' contact details in case they're needed later. It's a good idea to ask guests as they arrive to switch any location settings off in their social media systems that might let people not at the party know where all those amazing photos are coming from, to avoid uninvited guests turning up at your door. You can at this point suggest you take people's bags to keep them safe, as a bit of an attempt to bypass any unwanted alcohol slipping in. This is also a chance to let guests know where an adult will be for the evening. Sometimes teenage party guests find they need to take a bit of time out and spend some quiet moments with a responsible adult.
- **Food**: It's a good idea to limit the amount of food out at any time so you can keep bringing fresh supplies into the room, which gives you an excuse to do a bit of unobtrusive mingling while keeping an eye on proceedings.
- **Drinks**: If you are having alcohol, stick to low-alcohol drinks like beers or lagers, or some of the lower-alcohol mixers, and make sure there are plenty of soft drinks available as well as water. Some parents issue raffle tickets with one or two drinks per guest. Others set up a 'bar' with one of their adults as bartender, who can keep an eye out and maintain control, or even make cocktails, which can be mostly or entirely non-alcoholic, and definitely get less alcoholic as the evening wears on and spirits rise. If you have an unsupervised bar area, put out small amounts at a time, and avoid open drinks like punch which are easily spiked.

Staying safe on the road

The most recent government data shows that in 2018, in Great Britain, an estimated 240 people were killed, and 8,440 injured, in an accident on the road where at least one driver or rider was over the legal blood alcohol limit.[3] Even a small amount of alcohol can affect coordination and judgement sufficiently to make driving hazardous, so it's always safest not to drive if you've had a drink, and the same goes for drugs, for just the same reasons.

It's just as important not to be the passenger of a driver who has drunk alcohol or taken drugs before getting in the car. The total number of people killed or injured in 2018 was 8,680, but the total number of accidents was 5,890, which means that more than one person was killed or injured on average per accident, and some of these will have been passengers. It's also worth drivers thinking about whether intoxicated passengers may affect their ability to drive safely, because if this is the case they need to know they can say no, ideally helping them find a safe alternative means of getting home.

Cannabis is unusual among substances in its ability to have a psychoactive effect on non-smokers through second-hand exposure, especially in a place that's not well ventilated, such as a house party, car or a friend's bedroom. The greater the THC levels, the more people are smoking it, and the more confined the space is in which it's being smoked, the more likely it is that someone sensibly not smoking before driving nevertheless has their functioning impaired. They could potentially fail a roadside test, too.[4] The way cannabis works on the brain means it can affect reaction times as well as motor function, both of which are needed to get yourself safely somewhere in a car, or on a bike or a scooter, for that matter.

---

[3] Department of Transport (2020) Reported road casualties in Great Britain: final estimates involving illegal alcohol levels: 2018 [online]. *Gov.uk*. Available from: <assets.publishing.service.gov.uk/government/uploads/system/uploads/attachment_data/file/912948/drink-drive-final-estimates-2018.pdf> (accessed November 2020)

[4] National Institute for Drug Abuse (2020) What are the effects of secondhand exposure to marijuana smoke? [online]. *NIDA*. Available from: <www.drugabuse.gov/publications/research-reports/marijuana/what-are-effects-secondhand-expo-sure-to-marijuana-smoke> (accessed November 2020)

Talking point

Remind children who drive not only how important it is not to drive with any alcohol or drugs in their system, but also not to feel they have to accept passengers under the influence of drink or drugs who may affect their ability to get them and the car, and any other passengers, home in one piece.

Remind children getting lifts from friends not to get in the car if they have any concerns about the safety of their driver at the end of the evening. Make sure they have alternative means of getting home in case this happens.

Remind children that if they've spent time around people smoking cannabis, especially in a confined space, this can affect their own judgement, reaction times and motor function, and make them less safe on the road despite abstaining themselves.

Sex, drugs and safety

We've already looked at the links between substance use and sex in relation to the law in Chapter 5, but of course there are important implications with regard to personal safety as well. Common sense would lead most of us to assume you are more likely to take sexual risks if your judgement is impaired because of drink or drugs, and various studies have backed this assumption up. One such study found that 16–24-year-olds who reported frequent binge drinking or recent drug use were more likely to have had unprotected sex with more than one new partner in the previous year, sex with their last partner for the first time after only just meeting, to have used emergency contraception in the last year, and received a diagnosis of a sexually transmitted infection in the previous five years.[5] Understandably, someone is more likely to take sexual risks if they're someone who's taking risks with substances, but whatever the personality type or

5   Khadr S.N., Jones K.G., Mann S., et. al. (2016) Investigating the relationship between substance use and sexual behaviour in young people in Britain: findings from a national probability survey. *BMJ Open* [online]. 6:e011961. Available from: DOI: 10.1136/bmjopen-2016-011961

propensity for risky behaviours generally, the effects of the substances taken can potentially lead to risky decisions about sex. Most psycho-active substances alter the judgement and perceptions of the person who has taken them, and as we have seen already, some substances (such as cocaine, MDMA and alcohol) can directly influence sexual behaviour.

You are also more vulnerable to non-consensual sex, or sexual assault, if your judgement and perception is clouded by alcohol or drugs. In 2013 the Global Drug Survey started to explore the world of drugs and sex, and among other things asked whether people had been taken advantage of sexually while they were under the influence of alcohol or drugs. One in five people reported that this had happened to them at some point in their lives, and one in 20 said this had happened to them in the previous year. In addition, 14 per cent reported that they believed they had been given drugs or alcohol by someone intending to take advantage of them.[6]

Talking point: sex, drugs and safety – advice from the Global Drugs Survey

Questions to keep in mind, if drugs and sex get combined:

1. Am I doing what I want to do? Do I feel safe, happy, comfortable? Do I feel I could tell the other person if I don't?
2. Do I know what the other person wants? Have I asked? Have I checked again?
3. How might the substances I've taken affect how I'm feeling sexually? Has the person I'm with also taken something, and if so, how might this be affecting them? Is it likely to be different?
4. Does anyone know where I am, and who I'm with?
5. How will I make sure any sex that takes place is safe? Are there condoms?

---

[6] Aldridge, A. & Winstock, A.R. (2019) GDS 2019: Intoxication, sexual assault and consent [online]. *Global Drug Survey*. Available from: <www.globaldrugsur-vey.com/gds-2019/gds2019-intoxication-sexual-assault-and-consent/> (accessed November 2020)

Staying safe at festivals

A study published in 2019 revealed that more than half of all festival goers say they take drugs while they're there, and more than half of these report taking a greater quantity, and a wider variety, than they usually would.[7] That same year, five young people died over one weekend at UK festivals. The study's author, Fiona Measham, said her research showed that festivals are sites of 'atypical intoxication', where drug use is 'both more widespread and more risky than elsewhere'.

If your child is heading off to a festival, it's important they're aware of this context, because drug use will be more open, visible, widespread and consequently seem more normal than it may ever have before for them, unless of course it's not their first festival. Conversations about drugs and harm reduction are essential before they go, even if they've been many times before. There are a number of practical measures they can put in place to reduce any risks to them and their friends, however, and make sure they have a great time.

Talking point: festival safety tips

- **Locate the medical tent and welfare area**: This is something they should do as soon as they arrive, settle and start to explore.
- **Stay with their friends**: This is essential, but they can't rely on doing this by phone if they get separated. The signal is not always great, smart phone batteries can run flat quickly, and charging points can be busy and expensive. They could, however, take a big battery pack, or an old 'brick' phone with a battery that lasts for ages (and is also less likely to be stolen).
- **Having a meet up point and time**: Agree a place they'll meet up, and times to do this, in case they do get separated or just want some separate space, and can't make phone contact.
- **Festival harm reduction**: In addition to all the harm reduction advice included in this chapter, it's good to be aware that heat,

---

[7] Turner, T. & Measham, F. (2019) Into The Woods: Contextualising atypical intoxication by young adults in music festivals and nightlife tourist resorts, in Conroy, D. and Measham, F. (eds), *Young Adult Drinking Styles: Current Perspectives on Research, Policy and Practice*, London: Palgrave Macmillan, pp.87–114.

> dehydration and lack of sleep and food can all change the effect substances can have.
> - **Drug checking**: If there's a drug checking service available and anyone in their group has plans to take anything then using this service is vital (see below).

Drug checking, harm reduction and The Loop

As we saw in Chapter 3, The Loop offers a confidential drug-checking, harm-reduction service at music festivals and an increasing range of other settings, with full support of local police and other stakeholders. Qualified chemists test substances of concern submitted by service users and provide results along with a personalized counselling and harm reduction session for the individual and their friendship group by trained healthcare professionals. This second part of the service is essential. People need to know what the results actually mean, and to understand the complex range of factors that affect the risks to them if they choose to go ahead and take the drugs they've had tested, and how those risks can be reduced. The Loop has had very positive results with over half of service users discarding or handing substances to the service for onward safe policy destruction if the test identified the substance to be other than expected.

Sometimes seen as controversial because of concerns it condones drug use, or sends the message this makes drug taking safe, this is nevertheless the last line of defence for anyone with drugs and an intention to take them, and the first and last message is always that the only way to reduce drug-related risk to zero is not to take drugs. Once people had seen their test results and had a chat to counsellors, around one in five people decided not to take their drugs at all, and about half decided to take less, or take them more slowly. For all the controversy, drug-related harms are significantly lower at the festivals they've been at and there has never been a drug-related death, and that has to be a good thing.

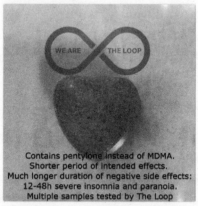

The Loop
@WeAreTheLoopUK

Following ⌄

We have tested 2 pills & 1 crystalline powder of n-ethylpentylone sold onsite @BoomtownFair today. Don't trust onsite dealers, bring substances of concern for free testing 12-8pm (Down Town) & seek medical attention if unwell.

Contains pentylone instead of MDMA.
Shorter period of intended effects.
Much longer duration of negative side effects:
12-48h severe insomnia and paranoia.
Multiple samples tested by The Loop

6:18 PM - 9 Aug 2018

The Loop's Twitter warning about ecstasy pills found at Boomtown festival in 2018 containing N-Ethylpentylone (provided by The Loop)

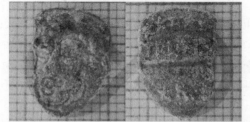

ALERT
Lilac Donald Trump pills
circulating onsite at **Lost Village** 2019

High Strength - contains 300mg+ MDMA
Over 3x common dose
Already associated with hospital admissions
across the UK
Take care & seek medical help if unwell

#JustSayKnow #TimeToTest

The Loop's Instagram warning about high strength ecstasy pills found at Lost Village festival in 2019 (provided by The Loop)

Talking point

With older teens, look on The Loop's website or social media for their drug alerts, which flag up particular pills or other substances that test results have shown are either very strong or have risky adulterants. It's a good way of reminding your children of the random risks of drugs from an illegal source, as well as making sure they know where they can find current information and advice.

Drug testing kits

Commercial kits can be bought online that can identify drugs from a certain range, and these can provide some degree of information that can help people make informed choices. However, they need to be used with some caution because the range of substances is inevitably much more limited than the growing array of synthetic substances that could potentially be present, and they are also generally limited because they do not provide information about the strength of any of the ingredients or the contents of mixtures. They also miss out the important, tailored harm-reduction advice a drug-checking service like The Loop can provide, which enables people to know how these results might translate into risk if they were to go ahead and take whatever it is. That said, with all these provisos in mind, they can provide some limited information which can inform safer decision-making and their particular value is in identifying if the substance of concern does *not* contain their desired drug.

Drugs and harm reduction – some general principles

As with all conversations about drugs, conversations about drugs and harm reduction will depend very much on your child, their age, and your family, but it can make it more comfortable if you focus on talking in terms of supporting a friend they may be with, rather than to suggest they might take something themselves. If you know they are taking drugs, then these harm reduction conversations are essential, but we'll look at that in the following chapter.

The following is general advice we give to older students at workshops, as well as to parents to bring into their conversations at home.

Talking point: Ten top tips for friends

(based on Global Drug Survey advice 2018)

If you're with a friend who's taking drugs, you are the best harm reduction measure they have. Here are some ways you can help.

1. Remember, the only way to reduce drug-related risk to zero is not to use drugs.
2. Make sure they have good information about anything they're taking, including harm reduction information specific to whatever it is.
3. Stay together and check in with them regularly. Look for physical signs (see the first aid advice below) and get them to tell you if they're not feeling right.
4. Don't mix anything – either alcohol or other drugs – because of the way it can alter the effects and the risks.
5. Start low, go slow – remind them just to take a little, and wait an hour or more before deciding to take any more, to see what effect it is having.
6. Be aware of the variable factors that affect risk, relating to the substance, the individual and the environment.
7. Keep any possible legal consequences in mind.
8. Think about whether food or water might help reduce risks, which will depend on what they've taken or are planning to take.
9. Remind them if they're feeling below par physically or mentally this can change the effects drugs have and alter the risks.
10. Don't be afraid to call 999 if things start going wrong. Check out the first aid advice below.

Drugs and alcohol first aid

On New Year's Eve a few years ago a 16-year-old boy was at a party with friends where he drank a 700ml bottle of vodka, collapsed, and – while he was lying unconscious – his friends drew on his face, poured water on his crotch, and took photos of him as a joke. Although they were unable to rouse him, they carried on with the party and one of them went off to play XBox, and when they realized they were still unable to wake him up they put him in the recovery position on the living room floor and went to bed. It wasn't until 11 am the following morning that a friend found the boy's arms were stiff, realized he was dead and ran to get his dad. The boy's parents were at home, one door down, and his dad called 999 immediately, but by then it was too late. His son was pronounced dead at 11.38 am on New Year's Day.

It is utterly heartbreaking for his parents that his friends behaved as they did, and I'm sure it will haunt these friends for the rest of their lives, but it's sadly not the only story of a young person whose friends could have made a literally vital difference in a time of crisis but didn't, for a whole host of reasons. There are plenty of other stories where friends have panicked and run off, where they'd being drinking or taking drugs themselves and weren't able to think clearly, where they hadn't realized how serious it was or just didn't know what to do.

It can be very frightening for a teenager if something starts going wrong for a friend. They may be the only one to pick up that something is going wrong because they know their friend so well, they may be the only person with a clear head around and there may not be a responsible adult on hand. It's all the more frightening if you're not quite sure what's happening and you don't know what to do in a crisis, or even what the start of a crisis might look like, and many teenagers don't. However, knowing what to do not only makes that crisis less scary but could stop things getting worse, and even save a life.

Talking point: the recovery position

If your child doesn't already know the recovery position, or you think their knowledge may need refreshing, there are useful videos online, for example on the NHS and St John Ambulance websites. Watch these together and have a practice at home.

Alcohol first aid

As well as all the vast array of possible injuries that might result from drinking too much, which may need various sorts of medical attention, alcohol poisoning is a risk to which teens and pre-teens are more vulnerable than adults. Their liver is not yet fully developed, levels of tolerance are lower and drinking too much in too short a space of time overloads their system, resulting in overdose.

Initial signs of alcohol poisoning can include:

- Being a little unresponsive
- Having a moist and reddened face
- Breathing deeply and noisily
- Having a strong and rapid pulse.

If it develops, they may begin to see the opposite of some of these signs, as parts of the person's system start to shut down:

- Shallow breathing
- A weak, rapid pulse
- Dilated pupils that react poorly to light
- Unresponsiveness.

If your child thinks someone has alcohol poisoning they should:

- Reassure them and cover them with a coat or blanket to keep them warm
- Check them for any injuries, especially head injuries
- Put them in the recovery position if they're unconscious or semi-conscious so that they don't choke on any vomit
- Keep a really close eye on them until they recover or until a responsible adult can take over care

If the person is unconscious, or if your child is unsure about how serious their condition is, they should call 999 for emergency help.

Drugs first aid

Advice on how to identify a crisis and then respond to that crisis is trickier with drugs because it depends on the substance, the strength, what else someone may have taken – including alcohol or medication – and many other variable factors, so it's best to respond to what's happening for them rather than second-guess or make assumptions. This is what paramedics do because, although someone may think they've taken (for example) ketamine, it may in fact have been something else altogether, or it may have been something else altogether that was in with the ketamine, that's causing the particular medical crisis.

In general, if the following things are happening to someone your child is with, they should keep a very close eye on them, and keep checking in with them regularly:

- Pale, cold and clammy skin
- Overheating
- Abdominal pain
- Nausea or vomiting
- Mood changes including excitability, aggression or depression
- Drowsiness
- Loss of coordination
- Confusion or hallucinations.

If someone's becoming anxious and panicky:

- Try to reassure and calm them
- Try to get them somewhere quiet and away from crowds, loud music or bright lights.

If they're hyperventilating, try to get them to relax and take long, deep breaths.

If someone's becoming drowsy:

- Try to keep them awake, but don't shake them hard or make them jump, because this could affect their heart, depending on what they've taken
- Never give someone who's drowsy coffee or an energy drink to perk them up. This can make the drug in them work even faster
- Place them in the recovery position and talk to them
- Call 999 if you think they might become unconscious.

If someone's becoming hot and dehydrated (warning signs of dehydration can include cramps, fainting, headache or sudden tiredness):

- Take them somewhere cool and quiet, perhaps outside
- Take off any excess clothing and try to cool them down
- Try to get them to sip water or a soft drink – but be careful of overhydration too
- If symptoms persist call 999.

Getting help

If they're concerned for a friend, are unable to get help from a responsible adult and want some medical advice, then they can call 111. **If it's an emergency, however, they must call 999.** Many young people are scared to call 999 in case they get in trouble or get their friend in trouble, but it's essential they make this call if they think it might be needed. If it's not needed the person on the phone will tell them, and they won't be in trouble, because if they were concerned, then they needed to ask for help. It's better to make the call unnecessarily, than to let a friend come to harm for fear of getting it wrong, or of getting in trouble.

When to call 999 *immediately*

If someone your child is with shows any of the following symptoms they must get emergency help immediately:

- Altered breathing pattern or breathing difficulty
- Choking
- Seizures or convulsions
- Unconsciousness.

Talking point

Stress to your children the importance of calling 999 if they have any concerns for someone they're with. Explain to them what will happen if they do:

The call will be answered by a trained emergency medical dispatcher who will calmly ask a series of questions to work out what the problem is and decide how they need to respond.

They need to give the paramedic on the phone as much information as they can, and it's vital they are totally honest, because this information will enable the person on the phone to make the best decision about how to respond. If your child can find out what substances the person they're with has taken and how much, when and how they took them, that's all important information.

If the person on the phone decides they need an ambulance they'll get one as quickly as possible. Young people sometimes worry about calling for an ambulance in case one isn't needed, but it's the decision of the emergency medical dispatcher, not theirs.

If they don't think the situation needs an ambulance, but they judge the person needs help, someone medically trained will talk them through what to do.

If an ambulance is on its way your child should:

- Observe symptoms closely. If the person's condition or location changes they must call 999 again to update them.
- Try to reassure the person by talking to them in a quiet, calm manner. If they're not fully conscious, they should put them in the recovery position and make sure they're not left alone.
- If the house number is unclear, or their location may be hard to find, they need to ask someone to be a look-out if they can, or flash the torch on their phone if there's no one else with them while they stay with the person.
- If any of the drugs they took are still around they should give them to paramedics.
- They should consider calling the police if the person's safety, their own or that of others becomes threatened.

Dan and harm reduction – how it could, perhaps, have reduced the harm

We'll look at where more detailed harm-reduction advice for specific substances can be found in the next chapter, but we'll finish this one by going back to where we started, with what I wish I'd known, and what I wish Dan had known, about how to reduce the harm done to him by the MDMA he took that night in January.

The problem for Dan, having taken the MDMA he was given that night, was that it was just so incredibly strong. Because of this, its effects were incredibly strong, and the impact on his body was rapid and intense. There was no way of him knowing exactly what was in that little bag of crystal, or the strength of any of those ingredients. This is always the case with drugs from an illegal source, as we've stressed before, and without the sort of professional testing we've just been looking at it's impossible for someone to know exactly what it is they have in their pill, little bag or little bottle of liquid. And organizers of illegal raves are unlikely to ever invite drug-testing, harm-reduction organizations like The Loop in to offer their services, so this wasn't something Dan could have called on. He was stuck with a substance of unknown quantity and quality.

This is why basic harm-reduction advice for anyone taking anything is to recognize that in doing so they are testing it on themselves. They are the guinea pig for that particular dose of whatever it is, taken by them as an individual in that particular place and at that particular time. Risk is complicated, as we've seen. They don't know what else might be in it, they have no idea how strong it is, or how it'll affect them on that occasion, so if they do go ahead and take something, they need to take it easy. Start low, go slow. The Loop's 'Crush, Dab, Wait' campaign launched in 2015 and reminds people taking ecstasy to start with a quarter of a pill, or to crush a small amount and dab it on their gums or tongue, and then to wait at least an hour and ideally longer to see what effect it has on them before having any more, if they do.

With MDMA crystal, similar harm-reduction advice is to dissolve it in water and then sip it slowly, which is exactly what the boys with Dan did. Whether they knew this was good harm-reduction advice, or whether it was just what they did, I have no idea, but if Dan had known this, he wouldn't have swallowed his down in one. His harm-reduction strategy was to watch these other boys for the hours it took to get across London, to see how the MDMA was affecting them. They were fine. They were probably having a great time. Feeling happy, buzzed, loved-up. So he drank his, downed it in one.

It breaks my heart to think of that swallow. That fatal swallow. The picture of it has flashed through my head so many times, and every time it makes me literally shudder. I want to shout at him to stop, to grab it from his hands, to stand in the way of the oncoming train. Once it was downed, there it was, in his system, MDMA at levels 12 times stronger than had caused fatality in the past.

For Dan, from that moment, the night was never going to end well, but it may not have ended with the ending of his life. There were still things he could have done, if only he'd known. Did he know how important it was to drink water to reduce the effects of the dehydration MDMA can cause? If he had, there was nothing he could have done. There was no water at that rave, either for sale or for free. However, if he'd known, and known there was unlikely to be any freely available at an illegally organized event, he could have taken a couple of big bottles up with him. A pain to heft across London, but more of a pain to suffer the effects of dehydration.

Harm-reduction advice for MDMA is to sip water slowly, ideally around 250 mls per hour. An eight-hour session needs two litres of water. A four-hour one, a litre would do. Too much, though, and this can also be harmful, and potentially fatal. Early harm reduction advice for ecstasy was to drink plenty of water, which was just what Leah Betts did before she died in 1995. The worse she felt, the more she drank. She ended up drinking around seven litres of water in less than 90 minutes, which caused water intoxication and hyponatremia, which in turn led to serious swelling of the brain, irreparably damaging it, and Leah sadly died, not from the ecstasy she'd taken but from the water she drank to reduce the risks of the ecstasy. Leah's is a tragic example of why young people's access to accurate, evidence-based harm reduction advice is vital.

I know Dan had wanted some water that night, whether or not he knew he needed it for harm reduction reasons. He'd gone off with another boy from the group to try to find some. That's how he ended up separated from his friends, and why, when things started going badly wrong, there was nobody who knew him on hand to help. The rumour they'd heard, that there was some somewhere in that disused industrial unit, was perhaps from other hopeful dehydrated rave-goers. The other boy made it back. Dan didn't.

Something else that may have helped Dan, if he'd known, would have been to take regular breaks to rest and cool down. Perhaps his body temperature wouldn't then have reached such fatally high levels. The stimulant effect of MDMA means that someone who's taken it can do something energetic like dancing a lot more vigorously, and for a lot longer, than they would naturally be able to do. Under normal circumstances our body feeling tired sends us a message that we need to take a break. Our body feeling hot tells us we need to cool down. Psychoactive substances that cause these effects unnaturally can switch off these natural reminders, and so anyone taking something that has these effects has to remember for themselves. Take a break, get outside, cool down. It might have been that the effects of the MDMA were so rapid and powerful for Dan that even if he had known this, he didn't have chance to act on it. I know he was hot. He'd taken his shirt off, Jack said, and was waving it around in the air as he danced. He was happy, but he was hot.

Into the finer details of harm reduction, if Dan had known taking magnesium tablets might help reduce jaw clenching, perhaps he could have stocked up at the chemist beforehand and had some in his pocket. If his jaw hadn't been so tightly locked, the vomit could have come out and not gone back into his lungs and caused the pneumonia which stopped him being able to breathe without a ventilator. It would also have meant his teeth wouldn't have been so tightly clenched the paramedics were prevented from getting a tube in his mouth, and would have been able to get oxygen into his system more quickly, and reduce the damage to his poor, clever, curious brain.

There are more of these finer details – vitamin and mineral supplements that can reduce some of the side- and after-effects, drinking sports drinks as well as water to replace lost electrolytes caused by the anti-diuretic effect of MDMA, making sure you get plenty of sleep when you get back home to recover from the exhaustion, plenty of healthy and protein-rich food to replace lost nutrition, plenty of water to keep that rehydration process going, and a plan for a way to get through blue Tuesday, the down in the wake of the up.

But Dan never had to worry about any of these.

8

I wish I'd known he'd tried drugs

What to do if you have concerns

Signs of teenage drug use can be hard to spot. There are various reasons for this. Young people can be very adept at making sure parents don't see things they feel they're better off not seeing. Some of the signs of drug use can easily disguise themselves as perfectly normal adolescent behaviour. And sometimes there'll be no signs in the first place. When Dan died someone asked, *had I seen any signs?* Signs of his descent into degeneracy? Signs of his decline into dependency? Is that what they meant? If so, no I hadn't, because he wasn't descending or declining, he was doing really well. We'd seen lots of signs of change and they were all good ones. Signs of working hard, taking responsibility, growing maturity. Someone who'd just turned down the opportunity of a shorter, quicker paper round that would have given him much more lucrative tips that Christmas because he was too fond of all the old ladies on his own round to leave them. Someone obsessed with making the perfect pot of tea, offering endless cups in the hopes that the warming of the pot or the adjusted ratio of tealeaves to boiling water or the sequencing of milk this time would have made that vital improvement. *Yes, Dan, I'd love another cup. I haven't quite finished the last one, but that would be lovely...*

Even the most open-minded, free-thinking, easy-going among us can have preconceptions about the sort of person who uses drugs and the journey they must be set upon having put their foot on that path, a path that can only lead downhill. This question was asked of me by a very sensible, level-headed, intelligent and compassionate friend, but one who as a parent herself was deeply concerned, for totally understandable reasons, to know how her own children could avoid the fate that befell Dan. And perhaps all she meant was had I seen him looking a bit the worse for wear on occasion. Perhaps I was jumping to conclusions from my own preconceptions, over-sensitive and protective. As parents we may need to shine a light on some of our assumptions, shake any off that might lead us astray, and reset our radars if we're to be sensitive to signs of drug use in our families, and offer our children the support and advice they might need – and take care of ourselves in the process.

How can you tell if your child is using drugs?

Like many others, Dan's journey with drugs was very short. It lasted about six months. A smoke of someone's weed at the after-prom party, a sip of someone's MDMA at a gig, then some of his own just once before that very last time. For many young people, if they do take anything, it'll be the sort of dip of the toe that Dan did, and nothing for a parent to see. In and out, and usually no harm done. However, a dip of the toe can be incredibly risky, as we know to our cost, and that's where those more general, preventative conversations come in that we looked at in Chapter 6. One day all may be revealed, perhaps from the safe far shore of independent adulthood, but either way, in the here and now of teenage toe-dipping, as a parent there may be nothing to go by. If Dan hadn't died, would we ever have known?

You may not have to do any detective work, however. The most reliable way of knowing if your child is using drugs is if they tell you they are. It could be they're so comfortable talking to you about drugs that this is all part of the natural flow of a conversation at home. It could be because they've become concerned about the way it's affecting them, or has affected someone they were with. It could be it's reached a point where they know they need help.

Between nothing to spot and full disclosure there are, however, various signs for which a parent can be vigilant. You may find drugs or some of the paraphernalia associated with drug use in your child's bedroom, trouser pocket or around the house. Check back to the table and photos in Chapter 2 to remind yourself what some of these might look like if you're not sure. They may not belong to your child but they warrant a conversation. You may see changes to their behaviour, mood or appearance which might raise questions and cause concerns. As I've said, some of these are perfectly normal in adolescence, so it's more useful to keep an eye out for patterns of change, but in any case many of these are things you'd want to have a chat about, whatever may lie behind them.

Types of drug use, signs to spot and conversations to have

There are different types of drug use, but not the orderly, inevitable progression from one to another that many imagine, and perhaps fear, if it's their child who's using drugs. With substance use there's nothing as simple as a clear starting point, a predictable journey and an unavoidable final destination, lost in addiction. There's definitely not a simple binary in or out, clean or addicted, which can be a concern for some parents if they suspect, or know, their child has been taking drugs. Drugs are complicated, drug use is complicated, people are complicated and teenagers the most complicated people of all. That said, it can be helpful to identify different types of drug use, always with the proviso this is simplifying the complex.

Occasional, or experimental use is the most common type of use by young people who do at some point use drugs, and if it begins at all this is where it will also most likely end. It'll often be prompted by the curiosity – this, we saw, was the biggest motivating factor for all those 11- to 15-year-olds in the government's school survey – or the desire to experience the effects substances can create. It could equally be just wanting to join in, or not wanting to miss out, or feeling the pressure of that 'social risk' factor. There are of course risks associated with any sort of drug use, but the risks that are more common with experimental use relate to lack of experience and lack of knowledge, as well as lower levels of tolerance than perhaps others around them. However, some young people will have done their research and brought a good level of understanding to bear in the decisions they make. It'll often stop because curiosity is satisfied, or a friendship group changes, or the experience wasn't as good as they'd been led to believe, or not as good as it was that first time, or a bad experience happens around them, or they just decide the risks aren't worth the reward.

Talking point: possible signs of occasional drug use

Other than finding drugs or paraphernalia, you're most likely to become aware your child is using drugs occasionally if the effects of the drugs they've taken are still evident. These may be physical but may also cause them to behave in ways that are unusual or out of character.

Physical changes can include:

- **Smells**: Unusual smells on breath, body or clothing are something to be alert to, always with the proviso the latter could be a legacy of that afternoon's double-chemistry lesson, and the former something new from the sweetshop shelves. Smells on skin or clothing are more likely to come from drugs that have been burned or heated in some way. That strong, somewhat sweet scent of cannabis can linger for a long while, and of course vape liquids come in many and various flavours and aromas.
- **Eyes**: Changes to the eyes can be caused by certain substances, for example pupil dilation and rapid eye movement can be caused by some stimulants, and cannabis can make people's eyes bloodshot shortly after use.
- **Nose**: Snorting drugs can lead to a nose that's often blocked or runny (though this could also be allergies or a recurrent cold), along with nosebleeds and redness around the nostrils.
- **Drowsiness, slurred speech and loss of coordination**: Most adults are familiar with alcohol causing these effects, but they can also be caused by benzodiazepines or other sedative or dissociative drugs.

Behavioural changes can include being:

- unusually energetic, confident, upbeat, talkative
- unusually affectionate, uninhibited, euphoric, happy
- unusually aggressive, anxious, agitated
- unusually relaxed, calm, chilled
- giggly, dream-like, experiencing distortions to senses.

You could also be alert to the after-effects of drug use – the down that can follow the up – if it's out of character. They may feel tired or low, soon after or a couple of days after taking a drug. There could be many other reasons for this, but it'd be something to warrant a concerned chat to check in with them and see what might lie behind it. Have a look back at Chapter 2 for the effects different substances can have.

Conversations if you think or know your child is experimenting with drugs:

- If you've seen any of these signs, or have other reasons for concern, check back on the general advice in Chapter 6 about how to make conversations work best.
- Depending on what you've seen and the level of your concerns, a more general conversation about drugs may test the waters, and it may give your child the opportunity to speak to you about their drug use. However, this degree of honesty depends on so many factors and is a tough one for most teens, whatever their level of use and however open they are with their parents, so don't hold your breath for this to happen.
- If you've seen clear signs, then you have every reason to tackle this head-on. You found this bag of pills, their behaviour when they came in last night was totally out of character, you need to talk. Make sure you listen to their answers, however angry, disappointed or worried you are, even if they're defensive and deflecting of blame.
- Whether there's a denial or a confession, a conversation checking their understanding of the risks of whatever you suspect or know it is, or the risks of drug use more generally, is important. It's also important to talk about strategies for staying safe and reducing harm – depending on the age of your child – as well as revisiting your family's values and boundaries. Where you take this from there will be dependent on many factors.

Regular use can develop for various reasons. Sometimes this can be down to drugs and alcohol becoming part of a young person's pattern of socializing. Perhaps every Friday they all pile over to somebody's house, or every Saturday there'll be a party somewhere, or it's just what this group of friends does when they're together. It can also begin to become more regular if it's helping solve a problem – if they're finding that taking this particular substance is helping them cope with this particular situation, or manage these particular emotions, or just keep going. Drug use may be more frequent but it won't necessarily interfere with their general functioning, they won't necessarily stop doing other things they do and it won't necessarily mean they can't cut down their use or stop altogether when other things change for them or they choose to do so.

However, there are risks, especially in adolescence, from more frequent use. As well as all the regular risks, it can sometimes lead to riskier use despite the increased levels of experience. As confidence grows, more risks might be taken, the range of substances might expand, and these may be mixed together in ways that increase the risk of harm. The more often a substance is used, the greater the impact can also begin to be on the physical and mental health of the person using it, depending on the substance. As we've seen, psychoactive drugs have the effects they do by changing the natural patterns of connection and communication in the brain, and the more frequently this happens, the longer it can take for the brain to restore the normal order of things, particularly in adolescence when so many changes are already taking place. This can begin to affect useful things like concentration and memory, and to lead to (or exacerbate) differing degrees of mental illnesses such as anxiety, depression or paranoia. Regular use can also begin to take a physical toll on the organs affected by the drug being used; whether the bladder with ketamine, the heart with a stimulant like cocaine or the kidneys with various drugs as they have to work harder to remove increased levels of toxins.

More frequent use can also risk creeping into addiction through various routes. If the substance is helping the person using it to cope with difficult or painful things in their life, they might begin to feel they can only cope with this source of help. Drug use may also, imperceptibly, begin to become the young person's principal recreational activity; their other social and personal functioning can start to decrease around it, and although they can still fulfil most roles and responsibilities, this might start to drop away. Additionally, the build-up of **tolerance** that increased use will often bring can lead some young people towards problematic and dependent use. Regular drug use causes the brain to change over time, as it adapts to whatever the effect that particular substance is having, and adjusts its natural processes to cope with the increased influx of chemicals. Those normal, natural, happy highs are harder to come by, and start only to be found through the artificial process, which itself has to be increasingly intensified to achieve the same effect.

Talking point: possible signs of regular drug use

More regular use of drugs can introduce changes that can affect your child physically, or that begin to be evident in their behaviour or patterns of socializing. You may also see changes in their mood. You may not notice, though, or be sure of what you're seeing, because these sorts of changes can be small and incremental, and identical to what might be seen in a person who's not touching a thing but just happens to be a teenager. A friend or relative you trust and who visits relatively infrequently can be a useful resource, if you have such a thing, bringing a bit of distance and time-lapse to their observations. Or try to think back to how things were six months or a year ago.

Physical changes:

- **Too much or too little sleep**: Everyone is familiar with that typical teenage sleep pattern, staying up far too late and lying in far too long, caused by shifts in their circadian rhythm that come along with the changes to their brain during adolescence. Problems with sleep can have many causes, from depression and anxiety to chatting on social media or gaming with friends into the early hours. However, certain drugs can also affect sleep patterns, for example, the use of stimulants such as cocaine and MDMA can lead to insomnia, whereas benzodiazepines calm down brain activity and, if taken at night, can lead to a drowsiness that lasts into the next day.
- **Energy levels**: Increased lethargy could, again, be perfectly normal – being a teenager is exhausting work after all – but it could also be a sign of more regular use of a stimulant drug, for example, especially if there's a pattern of fatigue following a night out that seems to do with more than just an energetic evening of socializing and a later than usual bedtime.
- **Unexpected changes to weight or build**: Adolescence is of course a time of multiple physical changes. In addition to this, acute bodily self-consciousness can lead to teenagers wanting to change the way they look, most often to slim down or muscle up. They will often take their own, natural – though not necessarily healthy – approaches to achieve this. However, a rapid loss of weight could be a sign of something like cocaine use, which can

affect appetite and also cause metabolic changes that affect the intake and storage of fat.[1] It could also indicate the use of diet pills which can easily be bought online. A bulking up of muscles that's out of proportion to the amount of time spent doing sports or working out could be down to the use of steroids.

Social/behavioural changes:

- **Sudden change in friendship group**: Falling out with current friends, or falling in with new ones, can all be perfectly normal in the emotional upheavals of adolescence, but could be a sign that their behaviour and choices around drugs have changed and no longer align with those of their old friendship group, and fit more comfortably with a new one.
- **Associating with people who use drugs**: A group for whom drug use is normal increases access to drugs as well as making it acceptable behaviour. However, although it's a risk factor, not everyone in any group inevitably joins in with everything the rest are getting up to.
- **Talking about drugs with friends**: Drug-related subject matter might be overheard when they're chatting with friends, or overseen in messages on their phone or on their social media. This could be said to impress, and based on nothing, but is worth a chat.
- **Lethargic or increasingly disruptive in class, particularly after weekends**: This could be caused by the down following the up, as the brain and body restore their natural balance.

Psychological changes:

- **Irritability, anger or aggression**: This could be down to a natural surge in testosterone, stress about an exam or any number of other factors in those turbulent teenage years. However, an increasing pattern of any of these behaviours would be something you'd want to talk about as a parent, to see what lies behind it, just in case it is the use of a drug like cocaine, which can lead to impulsivity, arrogance and aggressiveness.
- **Depression, anxiety and panic attacks**: All of these would be valid sources of concern for a parent, whether caused by drug use or not.

---

[1] Ersche, K.D. (2013) The skinny on cocaine: Insights into eating behavior and body weight in cocaine-dependent men, *Appetite* [online]. 1 December; 71: 75–80. Available from: DOI: 10.1016/j.appet.2013.07.011

More regular use of drugs can lead to changes in mental health, or exacerbate mental illness, and people can use drugs to help them cope, as we've seen.

Conversations if you think or know your child is using drugs regularly:

- As with occasional use, if you've seen any of these signs, or have other reasons for concern, check back on the general advice in Chapter 6 about how to make conversations work best, including tips for how to keep your cool and to listen.
- If you have suspicions and concerns, it's good to test them out before making drug-related assumptions. This is not just because you may get a defensive response that shuts the conversation down if you jump straight in talking about drugs, but there may be other causes altogether. Whatever these are, if you're worried then there's probably a reason that your parent-radar has detected something, which may be big (or may be small), and which may (or may not) be something that your child needs your help with.
- Focus on what you've seen and why this has concerned you. 'I've been noticing you seem to be really wiped out a lot of the time these days...',; Your little brother seems to be driving you mad a whole heap more than he used to...'.
- If you have good grounds for concern, then this can be talked about more directly. 'I couldn't help overhearing your conversation this morning and I was concerned to hear you talking about...'.
- Try to stay calm, try to understand, and listen. Keep that conversation open, because if your child's drug use has become more regular then it's a conversation that will need revisiting.
- Both the 'harder' and 'softer' conversations we looked at in Chapter 6 are important here – the 'hard' work of reinforcing or renegotiating rules and boundaries, and the 'softer' approach: talking through risks, consequences and managing decisions safely.
- Harm reduction information, as well as all the practical strategies for staying safe, is also essential (see below).
- Discussing, negotiating and agreeing some strategies, goals and boundaries around reducing or ideally stopping their drug use can help reduce risk and prevent problematic drug use developing. These could include a shift in friendship groups, support to reinstate activities they used to enjoy or a toolkit of excuses to get out of situations where they may feel pressured, or tempted, to use drugs.

Jack's story

I met Jack in 2018 when he was in sixth form college and was speaking on the panel at the parliamentary launch of Volteface's research paper, The Children's Inquiry,[2] which explored the impact of cannabis on young people. He spoke with such eloquence and honesty about his own experiences with cannabis, and those of his peers, I asked if he'd do some filming with us for parents, which he very kindly did. This is a transcript of one of these interviews, with the last paragraph added two years on, written especially for readers of this book.

'It was the half term in between my year 11 mock exams. I'd done half of them and I was going to do the next half when I got back. I went to a house party and someone had put a line out on a bathroom surface, and they told me it was MDMA, and I did it, then they told me afterwards it was actually coke, which is a bit of a weird one, mostly weird because it's, like, ten times more expensive. And then afterwards I did some bombs, and yeah, sort of went from there.'

Jack started getting drunk in year 9, smoking weed in year 10 and tried Class A drugs in year 11.

'It's very attractive to take a risk, and it's also very attractive to do something you know you're not meant to do, and it's also very attractive to do something that's different. I mean, you can only get drunk so many times.'

'I very quickly started doing it more and more – started smoking weed daily. Drinking alcohol every day would have seemed really bad, but people my age don't really see weed as a psychoactive substance. Smoking weed every day just doesn't have the negative connotations daily drinking would. It escalated, escalated more and more. At its peak I was probably smoking more than a gram of weed a day, which is very expensive, but also really bad for me.'

Jack's mum had no idea.

'I think a lot of young people are very savvy about how to hide their substance use and possession. I think a lot of the time unless a parent

---

2   McCulloch, L., Matharu, H, North, P. (2018) *The Children's Inquiry* [online]. *Volteface*. Available from: <volteface.me/app/uploads/2018/09/The-Childrens-Inquiry-Full-Report-2.pdf> (accessed November 2020)

is very savvy themselves, which is usually only a result of having been in the same position themselves, they're very unlikely to catch their child unless their child is very sloppy. I mean, for me, I was smoking for three years and I've still never to this day actually been caught smoking by my mum or anything like that. So it just goes to show that just because you don't think it's happening – like she didn't think it was happening – doesn't mean it isn't actually happening.'

Surely his mum noticed some changes?

'In retrospect I think my mum noticed a couple of things, but things that most parents could also just put down to being a classic teenager – a bit rude or moody, dirty dishes, lots of food, not wanting to speak to her, ignoring her. A lot of the time I'd get home and I'd be high and I'd just go straight to my bedroom, I'd get changed, I'd go downstairs, get loads of food, eat loads of food, jump in the shower then go and play some video games. I'd have as little interaction with my mum as possible so there was as little chance as possible of her actually realizing I was high.'

How did Jack pay for his drugs?

'The thing is with a lot of young people they'll have a friendship group or multiple friends or know lots of people who smoke weed so you don't even have to buy it every day to smoke it. One day someone will buy it, the next day someone else will buy it. I got pocket money off my mum every week, and then I'd also get food money for school because I go to college, and they have a cash part of the sixth form cafeteria, so I'd get a certain amount of cash for that per week as well. I would then just make my own food before I went to school, so that's like a straight £30-plus a week. Plus any other sort of money I could get from various things. I mean, a lot of young people, when they're at the height of their addiction, tend to sell their own property to buy things. I mean I had an iPad air – sold that. I had a PS Vita – which was like a pretty expensive hand-held console – sold that. I sold a lot of video games.'

How did Jack's mum finally find out about his dependency?

'Eventually I stopped wanting to hang around with the same people. An incident occurred where I was attacked by these people and so after that point I was, like, I need to speak to my mum about this. Obviously the drugs is part of what's occurring here. So I came clean to her and told her about every single drug I'd tried, how many times I'd done them, where I'd tried them, how old I was. From the perspective of a child, coming clean to your parent and telling them all the drugs you've done is exceptionally difficult. It's exceptionally scary. You're terrified of what your parents are going to think of you after that point. But the one thing that helped was that she just, like, accepted – right, well, you've done that now. There's nothing that she can do, but now that she's aware of it she can give me support to try to tackle the issues that I was using drugs for in the first place. That meant I got a drugs counsellor, which helped me to reduce and get rid of my dependence on weed.'

Jack says drugs are commonplace.

'Drug use is exceptionally normalized among young people now. Partly that's due to everything from movies, TV shows, video games, but young people are more and more aware than ever that these drugs are available, they're out there.'

Why do young people take drugs?

'Most Class A drugs people use exclusively recreationally. There are people that become dependent on them, but the vast majority of people who do Class A drugs do them at parties, festivals, gigs, that kind of thing. When it comes to weed, which is by far the one that most young people become dependent on, I'd say if people smoke regularly, upwards of 50 per cent of people who smoke regularly, at least in my age bracket, are doing it, whether they're aware of it or not, as a form of escapism. It's essentially how they take a break from whatever's going on in their life. Another problem that comes along with that is that if you take a break you're just ignoring the issues which just pile up and pile up and pile up. For me, when I was doing my GCSEs was probably when my substance use started to skyrocket the most, just because I was terrified about how my exams were going to go, really paranoid I was going to do badly, so it was essentially, among other things, a built-in fail-safe, essentially so if I failed I could say it was because of my drug use. I ended up doing pretty well, which I definitely didn't deserve to. But it's very much something that young people will turn to when they're at a low point. And that's when it'll get you.'

So, what does Jack think would help?

'Ultimately, ignorance about the reality that weed, like any other substance, can be misused and lead to an addiction, can easily be avoided with basic – and more importantly, early – education. The age at which most young people are exposed to drugs and the culture of substance use is far earlier than that of their parents' own experience, and with many parents feeling ill-equipped to discuss these topics, in many cases due to a lack of knowledge or experience themselves, early intervention with drugs education is key to prevent these problems. Given the mental health crises of this generation, substance use as a coping mechanism only becomes more likely.'

Addiction – how does it work?

Dr Suzi Gage has a useful definition of addiction:[3] 'Broadly speaking, a behaviour could be considered to be an addiction when an individual changes their life to fit around the consumption of a particular drug. It's not necessarily the quantity of the drug consumed, or even the regularity of use that would define a problem, but the way that use impacts on your life.[4] Drug use is now the dominant dynamic in someone's life, it's causing them harm, and it's much more difficult for them to reduce or stop its use. Sometimes there's a definite point at which an individual realizes their drug use is no longer under their control; sometimes it's a growing realization; often the people around them become aware of an issue long before they do themselves; but however that happens, there won't have been an identifiable point in time when the control they once had became lost. Addiction exists on a continuum, and there are various factors at work, interacting in often complex ways, that lead some but not others along this particular path.

It's reassuring for parents to know that most people using any substance won't develop an addiction to it. This is naturally one of the biggest fears parents have if they discover a child has been using drugs, but only a small number who use drugs or alcohol will develop problems that need help unravelling. The main exception to this is nicotine.

---

[3] See note in introduction for explanation of the use of the term 'addiction'.

[4] Gage, S. (2020) *Say Why to Drugs*, Hodder & Stoughton.

A study from St Mary's University found that at least 61 per cent of people who try their first cigarette become, at least temporarily, daily smokers, but that's unusual for most substances and most people.[5] As we've seen, the substance responsible for the vast majority of professional help provided to young people, however, is cannabis, which is surprising to many because it's often not considered to be an addictive substance. Nicotine can arguably play a part in this, because most people who smoke cannabis mix it with tobacco, but cannabis seems to cause addiction in some people all by itself. The strength of THC, the age of the user and the frequency with which they're using it are all relevant. Data from the US suggests that around one in six (17 per cent) teenagers who use cannabis will develop an addiction to it.[6] This means that five out of six won't, but nevertheless it's a higher number than most weed-smoking teens might imagine.

There are neurological factors at work in addiction. Addiction is associated with pathways of reward and reinforcement in the brain, and in particular with the neurotransmitter dopamine. But there are also dynamics relating to an individual's environment, circumstances, mental health, personality and genetics, which can make certain people more vulnerable, and others less so. In adolescence there are, however, developmental changes back in that teenage brain which can mean it's a period of life when the risks are a little higher.

The adolescent brain and addiction

Teenagers are wired to learn. This may not always translate into getting full marks in a test, or remembering it's their dad's birthday, but nevertheless their capacity to learn reaches a peak in their late teens. Babies are born with everything yet to be discovered, and there's a period of rapid growth of neurons and synapses in those early months, many of which aren't then needed. Those that are

5   Queen Mary University of London (2018) At least 3 out of 5 people who try a cigarette become daily smokers [online]. *Science Daily*. Available from: <www.sciencedaily.com/releases/2018/01/180109214939.htm> (accessed November 2020)

6   National Institute of Drug Abuse (2020) Is marijuana addictive? *NIDA*. Available from: <www.drugabuse.gov/publications/research-reports/marijuana/marijuana-addictive> (accessed November 2020)

unused get pruned away around the age of three, and the ones that are useful become strengthened. The next time a similar tidying up process takes place in the brain is in this critical period of adolescence. Just before puberty there's a second growth spurt, followed by another round of pruning, and a strengthening of those important connections and channels of communication in the brain. This is the synaptic plasticity we referred to earlier in the book.

It's the efficiency of teenagers' synaptic plasticity which means memories form more easily, and stay around longer, than they ever will again in their lives. It really is a time of life for making memories. However, as Frances E. Jensen points out, this gift can be double-edged sword, because 'it turns out that addiction is really a specialized form of memory'. Just like memories, not only can addictions develop more easily in adolescence, they can also be harder to lose.[7] That said, even in adolescence it's only a minority who will develop problems, but knowing there can be an additional risk of addiction in adolescence, and that there's a lot more hard work needed to come through it for teens for than for adults, is useful to be aware of as a parent, and to bring to your conversations – though as a risk factor it can be more difficult for young people to identify with an issue they are less likely to have witnessed unfolding in their friends, and they may see it as a bit of a niche possibility.

Factors in addiction

So, what else is going on? Suzi Gage refers to a highly influential US study into the substance use of American troops returning from Vietnam, amongst whom levels of drug use had been unusually high.[8] While they were out in a war zone many miles from home, around a third had been using heroin, and one in five soldiers showed signs of addiction. However, the vast majority of these stopped their heroin use when they got back home, and only 1 per cent of these reported becoming re-addicted in the following year. The primary reasons

[7] Jensen, F.E. (2015) *The Teenage Brain: A Neuroscientist's Survival Guide to Raising Adolescents and Young Adults*, Harper Collins.

[8] Hall, W. & Weier, M. (2018) Lee Robins' studies of heroin use among US Vietnam veterans. *Addiction* [online]. Available from: DOI: 10.1111/add.13584

the veterans gave for giving it up were the fear of addiction, fear of the disapproval of their family and friends and fear of landing up in prison. The bio-psycho-social model of addiction recognizes there are more dynamics at play than the power of the drug itself to make changes to the brain, which makes total sense to anyone who knows someone who has struggled with an addiction to drugs or alcohol. This also means that there is more to tackling addiction than just stopping the use of the drug, not that this is remotely straightforward in itself.

There are many theories, and many disagreements, around what these factors may be and the significance of the role they can play. One of these is family history. There does seem to be an increased likelihood that an addiction may develop if others in the family have also had problems with drugs or alcohol. Although the extent to which this is down to genes or environment or both is open to discussion, if this is part of your family story then it could be a potential risk factor – not an inevitability – for your child, and one it's useful for them to be aware of.

Arguably the biggest player, however, is mental health. We've already looked at how complex the relationship is between mental health and substance use, and the relationship between mental health, substance use and addiction adds another layer of complexity. Whatever the dynamics for an individual in relation to cause and effect – chicken and egg – the fact is that almost one third of under-18s entering treatment in 2018–19 had a mental health need[9] as well as more than half of adults.[10] There is increasing awareness in drug and alcohol treatment services of the importance of what's referred to as 'dual diagnosis'. For a long time people got stuck between services.

[9] Public Health England (2019) Young people's substance misuse treatment statistics 2018–2019: report [online]. *Public Health England*. Available from: <www.gov.uk/government/publications/substance-misuse-treatment-for-young-people-statistics-2018-to-2019/young-peoples-substance-misuse-treatment-statistics-2018-to-2019-report> (accessed November 2020)

[10] Public Health England (2019) Adult substance misuse treatment statistics 2018–2019: report [online]. *Public Health England*. Available from: <www.gov.uk/government/publications/substance-misuse-treatment-for-adults-statistics-2018-to-2019/adult-substance-misuse-treatment-statistics-2018-to-2019-report#mental-health> (accessed November 2020)

Mental health wouldn't work with them until their drug use was sorted, drugs treatment wouldn't work with them until their mental health was sorted. The truth is it's very hard to tackle one without also tackling the other because they're almost always deeply enmeshed, and by the time help is sought, almost always also deeply embedded. There have been huge improvements in many local authorities, however, especially for young people, but some areas still struggle, and of course budgets are under bigger than ever pressures which inevitably affect the services that can be made available.

Talking point: possible signs of problems

As with possible signs of occasional and more regular use there can be other reasons for many of the following, but most are signs that something's not right with your child, and a conversation is called for whatever the cause.

Physical changes:

- **Changes in self-care and hygiene**: This could be caused by other factors, in particular mental ill-health, but if drug use is becoming a primary focus then other priorities like looking good for the outside world can fall by the wayside. It could of course be a combination of both.

Social/ behavioural changes:

- **Social isolation**: A teenager becoming withdrawn is generally an indication that something's not right for them, and whether that's drug-related or not, it definitely warrants a concerned conversation with a parent to see what lies behind it and how they can be helped.
- **Too much money or nice new expensive things**: This could be a sign of involvement in drug dealing, or of the beginnings of exploitation into selling for others.
- **Too little money**: Asking for more money, money going missing from your purse, or things of value they owned disappearing, could be a sign that drug use is becoming expensive.
- **Keeping unusual hours**: Not out of the ordinary in adolescence, but staying out exceptionally long or late, popping out of the

house briefly but frequently (possibly to pick things up or drop things off), or no longer wanting to go out at all, could all be a cause for a conversation.

- **Significant unexplained drop in academic performance**: There could be many reasons for this but whatever they are, it's something you'd be talking about along with their school or college. Longer term use of certain drugs can begin to affect memory and concentration, mood and motivation, all of which can in turn affect the ability to do as well as they used to at school or college. Addiction leads to a loss of interest in much other than the use of the substance.
- **Persistent lateness, truancy or poor attendance**: Again, there could be other reasons for any of these, but lateness could be a sign that drug use is affecting sleep or energy levels, and absence from school or college could be the result of spending time with friends outside school who use drugs, or drugs becoming a primary driving force and superseding study in their list of personal priorities.
- **Unpredictable behaviour or self-harm**: Again, there could be many reasons, but these would be a cause for concern whatever lay behind them.
- **Loss of interest in previous activities, sports or hobbies**: Yet again, there could be many motivating factors behind these sorts of shifts in behaviour. It's not unusual at all for activities with which a child was besotted to become less appealing to their teenage self, for all sorts of perfectly understandable and natural reasons. However, a loss of interest in things that were previously of importance can indicate that drug use is taking precedence.

Psychological changes:

- **Paranoia**: The hypersensitivity of the average teenager to their peers can make the most stable and balanced among them more than a little paranoid about what the people around them might be thinking about them, or saying to everyone else. However, it could be a sign that cannabis use is beginning to affect their mental health. It can also be a side effect of drugs like cocaine and MDMA.

Conversations if you think or know your child has significant problems with drugs:

- As before, all the general advice from Chapter 6 about effective conversations – listening, keeping your cool, keeping that chat open – is a useful reference point.
- Make the most of times when your child seems more calm and more like 'themselves' to have conversations, because these are more likely to go well than when they are under the influence of drugs or alcohol.
- If you have suspicions or concerns and are beginning this conversation, focus on the cause of these concerns rather than making assumptions about what might lie behind them. Many of the signs described above need help whatever the cause.
- Remember that longer term, more significant drug use can cause changes to the way your child may behave towards you and the rest of the family. They may say hurtful things they'd never normally say, and do things that are very much out of character. Hold onto the fact they are still the same child and they still love you and need you, now more than ever.
- Understandable though it is, try to avoid slipping into a pattern of accusations, nagging and negativity in response to difficult behaviour.
- Try instead to maximize the positive – praise for the tiniest of good things, however hard they might be to spot, can make a huge difference, to the praiser as well as the praised.

It may be that you can negotiate and agree strategies, goals and boundaries that can enable you and your child to tackle their drug use together, but it may well be that by this stage professional help is needed – see below.

What can you do if they don't want help?

It's not unusual for it to take a while for someone experiencing problems with their drug or alcohol use to recognize that they are, but until they have it's difficult for them to engage with the help they may need. The old joke about how many social workers it takes to change a lightbulb is true when it comes to drugs and alcohol. They really do have to want to change. One of the effects of the reward pathways being strengthened in addiction is that the brain's routes to the pre-frontal cortex can start being pruned away. This means people who develop an addiction may find it harder to access that more rational, reflective part of their brain and so are often not aware that they have a problem for some time. This is especially so for teenagers at this stage of their life when this part of their brain is not yet fully connected in any case. You may need to tap into all your reserves of patience and persistence.

Talking point

The World Health Organization's definition of 'dependence syndrome' can be translated into some useful questions you could ask yourself if you have concerns, or you could perhaps work through with your child if it's difficult for them to see their behaviour may be causing problems for them and the people around them. In order to make a diagnosis of dependence syndrome, a clinician would be looking for three or more of these to have occurred together over the previous year, or for at least one month:[11]

1. A strong desire or sense of compulsion to take the substance: how do they feel if they are unable to use their chosen substance or substances when they want or need to, or if they even think about not being able to?

2. Difficulties in controlling substance-taking behaviour in terms of its onset, termination, or levels of use: how long are they able to hold off taking something without it causing them stress or anxiety? How hard would they find it to stop, or to cut down their use?

3. A physiological withdrawal state when substance use has ceased or has been reduced: if they do stop or reduce their use, do they experience physical withdrawal symptoms? Have they found themselves using the substance in order to relieve or avoid withdrawal symptoms?

[11] World Health Organization. Management of substance misuse: Dependence syndrome [online]. *WHO*. Available from: <www.who.int/substance_abuse/terminology/definition1/en/> (accessed November 2020)

4. Evidence of tolerance: if they were to look back over the last few months, are they having to take increasing amounts of the substance in order to achieve the same effects?

5. Progressive neglect of alternative pleasures or interests because of psychoactive substance use: are they devoting more time to drug use at the expense of other activities they used to enjoy, or are they neglecting other activities in order to recover from its effects?

6. Persisting with substance use despite clear evidence of overtly harmful consequences: are they continuing to use drugs even though they recognize that they're causing them harm, either physically or mentally, or both?

Adfam, a national charity offering support to families with loved ones experiencing problems with drugs or alcohol, describes the 'cycle of change', which is a useful model for understanding the process people may need to progress through and what support is most beneficial at each of these stages. See their website for more details, and for other useful information, advice and support for families.

How to find help and what that might look like

Your **GP** is a good place to start if you have concerns about your child's drug use, or if they do for themselves. The GP may refer them to your local treatment service if they feel they need this, and they should also do a check of their physical and mental health while they're there.

You can go direct to your **local drug and alcohol treatment service**, however, if you prefer. You can find locally commissioned services on the Talk to Frank or NHS websites, and there are also **charities and private providers** who offer treatment and support in different areas. Your GP may be able to advise you about these as well.

Young people's services often offer a flexible range of support to young people, but whatever they do they would start with an **assessment** of your child's drug use, talk about what treatment options are available and any other health problems they may have, and then develop a personal care plan with them which is tailored to their needs. This would normally detail their immediate and longer-term treatment goals and is intended to be updated throughout their time in treatment as their needs and circumstances change.

Most treatment will involve some sort of **talking therapy**, whether that's individual or in small groups, in a centre, at the school, or somewhere your child feels safe. Some services have drop-in times and spaces where young people can come and have informal chats or just spend time.

For over-18s a similar process would happen, with an assessment feeding into a plan involving goals and actions. Adults can also access self-help groups, such as Alcoholics Anonymous or Narcotics Anonymous, or other set ups. The Adfam website has a good list of locally available support for individuals and families, and in Scotland the Scottish Families Affected by Alcohol and Drugs website.

Talking point: advice for parents

From Dr Cara Robinson, Senior Supervising Clinician and Nick Hickmott, Early Intervention Lead

Nick and Cara have over 30 years' combined experience working with young people and substances, and in total around 50 years working with vulnerable young people.

Some tips:

1. **Research**: Make sure you have a solid understanding of local service providers and what they can and can't do. This is an issue you don't want to attempt to cope with at 2 am on a Sunday morning in crisis. You can find information on Talk to Frank (see the end of the book for more information).
2. **Knowledge**: Feeling confident in your factual knowledge will help both you and your child. Use reliable sources, such as Frank, Crew 2000 or Drugs and Me (see the end of the book for more information).
3. **Finances**: Check whether you're perhaps unknowingly funding your child's habit. Keeping track of cash flow in an open and non-punitive way can be a way of picking up on risky behaviour that might otherwise go unnoticed.
4. **Timing**: Time and place are important for creating a positive, constructive conversation – a time when neither of you are in a

hurry, and a place where you both feel comfortable and where there are minimal distractions.

5. **Stay calm**: Try not to allow conversations to become arguments. Sometimes it's better to take time to calm down and try again when everyone is ready.

6. **Using**: If your child is already using don't panic. Try to stay calm and not get angry. Remind them that you love them and seek supportive help.

7. **Help!** Get help if your child is using substances and you're concerned. Your local young person's substance misuse service is there to help. They can give you advice, support, and explain the options available for your child and for the family as a whole.

Involving parents in young people's treatment

Research recognizes the key role families can play in substance use treatment, in terms of preventing and/or influencing the course of the problem, improving outcomes for the young person and helping reduce the negative effects on other family members.

Programmes should aim to:

- Deliver interventions that work with family members to promote the entry and engagement of the young person into treatment
- Support the joint involvement of family members and the young person in the treatment plan
- Deliver interventions aimed to support family members by equipping them with knowledge and skills.

Parents can provide invaluable information that can make a significant contribution to their child's treatment plan. They can describe their own perspective on their child's substance use and the behaviour they've seen arising from it. They can provide medical history, developmental history, information about schooling and protective factors such as hobbies and interests. They can provide information about their child's friendships, family history and relationships, including any significant life events such as bereavement or separation. Parents can also ensure appropriate parental responsibility is provided for the young person in treatment, and give their consent if this is required.

Sessions can be built around the voice of the parent and should provide an opportunity for them to express their concerns in relation to their child's substance use. These could include:

- Emotions and feelings around the young person being challenging to live with
- Concern about the young person's health/school or work performance/behaviour
- Financial problems
- Impact on the family
- Keeping the problem secret for fear of others becoming involved
- The young person disappearing from home for prolonged periods
- Police involvement.

Sessions can then focus on providing the family member with information and education about drug misuse. The family can also be signposted to other appropriate services that could offer them support.

There should always be an opportunity to bring the young person and the family member together to discuss the young person's treatment plan. Conducting part of the young person's assessment with a parent or carer is a good practice. This will allow young people to experience their parent's concern for their well-being. It can aid communication between family members and may help to put young people's and parents' anxieties into perspective. The parent can make a contribution to the young person's care plan and may identify ways of supporting their child through treatment. This could involve simple tasks such as reminding their child of their appointments or agreeing to transport them to sessions.

If the young person does not consent to treatment then the majority of services should still carry out parental work and explore other options with them to engage their child, such as early intervention group work, a local youth club or outreach delivery.

Taking care of yourself

If you have a child using drugs problematically then it's very important you find support for yourself. It's more likely to be a marathon than a sprint, and you need all the inner and outer resources you can call on in good working order if you're to help your child, as well as keep going for everyone else who needs you. Parents always blame themselves for anything that goes wrong in their child's life, and especially when it's something to which there is so much stigma attached, and it's easy to feel you don't deserve to take care of yourself. However, as the parent reading this book, you're someone who is standing on that frontline for and with your child, and in order to keep standing you need to be as strong as you can be.

- **Find people you can talk to**: It can feel very isolating, you can fear people are judging you, but think of people you know you can trust.
- **Make space to look after your mental health**: What helps you unwind, destress, restore your inner reserves?
- **Look after your physical health**: Make time to get some exercise, some good food and enough sleep.
- **Take a break**: Do something completely different. Any significant issue within a family can become all-absorbing, so take time out once in a while, by yourself, with a friend or as a family, or all three.
- **Get help and support**: Some young people's treatment services offer support for parents and families, and Adfam and Drufam both provide advice and support in various forms, including groups of people meeting locally who are experiencing similar issues and who will understand best. In Scotland this service is provided by Scottish Families Affected by Alcohol and Drugs (SFAD).

Stigma and drug use

Drug use is arguably one of the most stigmatized of all human behaviours, and this appears to be the case the world over. A review of international studies going back 20 years found the level of stigma was higher towards individuals with substance use disorders than towards those with other psychiatric disorders, another highly stigmatized area of our lives.[12] This stigma can come from public perceptions as well as public pronouncements and policy decisions at national level.

---

[12] Yang, L. et al. (2017) Stigma and substance use disorders: an international phenomenon. *Current Opinion in Psychiatry* [online]. September, 30(5: 378–388. Available from: DOI: 10.1097/YCO.0000000000000351

It can and often does come from the media, especially parts of the tabloid press, which demonize people who use drugs with shocking labels, headlines and images. All of this might translate into a sense of blame and shame that can prevent individuals accessing the support available and lead to isolation as well as an ongoing struggle, and this applies to parents as well as to young people.

We talked very publicly and openly about Dan dying from drugs from the get-go, but every now and then I'd have a wobble, wondering whether this was wise. People would of course judge me as a parent, though none could possibly judge me more harshly than I did myself, but what I couldn't bear was the idea that anyone might judge Dan, and make assumptions about the kind of person he was, all of which would be wrong. By then of course it was too late, it was out there, so I kept on talking, and one of the things that surprised me was wherever I went I'd find there were always people whose family stories involved issues with drugs or alcohol, often stories they'd never shared. There's more of this that anyone might realize, and that's good to remember if you're a parent feeling on your own and wary of letting anyone know your child is using drugs. There may be those who will judge, but this is sometimes something people do to try to make themselves feel safer, by 'othering' people whose problems are those they fear facing themselves. For all of these, there'll be other people who share your worries, and walk the same path, or have in the past, and though they may not say as much, they have experienced very similar things to you.

I wish I'd known the grief and stigma around losing a child to a drugs overdose

By Janine Milburn, mum of Georgia Jones (18)

Around midday on 26 May 2018 I said goodbye to my 18-year-old daughter Georgia and her big sister Danielle as they headed off to Mutiny Festival, about ten miles from our home. By 8.20 pm that evening she was dead. She had taken two ecstasy pills.

That afternoon and evening are a total blur. We'd raced to the hospital, spoken to hospital staff and police, and then we'd stayed with Georgia till about 11 pm, as long as we could. As we left, we found out another young lad from the festival had died, and that others had been treated in the hospital for drug related complications. By the time we got home I was ready to drop, but before I did I needed to head over to her best friend's house to let her know what had happened before she saw it all over Facebook. It was then that I thought I should put something on Facebook myself. The festival was going on all weekend, so if no one knew what had happened to Georgia and the others, more people might lose their lives. So that's what I did.

The next morning we woke to find the media at our door and my daughter's face everywhere. Within 24 hours people around the world had heard about what happened to Georgia. Even my uncle in Spain.

Because we spoke out, and because it was about drugs, I knew there might be the odd nasty comment or the odd look in the street. For about a week I remember staying glued to my phone, checking comments and seeing what people were saying about it all, but overall people were being extremely supportive. I'm thankful I'm very laid back and don't take many things to heart, though, because from time to time between the loving words there were some horrid things. Messages I would never repeat, ever. Some were saying what would happen to her in hell, others would say things like she deserved to die because she took drugs, or it's her own fault as she knew what she was doing, or she was an adult and has to take responsibility for her actions. Sometimes they would say it was my fault. I should have known what she was doing. I should have told her not to do it. I must be a rubbish parent because if I was any good, she would still be here.

When you're at your lowest possible point emotionally these comments can make you question yourself, but I never read these comments out loud or discussed them because in my heart I knew who my daughter was. I knew we had a brilliant relationship, I knew I had done my best for her, for all of them, and I knew I was so overwhelmingly proud of the person she was becoming. So I held tight to that, and asked myself what did it matter what other people thought? They weren't anything to me so what did it matter?

Georgia Jones, with permission from Janine Milburn

Psychosis and substance use

Although it's thankfully relatively uncommon, research over several years has established links between psychosis and cannabis use, especially in adolescence, and especially use of high-potency cannabis, but of course there is always some degree of disagreement about cause and effect. As we've seen already the relationships between drug use and mental illness are complex, especially in adolescence, not least because this is the stage of neurological development when some mental illnesses, including an illness like schizophrenia, begin to manifest. However, in a study undertaken by Kings College, based on evidence taken from across Europe and Brazil, and published in *The Lancet* in 2019,[13] researchers found that daily cannabis use tripled the

[13] Di Forti, M. et. al. (2019) The contribution of cannabis use to variation in the incidence of psychotic disorder across Europe (EU-GEI): a multicentre case-control study. *The Lancet* [online]. Available from: DOI: 10.1016/S2215-0366(19)30048-3

odds of developing a psychotic disorder compared with people who had never used cannabis, and this increased to nearly five-times the odds for daily use of high-potency types of cannabis.

Psychosis is characterized by paranoia, delusions and hallucinations, a loss of touch with reality as other people see it. It might be experienced as hearing voices, seeing or feeling things that aren't there, or believing things that aren't true and don't make sense. There can be a feeling you're being followed, watched or controlled by something or someone outside yourself. It can be very frightening. It can be a symptom of a serious mental illness such as bipolar disorder or schizophrenia, but it can also be drug-induced. As we've seen, it's possible for drug use to cause, exacerbate or trigger an underlying mental illness. It's equally possible for the emergence of mental illness to coincide with drug use without the drug use being the cause. Whatever the reason, it is a condition that needs help. Some people will just have one episode and never have another. For others it is a long-term, often life-long condition, but one that is treatable with professional help, and usually medication.

Identifying early signs of psychosis and getting help and treatment quickly can make an enormous difference to a young person's outcomes. As a parent the changes can come in small, unobtrusive, incremental steps, however, and easily get lost among other adolescent behaviour patterns and the busyness of life. The young person concerned may also be unwilling to engage with treatment because the nature of their illness can mean they experience their delusions as reality, and it can also create significant issues trusting others which can lead to barriers accessing help.

Early warning signs for psychosis can include a combination of any of the following changes to patterns of behaviour:

- A sudden, unexpected drop in performance at school, college or work
- Difficulty concentrating or thinking clearly
- Paranoia, suspiciousness and mistrust of others
- Social withdrawal and isolation
- Speaking rapidly and constantly, switching suddenly from one topic to another, or losing a train of thought and stopping abruptly
- Strange, intense new ideas or feelings, or becoming emotionally detached

- Decline in self-care and personal hygiene
- Difficulty differentiating between fantasy and reality.[14,15]

Treatment for psychosis will usually involve a combination of antipsychotic medication and psychological therapies, including CBT, family therapy and self-help groups. If it relates to drug use then treatment services should also be involved. Psychosis can be as frightening for those witnessing its effects on someone they love as it is to the person experiencing it themselves, and it's important help is found for everyone who needs it. **If you have any concerns, speak to your GP as early as possible.**

Things I wish I had known: Jane's story

I wish I'd known how dangerous cannabis is.

Josh's father and I had both dabbled with drugs as older teenagers and we felt smoking cannabis was relatively harmless. That said, my relationship with his father had broken down in part due to his cannabis use. It was one of many things that I struggled with so I did know it could be destructive, but I had no idea just how destructive it can be.

I can't remember exactly how old Josh was when we realized he was smoking cannabis, or how we found out, because the journey since has been so long, but it was probably around 15 or 16, and possibly because we smelt it on him. I'm still not sure how old he was when he first started, but I'd guess around 14. We talked about the risks, and we talked about the fact it was cannabis that had been partly responsible for the problems with his father, but my main concern at the time was the risk that he might try other drugs if he was mixing with people who did these things. We talked to him about this and he seemed to understand. We felt that if we were open with him about what he was doing, he wouldn't be sneaking off behind our backs to take drugs. If I had known how dangerous cannabis was, though, I would have approached this very differently.

---

[14] National Institute of Mental Health. Understanding psychosis [online]. *NIMH.* Available from: <www.nimh.nih.gov/health/publications/understanding-psychosis/index.shtml> (accessed November 2020)

[15] NHS. Symptoms: psychosis [online]. *NHS.* Available from: <www.nhs.uk/conditions/psychosis/symptoms/> (accessed November 2020)

I wish I'd known that Josh was taking other drugs.

There are two things tied up with this particular regret. The first is that his father was 'encouraging' his drug use by engaging in drug use with him, and not just cannabis. If I had known that I would have taken action to prevent it, or to prevent Josh seeing his father. I'm not sure how that would have looked, or even if it was possible, but at least I could have tried to educate Josh (and his father), and that might have helped. The second is that if I had understood more about drug use I might have recognized the signs that Josh had moved on from cannabis. If I had realized he was taking other drugs, including LSD and cocaine, I might have been able to try to prevent the degree of illness he went on to experience and the damage he has done to himself. I feel so guilty that I didn't realize and that I didn't do more to protect him from himself.

I wish I'd known how to get help.

Josh had always been self-conscious and very sensitive to what he felt others thought about him, but this became more noticeable as he got older and by the time he was 17, it was becoming a problem, and beginning to turn into paranoia. The point at which I realized something was wrong and that he needed help was when we were in the car one day, sitting at red traffic lights, and he was absolutely convinced the people in the next car were looking at him and talking about him. From then onwards his mental health deteriorated.

When Josh had done his GCSEs he went off to college for a year, but it was only when his mental health had really gone downhill that his tutors said they had been concerned about him and wondered if there was something going on. I was so angry with them for not sharing that concern with anyone earlier – me, safeguarding, anyone. I realize 17 is a difficult age when they're not really a child but not yet an adult, and I appreciate that the college was perhaps protecting his confidentiality, but he was not an adult and as his parent I needed to have been told. Although I had my own concerns, they were witnesses to different behaviours than we saw at home and, had I realized how pervasive those behaviours were, I would have pushed harder for support at an earlier time, and that may have made a difference.

As things got worse for Josh I remember how helpless I felt on so many occasions. I was totally out of my depth and didn't know what to do. It was terrifying. By the time things really started to unravel Josh had turned 18 and was an adult, and this made a huge difference to my involvement in his care. I couldn't force him to do anything and he often refused to see his GP or to go to counselling. After six months of arranging appointments with a counsellor, and him refusing to go at the last minute, I finally managed to get him to turn up at one but by then he was so paranoid that he was convinced everyone in the building could hear everything he said and wouldn't go back. I said we could get someone to come to our house, but by that stage his paranoia was such that he didn't feel safe at home either.

I was desperate. I wrote to our GP and eventually begged him to escalate support for Josh. He was finally assessed many months after I had first raised concerns about his mental health. Once he was in the system, we did get support, and initially that support was very good, but by then we were both broken. Over the years since then he's been sectioned and hospitalized on several occasions. He's got better and then relapsed back into taking drugs that have made everything worse, and every time his recovery has left more damage behind. He's now been on anti-psychotic medication for many years, and is finally stable, but unable to work, and lives a life that's very limited compared to what it should be for an intelligent, kind, sensitive person with a loving, supportive family around him. I know this would all have been so different for Josh if it hadn't been for cannabis.

I wish I'd known the cost.

I wish I'd known before he started this journey just how much it would take from him, and from us all. I feel I lost my eldest son to drugs and have a different version of him now. I know I'm lucky I still have him, but the trauma of losing him in the way I did is something from which I feel I will never quite recover.

Talking point

Finally, whether you suspect or know your child may be trying drugs every now and then, using them more regularly, or experiencing problems with their use, it's vital both you and they have a good grounding in how the risks they're taking can be reduced. Obviously the most effective form of harm reduction is to stop taking drugs, but if that's not happening then there are measures that can be put in place to increase their chances of staying safe. These are some useful sites with information about specific substances (details for these can be found at the back of the book):

- **Drugsand.me**: A social enterprise that provides services centred around drug harm reduction. Their website provides accessible and comprehensive guides about individual substances intended to help reduce their short and long-term harms. It also has information about the risks of interactions between different substances.
- **Drugscience**: Founded by Professor David Nutt, former Chair of the Advisory Council for the Misuse of Drugs, in order to provide independent, research-based information about drugs, including detailed information about individual substances.
- **Crew 2000**: A harm reduction and outreach charity working with young people in Scotland. Their website has an A-Z of substances with detailed information, including harm reduction advice, as well as downloadable leaflets about cannabis, cocaine and psychoactive drugs more generally.
- **Re-solv**: A charity working to reduce the harms of volatile substance abuse, including nitrous oxide, and providing information and advice.

9

I wish I didn't know what it's like to lose a child to drugs

The impact

We had watched Dan die. We had, eventually, left him in his little intensive care room. We had packed up the things we'd accumulated over those few days. We'd said goodbye to the family who'd been with us and with Dan in that little room, to the friends who'd waited outside, and we'd gone back home to our empty house. The house from which we'd rushed in the early hours of Saturday morning.

When we opened the door, there was a pile of cards on the mat. People were already learning that Dan had died. Right at the bottom of all the sympathy cards, from a time before sympathy cards were the order of the day, were some get well soon cards for Dan that his friends had put through our door. A glimpse back to a time, in this very short time, when there was hope that he might get well, and get well soon.

What do you do when you get back home after leaving your dead son at the hospital? I didn't know. I needed to do something, though. I unpacked our bags. I tidied. But then what? Some friends brought some soup. It was evening, so I suppose at some point we went to bed, but I couldn't rest. I hadn't slept since Friday; I was so tired, but my heart wouldn't stop racing and racing, and neither would my head.

Early the next morning the doorbell went. It was a reporter, the local paper. They were very sorry for our loss, and wondered if they could talk to us about Daniel? I was still in my pyjamas and I'd had very little sleep with my head and heart racing and racing, so I said it wasn't a great moment, perhaps they could come back later? What does one say to reporters who knock on the door when one's son dies from drugs? It was nice they were interested seemed like a polite response – it put it off till another time when perhaps I'd know what to do.

Then the doorbell went again. This time it was a press agency. They were sorry for our loss, and wondered if they could talk to us about Daniel? I said it wasn't a great moment, could they come back later? They went, but then the door went again. It was the *Daily Mail*, a reporter and a cameraman. This time I took their card and said I'd be in touch. I was getting the hang of this. But then it went again, and again. Another press agency. Someone else.

By this time people had started to come over too, friends from church, from work, my boss, and then at midday the police came. Thank goodness. Steve would know what to do, Steve always knew what to do, and he did. He said we could either say *no comment*, or we could write a statement and the police would send that to all the media people, or we could talk to them, and if we did that then the police press bureau (who knew there was such a thing?) would manage it for us.

In the meantime, Jacob had been searching online and found there were already headlines out there: 'Ecstasy teen dies at illegal rave'. They'd found a photo of Dan on his Facebook page, not looking his best, looking, in fact, like an 'ecstasy teen' who might 'die at an illegal rave' (he needed better privacy settings). They'd found a statement that must have been put out by the police about a boy dying from drugs, they'd found his headteacher's statement from the school website, and his uncle's Twitter post: 'Man down. Dan died this morning'. From that they'd constructed an article, and an article that made us want to respond, to say Dan wasn't an 'ecstasy teen' and he didn't make a habit of going to illegal raves. He'd never done either of these things before (as far as we then knew). And we also wanted to warn other parents. Perhaps they also didn't know how close this stuff is to all our doors, and how dangerous it can be.

We decided we'd talk. So, early that afternoon, the day after Dan died, in our small living room in Croydon, we sat with Steve and talked, to a roomful of reporters and the *Daily Mail* cameraman, who thankfully chose not to photograph two broken people who'd had little sleep, and instead to trawl my Facebook page for better photos from happier times. (I also needed better privacy settings.) It turned out they hadn't ever gone further than the end of our road, where they'd been waiting all morning. We talked about Dan, we talked about what happened – what little we knew at that stage – and then someone asked if I could remember the last thing he'd said to me. Of course I could. Dan's last words went on to form a headline in every national paper the following day, accompanied by his year 11 school photo (that they'd also found on his Facebook page), wearing on his blazer his football badge, his drama badge, and the Red Army badge he'd taken off the big furry hat he'd bought on the school history trip to Berlin, and put on his blazer especially in order to provoke a very right wing friend and prompt a few interesting political discussions.

I love you, Mum – I promise I won't die.

The police press bureau straight away put out a message to all the media to say that we were willing to talk, but they needed to go through the police. However, it seemed to take a good 24 hours and several reminders before that message registered. The doorbell didn't stop ringing – not just ours but those of my brother and his family, Tim's brother, his stepmother (whose mind was on Tim's dad, in his last days of terminal cancer), Alice, Jenna. We had two unusual names we'd united into one even more unusual name when we got married, and anyone who was either a Spargo or a Mabbs that could be tracked down got a knock, along with anyone else who looked interesting from Dan's poorly-protected Facebook page. I didn't need to wonder what to do with myself any more. I was too busy the rest of that first day politely fending off reporters.

Early the next morning the doorbell went again. It was the BBC: two people, one with a big fluffy microphone. They were very sorry for our loss, and wondered if Vanessa Feltz could talk to us about Daniel on her Radio Two programme that morning. I was, again, still in my pyjamas, again I'd had very little sleep with my heart still racing and racing, and so again I said it wasn't a great moment, perhaps they could come back later? And didn't they get the message it was all supposed to be going through the police press bureau? They were very sorry, but the programme was going live in about 20 minutes, they needed to know now. So there we were, 20 minutes later, two days after Dan died, sitting around our dining table, in our pyjamas, talking live on air to Vanessa Feltz. It was all so mad. But we needed to warn everyone: this stuff had got Dan, we didn't want it to get anyone else. If we hadn't known it was so easy to fall down this hole perhaps other parents might not, either?

I said earlier that this most awful of experiences, that of losing a child, has its own unique awfulness when the loss is caused by drugs, because of the incomplete narrative to which you have to resign yourself. But there's so much more to add to this particularly complicated version of child loss, which I hadn't credited until I was told some time later, when I realized why I was doing so much worse at this grief business than I felt I should be. This was the only child loss I'd experienced, so I had nothing to compare it with. Not only is it an incredible shock, which brings with it trauma and post-traumatic stress for many, but these added elements of press interest, police involvement and the whole criminal justice process keep poking a jagged stick into that deep open wound, digging around in it some more and re-traumatizing before the initial trauma has really had the chance to stake a claim.

And then there's a post-mortem, which you have to not think about too much if you can help it, then an inquest. For us this took a year and a month. A year and a month of waiting for the answer to that biggest of all questions, the one about why our son had died. We knew it was MDMA, we knew there was nothing else of significance there, all of that had been needed for the trial, but we had no idea why four had lived and one had not. It wasn't until we were sent the toxicology report a couple of weeks before the inquest, along with all those other upsetting papers, and had found someone who could interpret the words and numbers for us, that we learned the little bag of MDMA Dan got had just been incredibly strong.

In the meantime we waited, not knowing how long that waiting would be, or how we'd be told, or by whom, or even where it would be held so we could give them a call and ask. Dan had lived his life in Croydon, died his death in Lambeth, but collapsed in Hillingdon from where everything else had been led. As we knew he would, Steve had stopped being our Family Liaison Officer and source of all strength and safety and sorting things out as soon as the trial was over, and so we were on our own. Who could we ask? There it was – that powerlessness of which I spoke before.

Somehow, eventually, I can't now remember how, I was finally able to find out which coroners' court it would be, and to speak to someone there, and eventually, finally, to get a date. And once we'd made contact, it was all as good as something so bad could be. They were all incredibly kind. I was able to visit the court and speak to someone there, I was able to sit in on another inquest, one very unlike ours, so I knew what would happen, and I was prepared when the big brown envelope arrived in the post, the one filled with all the papers that accounted for every medical detail of the death of my son Dan. Whereas at the trial we had been invisible, squashed into our six plastic seats, at the inquest we were centre stage. We were able to choose to sit where we'd feel most comfortable (or least uncomfortable), we were asked by the coroner before she began whether we'd rather she talked about Daniel or Dan, and there were tissues on all of the tables, which was handy because I cried through the entire hearing. I'd read all the papers that were being read out, I knew what had happened, but nevertheless I went through an awful lot of their tissues.

But the greatest kindness of all those that the coroner's court had done for us came two weeks after the inquest. It was my birthday, the second without Dan, another unhappy birthday. The phone rang: it was the coroners' officer. She'd been at the mortuary, and somebody there, somehow or other, had picked up on our name and had found they still had a sample of Dan's hair that had been taken at the post-mortem. Would we like this?

I had no idea there was any of Dan left anywhere. When a tiny baby dies, hospitals are generally so good at making sure parents have a little handprint or footprint and a lock of hair, if they have any, and often a special memory box and other lovely things, but with great big enormous teenagers who die there aren't always the same systems set up and it had never occurred to me in the flurry and shock of those last awful hours to take a lock of Dan's hair. But there it was, the best birthday present I had ever had.

In between that first day back at home without Dan and the inquest, in and around the press interest (which never went away), and the court hearings, trial and sentencing, life went on. Life goes on, whether you like it or not, and I didn't like it a lot of the time. I had a problem with time, along with a whole heap of other things. I hated the way it just moved relentlessly on, one day turning into another, taking me further away from the day when Dan was alive, and well, and safe and sound, and things made sense. I hated falling asleep and held out as long as I could every night, not wanting to let go of another day, knowing I'd wake up and it would be gone forever, and here I was in another one that had taken me a little bit further away from Dan, even though I hadn't asked it to.

I could write so much about those early days, weeks, months. That numb haze of confusion, the blank clouds of disbelief that occasionally parted with a flash of something too awful to look at for more than a moment. That exhausting, endless, impossible task of trying to make sense of something that made no sense and which occupied all my poor busy brain's processing capacity and stopped it taking in or taking on board anything else – anything anyone said, anything I tried to read, any decisions to make. And there are so many decisions to make when someone dies, and when a child dies the decisions are ones for which there is no reference point, no prior experience from which to work. And they all have to be made so soon.

What should he wear in his coffin? The funeral director offered something in white nylon and lace. Not sure Dan would have gone for that, even though he did always love a bit of dressing up. Eventually we decided something comfy seemed best, his favourite sloppy t-shirt and baggy tracksuit bottoms, but honestly, what a ridiculous decision to have to make, almost as ridiculous as which flowers he'd want at his funeral, which was another one. Burial or cremation we knew about (*thanks, Dan*) but which cemetery? We visited the ones with available spaces, and only one felt not too awful. But then which plot? We were shown a few options, all shared with someone else deeper down below who'd been there a while, because they were tight for space. None of them felt right, but then how could something so wrong possibly feel right? But then we were shown one right at the back of the cemetery, where the ground was awash with purple crocuses, and an enormous tree watched over all the surrounding headstones. This was the right place for this very wrong thing.

And so that was where we buried our boy, three weeks and a day after he died, in the pouring rain and driving wind.

The funeral is the last thing I'll write about, otherwise my story will never end.

The morning of the funeral, as the house filled up with family, and with Jenna and her family, and with Steve, I waited, knowing at some point there would be a hearse that would pull up outside, and inside the hearse would be a coffin, and inside the coffin would be Dan. Numb haze. The moment arrived, my sister in law came into the kitchen and said, *Fi, it's here*, and there it was. There was Dan. *Oh my goodness.* Off we all went, into the car that followed the hearse that carried Dan to the cemetery. But before we reached the cemetery, we'd arranged to drive past Dan's school. One last journey to school for Dan. The rain had started pouring and the wind was driving and, as we turned the corner into the road where his school was, we saw what appeared to be the whole road lined with pupils, teachers, staff, governors. The funeral director stopped the hearse, got out and put on his tall hat, and walked slowly in front as it drove past the school, and they all watched Dan pass, standing there in silence, in the pouring wind and driving rain.

Our road had been closed, the school road had been closed, and all the way there, from the house to the school, from the school to the cemetery, we had two police outriders on motorbikes, weaving in and out and stopping the traffic to let us pass. Steve had sorted this out, something to do with the press involvement, I think, or the fact there had been a crime, I'm not sure what, but whatever the reason, Dan would have been so impressed. For that morning, for those moments, Croydon stopped to let Dan through. He was the most important person at that time, in that place. The trams, the cars, the busiest of junctions, everyone stopped as Dan drove slowly through, in the hearse that carried his coffin.

The press had been told the burial was private, family only. They could be at the church for the service but only outside. They'd been huddled at the end of Dan's school road, and caught photos of everyone standing there in silence in the wind and rain, all those school uniforms and teachers, watching Dan pass. And there they were, outside the church, waiting, cameras at the ready. There were police out there too, watching over it all. One reporter got in and wrote up the service, wrongly and upsettingly referring to Alice, who did one of the tributes, as Dan's girlfriend Jenna. And as we left the church that had been jam packed with teenagers, teachers, family and friends, friends I hadn't seen for years, colleagues from work, so many people from so many places in our lives, there the press were, cameras ready and waiting.

And so that was it. We took Jacob back to university that weekend to make a start on his second term, a good few weeks late. A week or so later Tim went back to work full time, having been back part time since early on. My parents, who'd moved in at the very beginning, moved out and went back to their own home. And life went on, and night followed day, whether I wanted it to or not.

Along with so many of the chapters in this book, the subject of child bereavement is one that has many a book and website dedicated to it already, though not many are specific to a death from drugs. Losing a child to drugs is, thankfully, a relatively uncommon experience, but it's also a uniquely difficult experience. It's one that's often classified along with suicide, murder and road traffic accidents as a sudden, violent death, one that brings with it police, press, courts and coroners, and a different order of grief altogether. Kathleen O'Hara, who had been a practising psychotherapist in the US for several years before her son was found murdered at college, writes:

> 'Overcoming the violent death of someone you love is the most harrowing journey of them all. Your grief is a grief like no other, and one which you would have done anything to avoid. But here you are – you must make this journey or perish. When violence strikes, your familiar, safe shores vanish, throwing you into a vast ocean of grief and loss. In that ocean you will be tossed and battered and nearly destroyed. You will encounter the storms of anger, isolation, fear and pain; try to find comfort and hope wherever you can; and suffer alone when you cannot.[1]

I hope this chapter will not only help other parents who've lost a child through drugs or alcohol, but also those who have family, friends or people in their wider community who have, for whom the understanding and support they can bring could make an enormous difference. I also hope, along with the other chapters, and especially the stories they contain, it can help in the conversations you have with your child at home. The impact is bigger, and wider, and more far reaching than many would ever imagine.

---

[1] Kathleen O'Hara (2006) *A Grief Like No Other,* Marlowe & Company.

In writing about bereavement, it probably doesn't need saying, but there really are no rules, no simple solutions, nor straightforward responses. Grief is a messy business, and everyone grieves in their own way and at their own pace. Even when it's relatively straightforward – an elderly aunt who dies peacefully at home in her sleep after a long and happy life – her loss will affect the people who loved her and it will do this differently. With the loss of a child, and a loss due to drugs, the messiness and unpredictability of it can tip off the scale. What one person needs can be wildly different to another, and what that one person needs on one day, or in one moment of one day, could be wildly different from what they might need on another day, or in another moment. And generally speaking, we're all learning as we go, from the inside and the outside.

That said, there is some excellent support available, and I've done my best to signpost to some of this below. Over, above and through all this, though, what bereaved parents need more than anything is kindness, and patience. They need to be kind and patient with themselves, and they very much need the people around them to dig deep and do likewise.

Talking point

There are a few charities offering support to bereaved parents, including some support tailored specifically for those who have lost children to drugs or alcohol. I've signposted particular aspects of this support below in relevant sections, but more extensive support is available on their websites:

Care for the Family's Bereaved Parent Support offers a range of **information** on their website. They organize **events** throughout the year bringing bereaved parents together. They also offer a telephone **befriending service**, through which a bereaved parent can be put in contact with a trained volunteer who has also lost a child, in circumstances and of an age as similar as possible.

I've been speaking to my wonderful Care for the Family befriender Philippa since soon after losing Dan. She was one of my first lifelines in those early weeks, someone who understood in a way I didn't yet myself. Her own son had died from drugs, a few years older than Dan, and a few years ahead of him. We still speak regularly, now as friends. My journey would have been so much harder without her walking alongside me.

The Compassionate Friends (TCF) have an extensive range of **information leaflets and guides** on their website covering a wide range of relevant topics, including losing a child to drugs or alcohol, but also one for grandparents, schools, single parents, stepparents and more. They offer a **'Grief Companions'** service, which provides peer support from another bereaved parent in the first couple of years after a child's death. They also have a helpline on **0345 123 2304** and also offer support by email at <helpline@tcf.org.uk>. Both of these are staffed by trained volunteers who have also lost children. They coordinate **local groups** of bereaved parents that meet, and **events** during the year across the country.

Drugfam is a charity offering support to families affected by a loved one's drug or alcohol use, including those that have been bereaved. They offer a helpline on **0300 888 3853** which is open from 9am to 9pm seven days a week, and also provide support by email via the website.

The Child Death Helpline is staffed by trained volunteers and aims to provide a confidential freephone service to anyone affected by the death of a child of any age. As well as parents this includes grandparents, siblings, other family members, friends or involved professionals. They also have a telephone interpreting service and accept calls in any language. Their helpline is **0800 282 986**, their mobile helpline is **0808 800 6019** and you can also email <contact@childdeathhelpline.org>.

Supporting siblings

For parents who have lost their only child, this is a particularly rough road. Both TCF and Care for the Family provide support and advice for those that find themselves suddenly in a family without a child around, because this is another unique brand of bereavement (see below). For those with remaining children it's also hard. They've lost one child, and the children they have left are suffering. They've also have lost someone who was an integral part of their lives, that they assumed would always be there, that they loved, and for them this loss will also have had the added dimensions of shock and trauma. Their experience is different to that of their parents, it's an experience not many parents will have been through themselves, and it can be hard to know how to help them, however desperate we are to do so, especially when our own grief is so raw.

For children of any age the unexpected death of a brother or sister knocks their known universe totally off balance, and can make it seem like a very precarious place, which indeed it has proved itself to be. Older children, teens and young adults can feel they have to protect their parents, and often feel unable to talk to them about their own feelings for fear of adding to the burden of grief they can see them carrying around. They may feel they have to take on new roles and responsibilities within their differently shaped family. They may feel they have to try to replace their lost sibling somehow. And they may well feel very isolated, vulnerable and lonely. On top of all this they may have to cope with getting back to school, college, university or work, the questions and comments of others which could be intrusive or insensitive, and close friends who would inevitably struggle to understand, however kind and caring they are.

A return to routine, as much as is possible, can help. Giving them space to talk – or to switch it all off – if they need to, involving them in memory books or boxes or memorial events, can all help. In the early days when a parent's grief is too big and raw, and there's the business of police and press and paperwork to deal with, family members and friends can play a really important role, especially if there are little ones that need childcare, but also for bigger ones who need a clear-headed adult around. It can also help to make lots of spaces for very ordinary things. Someone whose younger brother had died when he was 14 said he spent hours at his best friend's house playing computer games and not talking about anything other than the game at hand.

Grief is a unique experience for every individual, and for children this will depend on so many more variables. There is a good amount of specialist support available to children and young people who have lost a brother or sister, and more that relates to child bereavement in general. This also provides very valuable insights for parents, and for friends and support networks of those bereaved families.

Talking point

Counselling is provided by many schools, colleges and universities, as well as privately, and sometimes through local bereavement services. You GP should be able to advise you. For teenagers Young Mind's messenger service can be a useful place to turn in a crisis – they just need to text **YM to 85258**.

Child Bereavement UK provides a wide range of information, support and advice for children and young people who have experienced bereavement, and for their families, as well as for parents who have lost a child. They also provide training for professionals working with bereaved families, and local support groups for children and families. They have a helpline on **0800 02 888 40**, Live Chat via their website, and email support on <support@childbereavementuk.org>.

Grief Encounter is a charity offering support to bereaved children, young people and their families, and to professionals working with them. As well as information and advice on their website for parents and professionals working with children and young people, and for young people themselves, they also offer a range of services including group activities, training, and counselling. They have a Grief Talk Number: **0808 802 0111** and a helpline email: <grieftalk@griefencounter.org.uk>.

Winston's Wish supports bereaved children, young people, their families and the professionals working with them. They provide a range of information, advice and support on their website, including an online tool specifically for teenagers, Help 2 Make Sense. There is a helpline on **08088 020 021**, online chat and email service which can be accessed via the website.

The Compassionate Friends has a leaflet for parents, 'Our surviving children', which provides valuable advice on supporting children through the loss of a sibling, and another for siblings themselves which is also useful for parents to read, or anyone else caring for someone who's lost a brother or sister, 'A sibling's grief'.

Care for the Family has a useful list of dos and don'ts, written by bereaved siblings.

Drugfam has a project called **Beyond**, formerly the Nicholas Mills Memorial Project, for young adults aged 18–30 who have been bereaved through drugs or alcohol. The focus is on death following addiction. They offer phone or email support, creative workshops and one-to-one support. See their website for more information.

> **For parents who have lost their only child**: TCF has a leaflet 'Childless parents – for parents who have no surviving children' and **Care for the Family** has an article, 'Helping parents to face the future when an only child has died'.

Formal processes: Child Death Reviews

In England and Wales, every time a child dies a formal review of that death takes place. The vast majority of these deaths are tiny babies, but it includes children up to their 18th birthday. Not all parents know this, but under revised guidance (in England) they should, and not only that they should also be allocated a key worker, a single point of contact who can advise and guide them through this process and signpost them to wider support.[2] In Scotland not every child death is currently reviewed, and practice is inconsistent generally across the country (as it has been in England), but work is underway to rectify that through setting up a National Hub, co-hosted by Healthcare Improvement Scotland and the Care Inspectorate.[3] In Northern Ireland there hasn't been a review system in place to date, but steps are being taken to bring that in line with the rest of the UK.

The purpose of the Child Death Review process is primarily to prevent future child deaths by examining the factors that led to each one and seeing whether any changes could be put in place that might reduce risks to others. They're not investigations – they don't look at who might be at fault or who is to blame for individual deaths – they focus on improvements for the future. Depending on the age of

---

[2]   H.M. Government (2018) Child Death Review statutory and operational guidance (England) [online]. *Gov.uk*. Available from: <assets.publishing.service. gov.uk/government/uploads/system/uploads/attachment_data/file/859302/ child-death-review-statutory-and-operational-guidance-england.pdf> (accessed November 2020)

[3]   Healthcare Improvement Scotland (2020) National hub for reviewing and learning from the deaths of children and young people: scoping exercise report [online]. *NHS Scotland*. Available from: <www.healthcareimprovementscotland. org/our_work/governance_and_assurance/deaths_of_children_reviews/scoping_ report_aug_20.aspx> (accessed November 2020)

the child and the nature of their death, different agencies might be involved. For the death of a teenager to drugs this would often include police, paramedics, hospital staff and school or college staff, as well as any other agencies that might have been involved with the family. In England, parents should be informed about the review process, given the opportunity to contribute to investigations and meetings, and be informed of their outcomes. Not all parents want this, but for some this can be an important part of their process of making sense of the senseless.

Talking point

- I was fortunate to have been able to work with NHS England on the production of a guide for parents about all these processes, along with other bereaved parents and professionals, 'When a child dies: a guide for parents and carers'. This is available on the NHS England website and is definitely worth reading, for families and for those supporting them in any capacity.
- 'Child Death Review: statutory and operational guidance (England)' is available on the gov.uk website. Chapter 6 covers 'Family Engagement and Bereavement Support' and is useful for understanding what is involved.

Legal proceedings

Most parents who lose a child to drugs will find themselves immediately thrown into a bewildering world of legal procedures that they have no choice but to navigate, ones which are generally totally alien to them, for which they have few reference points and about which the rules are a mystery. Like Tim and I, most will have had little, if any, dealings with the police, or encounters with the criminal justice system, or with coronial processes. And all of this is connected to the child we've suddenly found we have to start grieving. Legal proceedings intensify that grief and add layers of complexity to what was already incredibly complicated, while the length of time this can all take, which can be many months, and often well into a year or more after your child has died, serves to prolong it all. There may be unanswered questions, there may be feared answers, there may be new information about the events surrounding the death of your child you discover along the way, there may be anger towards the people involved, and whatever there is, there will be endless waiting.

Most of the time families will be assigned a Family Liaison Officer by the investigating police force, and as long as the criminal justice process is going on they should be able to provide information about progress and plans, and explain what's involved.

In addition to formal support, however, families going through all this need lots of support from the people close to them. They may need practical support in the form of lifts, childcare, meals, or someone to make difficult phone calls for them. They may need someone to sit with them in court, to ask questions of officials on their behalf and remember or record things they can't quite take in. They may just need someone to sit and listen to all their fears and frustrations before, and to listen to any anger, disappointment or confusion after, and if so they'll need to receive great patience, before, during and after this long process.

Talking point

The Compassionate Friends has several leaflets to guide parents through the legal processes: 'Coping with legal proceedings following the death of our child', and three covering inquests – 'Overview', 'Preparation' and 'The Day'.

Victim Support is a charity that provides services to ensure that victims are given the support they need before, during and after court, including taking Victim Personal Statements, managing witness care units and providing specialist witness support. You can call their Support line on **0808 1689111**, or access live webchat or email support via the website, where you can also find your local Victim Support Team.

The Coroners' Courts Support Service is a charity offering emotional support and practical help to bereaved families, witnesses and others attending an inquest at a coroner's court. They have volunteers currently providing support in 45 coronial areas of England in 68 coroners' courts (see their website for details). They have a helpline on **0300 111 2141** or you can email <helpline@ccss.org.uk>.

Physical and mental health

When Dan died, I lost weight rapidly. I felt sick for most of the first few years, sometimes in my stomach, more often as if something was filling my throat, less of the time as time moved on, but at difficult times it would come right back. I had a constant, sharp pain on the left side of my chest, just where my heart is. Again, this gradually eased, but often it would come back, and still comes back, on an anniversary, a birthday, Christmas. I had no idea all these metaphors to describe emotional pain and loss might arise from an actual, physical pain. Sick to the stomach, stuck in my throat, broken-hearted. And I had no idea it was just so very exhausting to be that sad. Still now there's a particular sort of exhaustion, a sudden draining of every single ounce of energy, that is unique to those moments of acute, intense, devastating sadness. It turns out these are some of the main physical symptoms that grief can bring, but there are others, too, and it can trigger or exacerbate other health conditions.

There is also, unsurprisingly, a huge impact on people's mental wellbeing. This sort of loss is like having a bomb explode inside your brain, knocking out every circuit and leaving a bunch of disconnected cables. It affects memory, concentration and the ability to process information. It can also lead to mental health problems, which can be short-term but can become protracted. Some time before Dan died, all managers across the council had received resilience training, and in my initial assessment I scored highly across all areas. I was, on the whole, a confident, optimistic, positive, resilient person, who relished a challenge as an opportunity to put a plan in place, take control and implement change. There wasn't a question about your son dying from drugs, though, and if there had been I'd have scored zero. My resilience in the face of Dan's death was rubbish. It turns out you can't plan your way out of this, you can't take control of very much, including your own emotions, and the change you most want to implement more than anything in the whole wide world is forever unattainable.

Not only do many parents suffer depression, there is also considerable anxiety for many – leaving the house, leaving a phone on, letting other children leave your sight. There is also, inevitably, a high rate of post-traumatic stress disorder associated with the loss of a child to drugs, and this can manifest itself in multiple ways depending on the individual, and can last for many years.

Talking point

A GP is the best place to start for anyone who has lost a child, especially in sudden and traumatic circumstances.

Anyone experiencing **physical symptoms** should get them checked out with their GP, just in case there's anything else lying behind them, or if they need an eye kept on them. 'Broken heart syndrome' is a recognized condition, technically known as stress cardiomyopathy. It mostly improves and mends itself in time, but can be serious, partly depending on other underlying conditions.

A GP should also be able to ask the right questions about **mental health** in the context of bereavement and trauma, and offer the best support, whether medication or counselling or both.

Counselling is something that's very individual. Not many can benefit from this very early on because it's all too chaotic. Some will have this for weeks, some for months or years, and some dip in and out. Some start having counselling only years after the event, and some never feel it would help. What is available in local areas, and how much it costs, is very variable. Most GPs will signpost to Cruse, which uses volunteer counsellors and is available for free. If someone does feel counselling would help, try to find someone who has a specialism in child bereavement, because this is a specific form of bereavement, and if at all possible, also someone experienced in trauma therapy.

AtaLoss.org is a charity that aims to provide a one-stop shop for anyone needing bereavement support including counselling. They have a search facility that enables you to filter by relationship, cause of death, age of person seeking help and location. They have a wide range of information and resources signposted on their website. They also provide online support through their Griefchat service.

Getting back to work

Returning to work is one of the many things that's different for different parents. For some, getting back to work is a welcome relief, a time when they have to put their head somewhere else, and give it a little break from the unbearable pain. For some, the routine and familiarity of the old normal is reassuring in the midst of the madness of grief. There can be more practical drivers, though – financial worries, fear of losing their job and concerns they might have about the extra workload on colleagues in their absence. For some, like me, the return to work takes a long time, and for some, like me, they never quite get there.

When Dan died, I'd been working in adult education for our local authority for the previous 15 years, and at that point I was managing a team of around 50 curriculum managers, project managers, tutors and sessional teachers. I worked closely with other departments within the council, and in partnership with local schools, early years settings, libraries, other community organizations, as well as various bodies across the UK, including a national network of Family Learning managers of which I was co-chair. I also taught for half a day a week, because that was what I loved best, and I always believed I managed teachers better if I myself taught too. I absolutely loved my job. I had a great team, a great boss. And then Dan died, and I broke.

I really struggled to get back to work, and I really struggled with the fact that I was struggling. For a long, long while I couldn't focus on anything other than Dan for more than a moment, and the effort to do so was exhausting. I couldn't make decisions of the most basic sort. *What plates do we need for the dinner someone's just brought round for us?* I remember how long it took me to write my first email, which was only to reschedule an examiner's visit. I had to re-read it so many times because I just couldn't tell whether I'd said what I needed to say, or whether I'd judged the tone right. And things matter differently when your son has died. It was very hard to care very much about performance data, or programme planning, or even Ofsted, in the grand scheme of boys being here and then not.

And it wasn't just the work; it was the social space in which that work took place. Very much like Dan, I loved to befriend the people I met, and to be friends with everyone around me. I chatted to anyone and everyone, but when Dan died, I totally forgot how to do that. What's the social chit-chat you need for the person in the shop as you hand over your money in return for your goods? I just couldn't remember. What about when you're waiting for the photocopier, or making a cup of tea, in a big open plan office with 30-odd other people? I had no idea what I used to say. And my poor colleagues were probably thinking, *how can I possibly chat to Fiona about what I had for dinner when her son has just died?* I was so incredibly fragile, I could break at any moment – so I had to carry an invisible protective barrier around myself which must have made me seem so unfriendly. Tim likened it to being an unset jelly in a mould. You can look to all intents and purposes the right shape, a jelly all set and ready to go, but if anyone gives that mould the tiniest of knocks, says anything at all to wobble that precarious mixture at that particular moment, then all is lost. Jelly everywhere.

It took me months to get back, starting with a very few hours, and I never quite made it full time, though to be fair I'd started running a charity which was taking up increasing amounts of my time, and almost all of my head and heart. Thankfully I had the most under-standing, supportive and patient boss anyone could possibly hope for, and the most understanding and supportive team who carried me through most of those first few months back. Others aren't so fortunate, however, and this is incredibly hard. There can be a heavy financial price to pay for the time off that you need, and even though there's now an entitlement to two weeks' paid leave for bereaved parents (see Jack's Law, below), which is a huge improvement on the minimal time previously given by some employers, many parents will need much more than this. Some may need to take unpaid leave to get this, others may need to change to part-time hours, even if only temporarily, and both have costs, not only to income but to National Insurance and pension contributions.

The loss of a child brings with it the loss of so much more, in fact pretty much all that made up the life that was lived when that child was alive and well, at least to begin with. Isolation can be a big issue for bereaved parents, and the social space of the work environment is part of most working adults' broader social lives. People need to take the time they need to take each next step, but sometimes they need practical changes to be made, where they can, to enable that step to be less painful. They also need bucketloads of understanding and patience. One piece of advice from Care for the Family (see below) is valid for every aspect of the life of a parent who has lost a child: Don't expect them to return to being 'their old self' – the trauma of their loss will have changed them forever.[4]

> ## Talking point
>
> **Care for the Family** has a really useful downloadable leaflet on the Bereaved Parents' Support area of their website, 'How you can help your employee when their child has died: dos and don'ts for employers'. They also have a couple of articles there that might be helpful to read, either for employers, employees, colleagues or friends: 'Grieving and employment – do they mix?' and 'Grief in your own workplace' for the self-employed.
>
> **The Compassionate Friends** also has a detailed leaflet for employers on their website, which would also be useful for colleagues, 'Helping a bereaved employee after the death of their child'.
>
> On 6 April 2020 the UK government confirmed that it would be statutory for employees to be entitled to a minimum of two weeks' paid leave in the event they lose a child. This is known as Jack's Law, in memory of Jack Herd whose mother Lucy campaigned for mandatory leave for grieving parents.
>
> The Act gives a statutory right to a minimum of two weeks' leave for all employed parents if they lose a child under the age of 18 or have a stillbirth from the 24th week of pregnancy. The right will exist irrespective of how long they have worked for their employer.
>
> Statutory Parental Bereavement Leave can be taken at any point during the 56 weeks following their child's death.
>
> Anyone classed as a 'worker' (for example a contractor or someone on a 'zero hours' contract) may not be entitled to leave but would be entitled to pay under this Act.
>
> For more information on Jack's Law see <acas.org.uk>.

---

4   Care for the Family. How you can help your employee when their child has died: some suggested Dos and Don'ts for employers [online]. *Care for the Family.* Available from: <www.careforthefamily.org.uk/wp-content/uploads/2014/08/Dos-and-Donts-for-Employers.pdf> (accessed November 2020)

Stigma that sticks

To add to the array of special features that characterize a loss of this nature, it's impossible to escape the stigma that unavoidably attaches itself to a death from drugs, both to the child and to that child's parents. This is something that troubles us all. Tim and I had talked so openly about Dan from the start, as I've said, but this was driven at least partly by the sense of a need to defend his character. He wasn't like *that*, he was like *this*, as if boys like *that* somehow deserve it and boys like *this* don't, which of course is shamefully false. But a lot of the reason I continue to say Dan was like this and he died from drugs, is because I know only too well those assumptions exist because they were mine, too, and I know they can lead to a false sense of security, which can lead in turn to inadequate protections being put in place. I want to make sure others don't trip up like I did.

That said, despite my openness about Dan and drugs within the safe confines of the charity, outside this I've managed to avoid, with almost complete success, any social situation where somebody might ask if I have children, because then they might ask how many, and if they do, I need to decide whether I say one or two. If I say one, I'm denying Dan's existence, but if I say two, will they ask me what they do, and then I'll have to say one's a writer/editor working for a really interesting charity, and the other one died? And if I say one died, I risk them saying *Gosh, that's awful, what happened?* And then what do I say?

Talking to other parents who've lost children to drugs, we all do the same. If it happens, and someone takes their questions that far, the reason often given, and given as vaguely as possible, is that it was an accident, and one that they'd prefer not to talk about. Most people are too polite to ask, but it's a risk worth avoiding, because if you mention drugs you envisage that cloud of judgement descending over their expression, whether it's real or imagined, and we all want to protect our dead child from judgement. They've suffered enough, paid the heaviest of prices. It's usually when you first meet someone and are making those polite early steps into conversation that the sort of questioning happens that might move into *So, how many children do you have?* It's uncomfortable on both sides, and on so many levels, and so we tend to work hard to avoid it.

Somehow the stigma seems worse that they died, which multiplies the unfairness of it all out of even more proportion. The other four boys who got to go home that night in January never seemed so shrouded in shame even though they all did exactly the same thing, perhaps because they weren't left stuck in that moment of drug-related decision like poor old Dan. There was always the chance to make other, safer choices, live good and healthy lives, rewrite themselves. Somehow it's worse if you not only take drugs but end up dead. We've talked about the stigma of drugs in general, whether dabbling or dependency. With death you're stuck with it.

Talking point

If you've lost a child to drugs, try to hold tight to the child you knew. If you know your child has struggled with drugs you will already have had to keep doing this, but for those who had no idea their child was using drugs, even if this was a one-off, or a very new thing, the shock of their death is complicated by finding out their child had been doing something they knew nothing about, and that something was drugs, and this can feel like a double loss. It can lead some to feel angry with their child, and others to feel they never knew their child at all. It's so important to remember the child you knew and loved is still that same child.

If you know someone whose child has died from drugs, try to challenge any assumptions that might naturally arise in your head, as they do for so many of us, and put them aside. It may help that person if you acknowledge you're aware that the sense of stigma is something that could make their loss more painful, because it's likely they'll be conscious of this, and concerned about the extent to which the people around them may be judging them, their child and their family. If so, it will help them to know that you, at least, aren't. And you can try to help them remember the special, precious person their child was.

The Compassionate Friends has a couple of leaflets which may be helpful: 'Bereaved through drug or alcohol use' and 'Coping with judgemental attitudes'.

Some of the things that helped me

- **Professional help**: As well as my Care for the Family befriender, a very wise and insightful counsellor and a more specialist trauma therapist, I was really fortunate that when a child dies at Kings College Hospital their specialist bereavement nurse Anne-Marie comes to you, and stays around for as long as you need her. Anne-Marie was there as Dan died, stayed with us in that little room in the immediate aftermath, and was then my frontline of support over those very early days and weeks, ringing to check in, being there for me to call if I needed, offering really wise bereavement advice but also a lot that was very practical. She advised me that if mornings were better, and I was able to make breakfast, to make a sandwich for lunch as well in case I didn't feel I could by the time lunchtime comes (which is what often happened). If I couldn't cope with all the intricate planning and decisions needed to make a shopping list for more than one day (which I couldn't for a fair while), shop one day at a time at the little local supermarket, buying just what's needed for that day. Anne-Marie organized for us to go back to the hospital to see the consultant a couple of months after Dan died when I realized I couldn't remember most of what he said, and really didn't understand what had been happening. And again, 18 months later when I got fixated on needing to know what the very last thing was that they switched off. Everyone needs an Anne-Marie, but sadly not everyone gets one. I was very blessed that Dan died at Kings.
- **Practical help**: To start off with we could do not the tiniest useful thing at all. Thankfully our family, friends and our incredible church community did everything for us. Our church immediately set up a rota and organized people to bring us an evening meal every day. If we had visitors, they'd bring more. In fact, there was always more than we could manage, and we ended up with a freezer full of leftover lasagne and had to borrow some space in a friend's. Between our church and our friends, all our laundry was done, and our shopping, they took the cat to the vet and cleaned the house before the next lot of reporters came round. One day we got back from wherever we'd been to find someone had filled an empty

trough at the front of the house with bright, beautiful primulas. When it came to the funeral not only did the church pay a big chunk of the costs, they also organized the service, which as you've read was huge and complicated by press and police. Apparently they had six spreadsheets of plans on the go, which included Dan's favourite cakes for hundreds of people. We were very blessed.

Talking point

Practical help, especially in those early days, is invaluable. My advice would be to take anything that's offered, though everyone's different, and some people need to shut themselves away.

Most local faith communities will be very committed to helping those in need and would be more than happy to offer practical help, as long as they're big enough to resource this. Ask someone helpful to ask around for you, if this would be useful.

If you have a friend or family member who's lost a child, then try to offer specific practical help, as well as general offers of whatever they need. It's hard to know what you need in the early chaos, but most people will need and welcome help of the most basic, practical varieties. Check the leaflets on TCF or Care for the Family signposted above for advice.

- **Family and friends**: My parents moved in for six weeks, looking after us all, in the midst of their own deep grief for the Dan they loved, and a daughter who was broken in pieces. Family came, friends came, people from work and from church came. In fact, because Dan's death was so public and everyone we'd ever known knew, and our house was full of people coming and going for weeks. At some points there was standing room only. People turned up at the door who I hadn't seen for years. The house filled with flowers. The postman had to knock because the daily pile of cards got so huge. It was mad, but it was a fitting madness. It meant so much that so many people cared, and that I didn't have to make myself a cup of tea for weeks. Again, we were very blessed.

Talking point

Although it was lovely having people coming and going, and dropping in unannounced in the early chaos, there comes a point when it can be good to call ahead. It may be a bad day, or just a bad moment, or the person may need time to get their head together, or get dressed. Try to be understanding, too, and not feel hurt, or offended, or take it personally if they feel they can't manage a visit, and do offer again. And if you're the bereaved parent, do know it's always OK to say it's not OK.

- **Bereaved parents**: However compassionate someone is, it's very hard to understand the loss of a child if you haven't lost a child yourself, and especially a loss under these circumstances, and I wouldn't want anyone to try too hard, to be honest. And so talking to other bereaved parents, and especially those who've lost a child in similar circumstances, has always been an enormous relief. Even then nobody's experience is ever identical, but it creates a space where there are things that don't have to be explained, or apologized for, and everyone gets it.

Talking point

Everyone's different and it isn't right for everyone – Tim didn't find it anything like as helpful as I did – but nevertheless I'd really recommend connecting with other bereaved parents if you can, whether a befriender through Care for the Family or events organized by them or The Compassionate Friends. If it doesn't help, you don't have to do it again, but if it does it can be an enormous source of support.

If you're the friend or family member of someone who's lost a child, perhaps help them make that contact, or go along to an event with them if it feels a bit daunting, which it can.

- **Reading and writing**: As someone who's always loved to put pen to paper and thoughts into words, I wrote and wrote when Dan died. I filled journals with endless failed attempts to articulate something I was desperate to make sense of, which I needed to try to capture and pin down, to explain, to myself first and foremost, but also to the people around me. I wanted to be able to say this is what it's like, this is why it's like this. I struggled to find the words I needed, perhaps because what I was trying to define was itself so elusive and formless, but I kept trying, and the trying did help. And although I found reading so hard (a sore point for a former English teacher) I found I could read the writing of other bereaved parents, and found it so helpful when there on the page were the words that had been escaping me.

Talking point

Reading

There are many autobiographies written by parents who have lost children in various ways. My personal top four – and it's very personal what anyone will find particularly helpful – were:

- *Michael Rosen's Sad Book* by Michael Rosen – although written for children, the simple, beautiful words of a poet who had lost his own 18-year-old son Eddie five years earlier, coupled with the illustrations of Quentin Blake, articulate for me, perhaps better than anything else, the true nature of grief.
- *See You Soon: A Mother's Story of Drugs, Grief and Hope* by Philippa Skinner – a reflection on Philippa's experience of grief following the death of her son Jim to drugs when he was 21. Philippa is a counsellor and has been my Care for the Family befriender since Dan died.
- *Lament for a Son* by Nicholas Wolterstorff – describes the progress of grief following the death of his son Eric in a mountaineering accident when he was 24. Nicholas Wolterstorff is an American philosopher and Professor of Philosophical Theology at Yale University.
- *A Grief Like No Other: Surviving the Violent Death of Someone You Love* by Kathleen O'Hara – a book which offers concrete, practical and compassionate steps for those who have been bereaved through violence, including drug overdoses. As mentioned above, Kathleen is a therapist whose own college-age son was murdered.

Writing

Kathleen O'Hara writes about the importance of telling the story when you lose a child to a sudden, violent death. This is important not just to try to make sense, and to feel less overwhelmed by it, but also because the nature of this sort of death means it's a story that will have to keep being told, to various people and for various purposes for some time to come, whether you want to or not. Having different versions ready at hand is a help, from the bare bones to the detailed narrative. If you're not someone who likes to write, tell it to someone else who can write it down for you, or record something on your phone. It doesn't have to be perfect first time, or ever, but finding a way to frame your story can help.

- **Hugs**: When Dan died I lost my grip of every boundary I'd ever had and found I had a need to hug everyone. I also told everyone all that was passing through my head (but that's another thing). I hugged everyone who came to the house, everyone I met outside the house, poor Steve was forever hugged, I even hugged reporters and presenters (though only the extra-nice ones). I'm sure I read something, somewhere, at some point, explaining that this can happen in grief, but I can't now find it to provide an evidence-base for my unboundaried behaviour. Dan was always a huggy boy, so perhaps that was why. The last thing I'd done was to give him a hug, so perhaps that was why. Whatever the reason, there were hugs aplenty when Dan died, and it helped me, even if it proved disconcerting for some on the receiving end.
- **Starting a charity**: This is perhaps what has helped me most, and for so many reasons, many of them wholly unhealthy, I'm sure. The complex motives that bring forth a charity out of a tragedy must be worthy of a lengthy PhD thesis. From time to time people have asked if having the charity has helped me, and to start off with I denied it, because I was wary of making it seem I'd done this for my own personal therapeutic purposes. But now I don't mind admitting that without having this positive focus, without feeling Dan's death was making a difference, without being able to do for others what I can't do for Dan, life without him would have been so much harder.

Advice for supporting someone who's lost a child – tips from other bereaved parents

'Definitely text or call before dropping in – and don't take offence if you don't want to see them just at that moment. Do try again, too.'

'People dropping by anonymous food was an incredible help in the beginning, because I couldn't even cook an egg for the first month.'

'For me it was ongoing support after the funeral. I found a lot of people seemed to back off and really that's when you need support more than ever – the small things like a text or just a random hug.'

'Always speak their names. I love hearing the stories off the tongues of people in Joel's life and the fun times they had with him.'

'If you can, tell me something about them I didn't know.'

'Don't feel uncomfortable talking about them – a lot of bereaved parents just want to talk about their child.'

'Don't worry about saying the wrong thing and avoid me. Avoidance is worse than saying the wrong thing. Just treat me the same as you always have.'

'One woman left flowers outside the house every week for about three months, and I didn't even know who was leaving them, but these anonymous gifts are like angels' assistance and make the unbearable just a tiny bit bearable.'

Ending (and beginning) with sycamore seeds

As you know, Tim and I talked and talked to anyone who would listen after Dan died, in a desperate hope that we might help others avoid the fate that had befallen us and Dan. We were also driven by the need to make this very bad thing do as much good as it possibly could. We couldn't make the bad thing better, or take it away, but we could make it do good things. We knew we could only do what we could do, though, and once our words had left our lips, what they did was only so much under our control. We didn't know where they might travel, or where they might land, or what they might do when they got there. All we could do was to talk, and to hope and pray that wherever they ended up they would do lots of good, make a difference, bear much fruit.

Of course, in growing a drugs education charity that process became much more managed, sophisticated and based on international evidence of what works best. But however effective, evaluated and evidence-based our approaches, there will always only be so much we can do through the best drugs education we can possibly muster to effect change in any one individual. And so, we also hope and pray.

After Dan died, we met a lovely couple, Ray and Vi Donovan, whose son Chris's story is included in Chapter 5. Some months after Dan's death, they invited us round for dinner. While we were there, they told us about Prison Fellowship and the Sycamore Tree Project, and the power of story in restorative justice. They told us about the impact the project has, the responses they'd had from prisoners to their story, and the story that lay behind it all. The founding principle is the story of Zaccheus the tax collector, as told in the Bible.[5] The story is one of forgiveness, restoration and reconciliation, and it centres around a sycamore tree. We were inspired, moved and interested in getting involved ourselves, and since then we've been telling Dan's story in prisons across the country, and not so long ago on the first Sycamore Tree course over the Channel in France.

But back to that evening. I'd been brought up in Sunday School, I knew all about the very little man who'd been taking far too much tax from his fellow Jews, who'd had to climb up into a sycamore tree when Jesus came to town so he could see him passing by, and how that encounter had led him to pay back everything he'd taken from others four times over, and to give half his possessions to the poor. But I'd never thought of the significance of the sycamore tree in the story other than a means of elevation, not as a powerful symbol of change for good.

The next day we were up at the cemetery, under the enormous tree that had sheltered and shaded Dan's grave for the last few months, and for the very first time we realized this tree was a sycamore. For us, that was a goosebumps moment, and from that moment the sycamore gained a huge significance. Its seeds spin around everywhere, land up in some very surprising places, and push up shoots where people least expect them, potentially growing trees that will

---

[5] Luke 19:1–10

shower the world around them with yet more sycamore seeds in turn. Bearing much fruit.

On the first anniversary of Dan's death we had a little memorial service in our church, which involved family, friends of Dan's and of ours, lots of candles and an enormous chocolate cake. And we gave everyone who came a sycamore seed from the tree up at the cemetery, and a little card, tied with a ribbon, with a photo of Dan and these words:

> This sycamore seed is from the tree that overshadows Dan's grave. Our prayer is that through our words, and through the Foundation that works in his name, the story of Dan will journey far and wide – just as the spinning sycamore seed does – and that where it lands it will bear much fruit, growing many good things from this very bad thing.

These words came to open and close the play that tells his story, and they close this final chapter now. My hope is that for you the good fruit this book bears will be children who live long, happy and healthy lives, and who never forget how incredibly precious they are, and how important it is they do all they can to make sure they get home in one piece.

Dan's year 11 school photo, 2013

I Wish I'd Known – a final word from Dan's Dad

The evening before the rave – there will only ever be one rave for me – I went into Dan's room to say goodnight. To be sure I would normally wish him a good night when the first of us retired to bed, but it was often called up the stairs, sincere but transient. Tonight was different. Earlier in the evening I had been to visit my father in the last stages of terminal cancer in a nursing home in Wimbledon. I had asked Dan if he wanted to come with me. He had puckered his face into a shape that clearly meant 'No' but had struggled with words. We had all been coming to terms with Dad's impending death since Christmas Eve. I said, 'No is fine, Dan. We all have to play this our own way.' This released him. 'You see, Dad, I want to remember Grandpa how he was.' So, I had gone on my own.

When I got back bedtime was approaching. Something nudged me out of my way and into Dan's. We must have talked but I can't now remember what we talked about. Presumably we talked about my father – he was on top form and Dan would have loved to have remembered him like that. It was utterly inconceivable to me that, though a week later my father would die in the night with his wife and children around him, by then Dan would already have been dead for almost four days. What else we talked about I have forgotten, and Dan isn't here to remind me. What I do remember after our check in was that, when the conversation reached its natural conclusion, I turned and looked him in the eye. 'Goodnight Dan,' I said. Dan returned my gaze, eyeball to eyeball, confident, assured, peaceful and warm. 'Goodnight Dad,' he smiled. Something at depth in me had made contact with something at depth in him and I think both of us recognized it. I turned and walked out of his room. 'Boy, that was good,' I thought to myself. 'I've got him for another 18 months,' (before university swept him away) 'I'm going to do that every time I can.'

What I wish I'd known is that life doesn't come with a guarantee. What I didn't know was that I had just experienced the last opportunity I would ever have to go heart to heart with him. Something that had only just started would be snuffed out just the other side of the weekend, before it had the chance to grow the way of my good intentions into something permanent. My first man-to-man inter-action with Dan (or so it felt) would turn out to be my last.

If I had known that it wasn't guaranteed that my children would bury me (and not the other way round) I would have taken every opportunity to document the special times, the birthdays, the outings, but also the ordinary times too. I would have kept a journal, I would have taken many more photographs, I would have saved programmes, postcards, in fact, anything that would have kept the memories alive. I would have acted as if every day counts, which of course it does. I would have started saying my heartfelt goodnights a lot earlier.

So, as this book comes to its close, I would urge you parents, if it needed saying, never to take anything for granted. Don't assume in 20 years' time you'll remember today just because you can recall it so vividly now. Jot down somewhere everything that made today special. And on top of that, let your children know how special they are, that come what may you are on their side, that nothing can separate them from your love. Set them free to return to you as they grow into independence. Set them up to live the best life they can.

Dan isn't here to live the good life that he was clearly growing into. The best we can hope for is that your children are, and will. We can't do it with Dan, but we want to help it to happen with as many others as possible. That's what joy looks like for us now.

Here's to the journey!

Tim Spargo-Mabbs

Tim and Little Dan, 1998

About the Daniel Spargo-Mabbs Foundation

DANIEL SPARGO -MABBS foundation

The drug education charity

Credit: The Daniel Spargo-Mabbs Foundation

The Daniel Spargo-Mabbs Foundation is a drugs and alcohol education charity founded by Tim and Fiona Spargo-Mabbs in the response to their son Dan's death from MDMA. The charity aims to support young people to make safer choices and reduce harm, through increasing their understanding of the effects and risks of drugs and alcohol, and improving their life skills and resilience. It works with young people, families, teachers and professionals in schools, colleges and community groups across the UK and overseas.

Drugs education for young people

The DSM Foundation's evidence-based drugs and alcohol education programme for students incorporates direct delivery by their specialist drugs educators, together with a spiral curriculum of planning and resources for teachers to deliver effective drugs education to their students, from 10 to 18 years. Sessions combine age-appropriate information about the effects and risks of drugs and alcohol, and discussion around issues such as motivation, the teenage brain, peer influence and resilience. Important practical and harm reduction strategies are included, especially for older students.

Student Workshop at Hayes Primary School *Credit: Clare Slade*

Everything is evaluated, reviewed and updated on an ongoing basis to ensure it reflects the latest research and guidance, and addresses current priorities for young people.

Drugs education for parents and carers

Working with parents has been a priority of the DSM Foundation from the start. Interactive workshops for parents and carers, whether in person or online, involve finding out about current issues for young people in relation to drugs and alcohol, decision-making and adolescent brain development, practical strategies, conversations and where to find information, advice and support.

Online resources are available for parents on the DSM Foundation website and Facebook page, including short videos and downloadable leaflets.

Theatre in education

I Love You, Mum – I Promise I Won't Die is a powerful verbatim play that tells Dan's story, and was commissioned from award-winning playwright Mark Wheeller by the charity. It was published by Bloomsbury (Methuen Drama) in 2017, and has been touring schools and communities as a professional Theatre in Education production since then, with performances followed by interactive workshops. A new production was filmed during the Covid-19 pandemic to enable it to continue to tour 'virtually' despite restrictions, and to further its reach.

Credit: Bloomsbury Publishing, PLC

From September 2022 *I Love You, Mum – I Promise I Won't Die* will be a set text on the Eduqas GCSE Drama syllabus, building on its rich heritage of being studied and performed by young people around the world.

Oli Webb as Dan, with permission from Chris Webb

Training for teachers and professionals

Training is available for a range of professionals working with young people, whether in educational or community settings. Training can be bespoke to individual organizations, developed in discussion with the DSM Foundation drugs education team.

Youth ambassadors

Having young people at the heart of the charity's work has been a key ingredient of the DSM Foundation from its beginning. The Youth Ambassador programme trains and supports 16 to18-year olds to be positive peer influences within their community and to support the work of the charity in a variety of ways, including in an important advisory capacity. DSM Foundation Youth Ambassadors have offered their advice for parents in Chapter 6.

To offer your support

The majority of the DSM Foundation's drugs education work is offered free of charge, because there are huge pressures on the budgets of state-funded schools, colleges and community organizations, and cost should never be a barrier to young people and parents accessing the best possible drugs education. In consequence, the charity relies heavily on fundraising and donations to keep going and growing. If you would like to offer your support, donations can be made via the website.

For more information see <www.dsmfoundation.org.uk> or email <admin@dsmfoundation.org.uk>
Facebook: @danielspargomabbsfoundation
Twitter: @foundationdsm

Further Resources

Information and advice about drugs

The Drug Conversation by Dr Owen Bowden-Jones (RCPsych Publications, 2016): Owen Bowden-Jones is a consultant psychiatrist and researcher with over 20 years' experience working with people with drug and alcohol problems. This book provides information about the effects and risks of the different drugs available to young people, case studies and examples, and practical advice for parents on how to prepare for and have conversations with your child.

Say Why to Drugs by Dr Suzi Gage (Hodder and Stoughton, 2020): Dr Suzi Gage is a psychologist and epidemiologist at Liverpool University. This is a very accessible, sensible and comprehensive book which covers a range of substances and issues relating to their use. She also has a very interesting podcast series by the same name.

Talk to Frank <www.talktofrank.com>: Set up by the Department of Health, the website provides information about substances that may be used by young people, including an A–Z directory of information about different drugs, and a menu of advice for young people and parents. Advice and support can be accessed by phone, text, email or online chat.

Know the Score <www.knowthescore.info>: Set up as a national drugs campaign by the Scottish Government. The website contains information and advice for young people and parents, including an A–Z of drugs and information on related issues. Advice and support can be accessed by phone, online chat or email.

DAN24/7 <www.dan247.org.uk>: The website of the Wales Drugs and Alcohol Helpline, funded by the Welsh Government, which has an A–Z directory of drugs, information about issues relating to drug use and free leaflets that can be ordered online by anyone living in Wales. Advice and support can be accessed by phone or text.

Drugsand.me <www.drugsand.me>: A social enterprise that provides services centred around drug harm reduction. Their website provides accessible and detailed guides about individual substances, intended to help reduce their short and long-term harms, and issues related to drug use, including advice for parents.

Crew 2000 <www.crew.scot>: A harm-reduction and outreach charity working with young people in Scotland, based in Edinburgh. As well as offering direct support to young people locally, their website has an A–Z of substances with detailed information, including harm reduction advice, leaflets that can be downloaded or ordered, and a self-assessment tool to identify how risky an individual's drug use is.

Drugscience <www.drugscience.org.uk>: Founded by Professor David Nutt to provide independent, evidence-based information about drugs. David Nutt is Professor of Neuropsychopharmacology and director of the Neuropsychopharmacology Unit in the Division of Brain Sciences at Imperial College London. The website provides detailed information about individual substances as well as research.

Re-solv <www.re-solv.org>: A charity working to reduce the harms of solvent abuse, including nitrous oxide. Their website provides information and advice, including for parents, and advice and support can also be accessed via phone, text, email or live chat.

Information and advice about alcohol

Drinkaware <www.drinkaware.co.uk>: An independent UK-wide alcohol education charity, aiming to reduce alcohol-related harm by helping people make better choices about their drinking. Their website has lots of information, including for parents, and various tools to enable people to be more aware of their own drinking, to reduce their use and improve their health. There is a helpline and online chat function for anyone concerned about their own or someone else's drinking.

Alcohol Education Trust <www.alcoholeducationtrust.org>: A national alcohol education charity that supports schools, parents, carers, health educators and youth outreach teams to ensure that young people of all abilities learn to stay safe around alcohol. Their website includes a parents' area, with a range of information and advice.

Their **Talk About Alcohol** <www.talkaboutalcohol.com>: A website designed for 11- to 16-year-olds to be used in AET alcohol education lessons, but many of the activities and resources are also useful for parents to look at with their children, including a series of videos.

Alcohol Change UK <www.alcoholchange.org.uk>: A charity working to reduce alcohol-related harm, focusing on five key changes: improved knowledge, better policies and regulation, shifted cultural norms, improved drinking behaviours, and more and better support and treatment. Their website has information and advice, fact sheets and interactive tools to help people monitor and manage their alcohol use.

To find local treatment providers

England

NHS: The NHS website has a postcode search to find local treatment providers in England.

Talk to Frank: The website provides a postcode search to find local treatment providers.

Scotland

Scottish Drug Services <www.scottishdrugservices.com>: An online directory developed to help people access contact information and details for over 200 agencies in Scotland who can help with drug treatment and care.

Scottish Families Affected by Alcohol and Drugs <www.sfad.org.uk>: Offers support to anyone concerned about someone else's drug or alcohol use, including through their helpline and Telehealth, a one-to-one support service. The website provides a service directory with postcode search for an extensive range of services for people living in Scotland, including mental health and family support.

Wales

DAN24/7 <www.dan247.org.uk>: Postcode search service for local treatment providers, and a bilingual telephone helpline for individuals and their families.

Northern Ireland

NI Direct <www.nidirect.gov.uk>: The website of the Northern Ireland Government provides information for parents concerned for a child including a link to local services via the **Northern Ireland Drugs and Alcohol Services Directory.**

UK-wide

Collective Voice: A consortium of nine national drugs and alcohol treatment providers, each of which provide information, advice and support to young people, adults and families, operating in different regions and local authorities across the UK. Have a look through their websites to find out more about what each service can offer. See <www.collectivevoice.org.uk>

They are:

- **Change Grow Live** <www.changegrowlive.org>
- **Changing Lives** <www.changing-lives.org.uk>
- **Cranstoun** <www.cranstoun.org>
- **Forward Trust** <www.forwardtrust.org.uk>
- **Humankind Charity** <www.humankindcharity.org.uk>
- **Phoenix Futures** <www.phoenix-futures.org.uk>
- **Turning Point** <www.turning-point.co.uk>
- **WDP** <www.wdp.org.uk>
- **We Are With You** <www.wearewithyou.org.uk >

To find local support groups for families affected by drugs or alcohol

Adfam <www.adfam.org.uk>: A national charity tackling the effects of alcohol, drug use and gambling on family members and friends. The website has lots of information and advice, and they bring together well over 200 support groups in local communities across the UK, which can be found by a postcode search on the website.

Scottish families affected by alcohol and drugs <www.sfad.org.uk>: A charity which exists to support those affected by the substance use of a loved one. It facilitates a Scotland-wide network of family support groups and runs a helpline service, as well as offering support by email.

Al-anon <www.al-anonuk.org.uk>: A charity offering support to people affected by someone else's alcohol use. They have over 700 support groups for family members operating across the UK and Eire, which can be found using the postcode search on their website. They also offer support via their helpline or by email.

Drugfam <www.drugfam.co.uk>: A charity that aims to provide a lifeline to families, friends and partners affected by someone else's addiction to drugs and/or alcohol and those who have been bereaved by substance misuse. They offer support via their helpline and by email, and also have a number of local support groups in the South of England that can be found on their website.

Information and advice about and for teenagers

Inventing ourselves: The Secret Life of the Teenage Brain by Sarah Jayne Blakemore (Doubleday, 2018). Sarah-Jayne Blakemore, Professor of Psychology at the University of Cambridge, explains how the adolescent brain develops through a fascinating and accessible introduction to neuroscience. She explores the ways in which this critical period of change affects teenage behaviour, and why it is both a period of vulnerability but also enormous creativity that should be celebrated.

The Teenage Brain: A Neuroscientist's Survival Guide to Raising Adolescents and Young Adults by Frances E Jensen MD (HarperThorsons, 2015). Frances E. Jensen is chair of the department of neurology in the Perelman School of Medicine at the University of Pennsylvania. She has written this book as a mother, teacher, researcher, clinician and frequent lecturer to parents and teens, to provide a practical guide and handbook for parents.

Blame my Brain: The Amazing Teenage Brain Revealed by Nicola Morgan (Walker Books, 2012). Nicola Morgan's carefully researched, accessible and humorous examination of the ups and downs of the teenage brain is written for a teenage reader, but also makes for an easy and engaging read for parents.

Why Every Teenager Needs a Parrot: Tips for Parenting 21st Century Teenagers by Alicia Drummond (Let's Talk Ltd, 2013). Alicia Drummond is a psychotherapist, parent coach, speaker and author. This is a positive and practical guide to parenting today's teenagers, helping parents find the right balance between letting them go and keeping them safe, and exploring a range of aspects of teenage life.

How to Grow a Grown Up: Prepare Your Teen for the Real World by Dr Dominique Thompson and Fabienne Vailes (Vermillion, 2019) Dominique Thompson is a prominent GP specializing in student mental health, and Fabienne Vailes is an academic and expert in wellbeing in education. This is a very practical guide for parents that aims to help them build their children's confidence and resilience so they can become a strong, happy and independent adult.

Care for the Family <www.careforthefamily.org.uk>: A national charity that aims to promote strong family life and help those who face family difficulties. As well as offering events and courses for parents, the website contains a range of information, advice and support for parents of children at all ages and stages. They also have a series of podcasts for parents of teenagers, *Raising Teens*, covering various important issues they may face.

Teen Tips <www.teentips.co.uk>: Run by Alicia Drummond, author of *Why Every Teenager Needs a Parrot*, Teen Tips works with schools and parents to help them meet the social and emotional needs of young people. Their live and interactive Wellbeing Hub has a wealth of resources including staff training, a parenting course, blogs, podcasts and interviews with experts to support all aspects of your parenting journey.

Family Lives <www.familylives.org.uk>: A national charity offering advice and support to families with children of all ages. There is lots of information on the website, including some useful videos, and they offer help and support via their helpline, online chat or by email.

Relate <www.relate.org.uk>: As well as offering advice and relationship counselling for couples, Relate also provides advice for parents and other family members to help families deal with difficult times. The charity has a network of Relate Centres across the UK and a group of licensed local counsellors who provide face-to-face counselling and support.

The Mix <www.themix.org.uk>: The Mix is a leading support service for young people, providing information and advice about a wide range of challenges they may face, from very practical concerns like finances, to mental health, drugs and relationships. It's a useful site for parents of teens, interested in finding out ways to guide their children through some of these issues. For teens there's advice available via their helpline, text chat and email, and also a crisis messenger service.

Mental health and wellbeing

Young Minds <www.youngminds.org.uk>: A mental health charity committed to improving children and young people's mental health and wellbeing. The Young Minds resources library on the website is full of useful toolkits, publications, reports and policy information about children and young people's mental health. The website has an area dedicated to parents with a wealth of information, and a parents' helpline for anyone needing to talk to someone about their child, as well as a crisis messenger service for young people.

On My Mind <www.annafreud.org/on-my-mind>: This section of the Anna Freud National Centre for Children and Families website was co-produced by young people for young people. It aims to empower young people to make positive choices about their mental health and wellbeing. There's an extensive range of self-help tips, advice about various issues, a crisis text messenger service and a youth wellbeing directory of local services.

Royal College of Psychiatrists <www.rcpsych.ac.uk/mental-health/parents-and-young-people>: This website contains detailed information for young people and for parents and carers covering an extensive range of mental health issues and related concerns.

MindEd for Families <www.mindedforfamilies.org.uk/young-people>: funded by the Department for Education and the NHS, MindEd for Families is intended to support parents and those caring for children and young people in their family when they're concerned about a young person's mental health or wellbeing. The website includes an area focused on young people, which aims to provide safe, reliable advice for parents about young people's mental health, created by experts and parents together. The website also guides people through stages of concern and what they should do.

Papyrus Trust <www.papyrus-uk.org>: A youth suicide prevention charity that offers confidential support and advice to young people struggling with thoughts of suicide, and anyone worried about a young person through their helpline, HOPELINEUK. They also deliver suicide prevention projects and training in local communities, and work to shape policy nationally. The website includes a downloadable guide for parents about young people's self-harm and suicide, which aims to provide information and guidance and to help parents cope with a young person who is struggling with thoughts of suicide.

Local mental health support for young people can be found via the NHS website or your GP: <www.nhs.uk/service-search/other-services/Mental-health-support-for-young-people/LocationSearch>

Child bereavement

Care for the Family Bereaved Parents' Support <www.careforthefamily.org.uk/family-life/bereavement-support/bereaved-parent-support>: This specialized area of support for families offered by Care for the Family provides a range of information on their website, and organizes events throughout the year bringing bereaved parents together. They also offer a telephone befriending service, through which a bereaved parent can be put in contact with a trained volunteer who has also lost a child, in circumstances and of an age as similar as possible.

The Compassionate Friends <www.tcf.org.uk>: A national charity supporting bereaved parents which has an extensive range of information leaflets and guides on their website covering a wide range of relevant topics. They offer a 'Grief Companions' service, which provides peer support from another bereaved parent in the first couple of years after a child's death. They coordinate local groups of bereaved parents who meet, and events during the year across the country. They also have a helpline offer and support by email.

Drugfam <www.drugfam.co.uk>: A charity offering support to families affected by bereavement through drugs or alcohol, as well as support for the drug and alcohol use of a loved one. They hold an annual bereavement conference, and offer support via the helpline and by email. They have a project for 18- to 30-year-olds called Beyond which offers support to bereaved young adults via the helpline and by email as well as through creative workshops.

Scottish Families Affected by Alcohol and Drugs <www.sfad.org.uk>: Offers free counselling to families in Scotland bereaved through drugs or alcohol, as well as providing support through their helpline and by email or live chat. There is also information and advice about coping with bereavement through drugs or alcohol on their website.

The Child Death Helpline <www.childdeathhelpline.org.uk>: Staffed by trained volunteers and aims to provide a confidential freephone service to family members affected by the death of a child of any age. They also have a telephone interpreting service and accept calls in any language.

Child Bereavement UK <www.childbereavementuk.org> Provides a wide range of information, support and advice for children and young people who have experienced bereavement, and for their families, as well as for parents who have lost a child. They also provide training for professionals working with bereaved families, and local support groups for children and families. Support is available through their helpline, Live Chat and email.

Grief Encounter <www.griefencounter.org.uk>: A charity offering support to bereaved children, young people and their families, and to professionals working with them. As well as information and advice on their website for parents and professionals working with children and young people, and for young people themselves, they also offer a range of services including group activities, training and counselling. They offer support via their helpline and by email.

Winston's Wish <www.winstonswish.org>: A charity that supports bereaved children, young people, their families and the professionals working with them. They provide a range of information, advice and support on their website, including an online tool specifically for teenagers, Help 2 Make Sense. They provide a helpline, online chat and email service.

Victim Support <www.victimsupport.org.uk>: A charity that provides services to ensure that victims are given the support they need before, during and after court, including taking Victim Personal Statements, managing witness care units and providing specialist witness support. Your local Victim Support Team can by found on their website. Support is available via their Supportline or by live webchat or email.

The Coroners Courts Support Service <www.coronerscourts-supportservice.org.uk>: A charity offering emotional support and practical help to bereaved families, witnesses and others attending an inquest at a coroner's court. They have volunteers currently providing support in 45 coronial areas of England in 68 coroners' courts (see their website for details). They have a helpline and offer advice and support by email.

AtaLoss.org <www.ataloss.org>: A charity that aims to provide a one-stop shop for anyone needing bereavement support including counselling. They have a search facility which enables you to filter by relationship, cause of death, age of person seeking help and location. They have a wide range of information and resources signposted on their website. They also offer support online through their Griefchat service.

Michael Rosen's Sad Book by Michael Rosen, illustrated by Quentin Blake (Walker Books, 2004): Children's author and poet Michael Rosen lost his 18-year-old son Eddie to meningitis five years before writing this book. Although ostensibly written for children, his simple, beautiful words, coupled with the illustrations of Quentin Blake, movingly articulate the nature of grief.

A Grief Like No Other: Surviving the Violent Death of Someone You Love by Kathleen O'Hara (Marlowe & Company, 2006): Kathleen O'Hara is a therapist whose own college-age son was murdered. This book offers concrete, practical and compassionate steps for those who have been bereaved through violence, including drugs overdose.

See You Soon: A Mother's Story of Drugs, Grief and Hope by Philippa Skinner (Spoonbill Publications, 2012): A reflection on Philippa's experience of grief following the death of her son Jim to drugs when he was 21 and working in Hong Kong.

Lament for a Son by Nicholas Wolterstorff (Eerdmans, 1987): Describes the author's progress of grief following the death of his son Eric in a mountaineering accident when he was 24. Nicholas Wolterstorff is an American philosopher and Professor of Philosophical Theology at Yale University.

5742 Days: A Mother's Journey Through Loss by Anne-Marie Cockburn (Infinite Ideas, 2013). Anne-Marie started writing this book just hours after the death of her 15-year-old daughter Martha from MDMA. Written in real-time, it charts the 102 days that followed the loss of Anne-Marie's only child, through to the party she held to acknowledge what would have been Martha's 16th birthday.

Index

2CB, 10

access to drugs, 12–13
  on social media, 13–16
accessibility, 15
addiction, 67–8
  alcohol, 170
  and the brain, 207–8
  cannabis, 46, 203–6, 207
  and mental health, 209–10
  nicotine, 47, 206–7
  seeking help for, 212–16
  signs of, 210–11, 213–14
  treatment for, 17, 216–17
  see also regular drug use
Adfam, 214, 215
advertisements for drugs, on social
  media, 13–16
age
  and attitudes to drugs, 11
  and laws on alcohol, 133
  and type of conversations about
  drugs, 154–5
aggressive behaviour, 127–30
alcohol, 10, 42–4
  and driving, 130–2, 177–9
  first aid, 186–7
  introduced at home, 170–1
  legal implications, 132–3
  mixed with other drugs, 60–2
  safety strategies, 168–73
  treatment for dependency, 17
  and violent crime, 127–30
Alcohol Education Trust, 44
amphetamines, 10
AtaLoss.org, 243
attitudes to drugs, 11–12
Australia, criminal records as barriers
  to entry, 136

BBC, documentary on social media,
  13–14
benzodiazepines, 9–10, 33–5
  see also Xanax
bereavement, 253–4
  effect on health, 242–3
  help and support, 235–9, 243,
  249–51
  reading and writing, 251–3
  returning to work, 244–6
Betts, Leah, 143, 192
Blakemore, Sarah-Jayne, 99
books on grief, 252
boredom, as reason for drug-taking,
  89
boundaries, 158–9
brain
  and addiction, 207–8
  adolescent, 79–80, 86–7, 92–8,
  147, 158
  functions, 27–8
broken heart syndrome, 243

cannabinoids, 29, 45
  synthetic, 113–14
cannabis, 10, 33–5, 44–6
  access to, 12
  advertisements on social media, 14
  attitudes towards, 11
  dependency, 46, 203–6, 207
  and driving, 178
  effects, 28, 33–4
  methods of taking, 59–60
  possession, 115–17
  and psychosis, 221–2, 223–5
  regular use, 203–6
  risks, 16–17, 34, 46, 59
  side effects, 34
  and violent crime, 128